10106

Mastering the art of performance

Mastering the art of performance
A Primer for Musicians

Stewart Gordon

OXFORD
UNIVERSITY PRESS
2006

OXFORD
UNIVERSITY PRESS

Oxford University Press, Inc., publishes works that further
Oxford University's objective of excellence
in research, scholarship, and education.

Oxford   New York
Auckland   Cape Town   Dar es Salaam   Hong Kong   Karachi
Kuala Lumpur   Madrid   Melbourne   Mexico City   Nairobi
New Delhi   Shanghai   Taipei   Toronto

With offices in
Argentina   Austria   Brazil   Chile   Czech Republic   France   Greece
Guatemala   Hungary   Italy   Japan   Poland   Portugal   Singapore
South Korea   Switzerland   Thailand   Turkey   Ukraine   Vietnam

Copyright © 2006 by Oxford University Press, Inc.

Published by Oxford University Press, Inc.
198 Madison Avenue, New York, New York 10016

www.oup.com

Oxford is a registered trademark of Oxford University Press

Library of Congress Cataloging-in-Publication Data
Gordon, Stewart, 1930–
Mastering the art of performance : a primer for musicians / Stewart Gordon.
p. cm.
Includes bibliographical references and index.
ISBN-13 978-0-19-517743-5
ISBN 0-19-517743-6
1. Music—Performance. 2. Performance practice (Music) I. Title.
ML457.G66   2006
781.4′3—dc22   2005010152

9 8 7 6 5 4 3 2 1

Printed in the United States of America
on acid-free paper

Contents

Prelude	Defining Performance	3
chapter one	Assessing Yourself, the Performer: Achieving a Positive Mind-Set toward Performance	13
chapter two	Why We Perform: Forging a Performance Philosophy	25
chapter three	Physical Support for Performance	33
chapter four	Conceptualizing and Scheduling Goals	41
chapter five	Keeping Preparation Fresh and Focused	55
chapter six	Dealing with Repetition and Drill	69
chapter seven	Techniques to Develop Secure Memorization	81
chapter eight	Ensuring Quality	91
chapter nine	Self-Regard at the Time of Performance	97
chapter ten	Managing Stage Fright	105
chapter eleven	Dynamics during Performance	117
chapter twelve	Evaluation after Performance	129
chapter thirteen	Performance and Human Interaction	153
chapter fourteen	The Career Challenge	159
chapter fifteen	Physical Challenge and Performance	179
chapter sixteen	Performance Careers in Retrospect	185
Postlude	Performance and Your Spiritual Life	199
Selected Bibliography		205
Index		207

Mastering the art of performance

prelude
Defining Performance

This volume is intended to serve as a series of thought-provoking exercises for those who strive to perfect the art of musical performance. Written by a musician, these chapters are intended to stimulate and assist other musicians as they prepare to perform music for an audience of listeners, attempt to realize artistic goals, and attempt to sustain a career as a musical performer.

Some musicians are attracted to the overall field of music because of the excitement inherent in performance. Perhaps they equate playing or singing before an audience to receiving admiration. In time, these musicians often find that their initial attraction to the rewards of performance becomes less important as a love for the music itself grows. Others are attracted to the music first. These musicians may find that their regard for performance often assumes increasing significance as they realize that performance is the logical goal through which they can share the music they love so much.

Thus performance and music study are intertwined. As a musician embarks on learning to play or sing a given work, somewhere in the back of his or her mind is the concept of *performing* that music. This concept envisions recreating the musical work as a whole in an act that sets forth the beauty, the excitement, the emotion, the humor, and the intricacy of the music. Many musicians downplay their interest in the spotlight, pointing to the worth of the music rather than their achievement in realizing the music. Yet, they also realize at some level that an awareness of oneself is almost inescapable. Moreover, most cannot completely eradicate from consideration the possible rewards from successful performance.

Having noted the close links between music study and performance, we are now faced with a paradox, for, while the two are inextricably linked, we almost always regard a performance as a distinct and separate goal. The act

3

of the performance is almost always set apart by some external formality: a concert, an audition, a recording session, or a social gathering. The performance is likely envisioned, moreover, as a single *event*, and as such contains elements of unpredictability. Such perceptions inspire various reactions in performers; these can range from excited anticipation to numbing dread.

Performance offers the possibility of an intensely satisfying experience. Yet, although complete fulfillment seems within grasp, it is never promised unconditionally and never fully realized. Notwithstanding these obstacles, musicians and performers continue to be drawn to performance as the consummation of their achievement. Moreover once a performance is completed, regardless of its degree of success or failure, they experience the drive to perform again and again, trying each time to make the performance better, more perfect, more deeply expressive. Thus they live with the frustration of never quite reaching the perfection they envision, but they are never free of their desire to pursue this Nirvana.

It is helpful for us to step back from the intensity of our pursuit. We should look around and realize that many of the processes and challenges we face in dealing with musical performance apply to a wide variety of activities, for *performance* is an integral component of every human being. Thus much of this book applies to a broad spectrum of activities that are, in fact, performance related.

To musicians performance suggests being on a stage, before an audience, or in front of a camera or a microphone. In reality performance is far less rarefied and far more frequently encountered. In fact, we perform all the time. Here are a few examples of the many performances that go on around us:

- Thanksgiving dinner at grandmother's house is an event to which the family looks forward. Children and grandchildren assemble, knowing that the holiday will be graced by a delicious meal. Grandmother plans her feast by shopping for food in the days leading up to the holiday, and the day before Thanksgiving she begins the lengthy process of preparing her complete menu, timing everything to be ready at the appointed hour. The holiday dinnertime arrives, and grandmother unveils a sequence of superb culinary delights, each presented at its moment of optimum goodness. Grandmother has given a successful performance.

- The final examination in a required course has a reputation for being tough and searching. A student has attended most of the classes and done most of the homework leading up to the final, but the prospect of taking the test makes him nervous because of its reputation and because it counts significantly in determining his final grade. Passing the course with a good mark is important to future goals. Two weeks before the exam the student begins assembling and organizing class notes. He rereads several key sections in his textbooks and makes two trips to the library to catch up on some supplementary reading. Three days before the exam, he begins to study hard, writing down on index cards key words or phrases designed to trigger recall of complicated information. He drills the correct, complete sequence of items that he tends to get mixed up by repeating them over and over. He checks the spelling of a short list of names and terms over which he tends to falter. As exam time approaches, he moves even more quickly from list to list, from key word to key word, checking his recall and accuracy. The appointed hour arrives, and as he works through the exam, he realizes that although he missed prepping for a few things, his hard work has paid off, for he is successfully meeting the challenges of most of the questions. He is nervous, but he also experiences some degree of satisfaction, a good sensation that becomes a feeling of command as he nears the end of the exam. He walks out of the exam room knowing that he has, indeed, aced the exam. The student has just given a fine performance.

- A young woman has been attracted to an individual for several weeks. She has no way to garner the attention of this person without seeming to be embarrassingly forward, although their paths cross every few days in the course of an activity in which they both participate. Unexpectedly she finds herself in a committee meeting as a result of this activity, and the object of her interest joins the group. She feels aflutter, but composes herself, turning her attention to the business at hand. In the course of the discussion she speaks several times, offering helpful comments. At one point she says something funny and everyone laughs. She manages to make eye contact several times with the person of interest as she speaks to the group. She is careful not to monopolize the discussion but knows she has given the impression of being an intelligent, imaginative, upbeat person. After the meeting the person she is interested in asks her out for coffee on the pretext of discussing in greater detail one of the points she made in the meeting. The young woman has given a successful performance.

From these examples we can see that giving a performance is a part of many activities in our lives. Indeed, a large number of routine undertakings have the potential of being transformed conceptually into performance challenges. Adopting such an attitude opens the door to perfecting skills that contribute significantly not only toward successful musical performance, but also toward achieving many of our other life goals. For instance:

- *Learning situations* (operating machinery, driving automobiles, running computers)

- *Testing* (in school, at work, or at the Division of Motor Vehicles)
- *Participation in sports* (Little League, bowling teams, golf, marathon running)
- *Playing games* (chess; bridge; quiz, board, or computer games)
- *Presentations* (classroom, conference, and sales)
- *Social Events* (weddings, religious services, installation and ceremonial events, any circumstance in which you wish to make an unusually good impression, such as first dates, meeting authority figures, proposals of marriage, hobnobbing with the boss, or socializing with important people)

This list should include, of course, activities built around performance as a musician: those in front of an audience, microphone, or camera, participating in theatrical presentations, concerts, recording, or film-making.

As musicians, we probably work with some aspect of music on a regular, perhaps daily, basis. We can regard what we do as a routine task or as a performance, depending on our perception of a number of external factors. Routine work begins to take on a performance orientation when we begin to identify any one or a combination of the following conditions:

- *Stakes:* If we perceive that our music-making will result in far-reaching, important consequences, we begin to regard successful execution as important to our long-range goals, desires, or well-being. Once that connection is made in our minds, that playing or singing tends to become transformed from a benign activity into a performance activity.
- *Time Frame:* If we perceive that the music we are learning to play or sing must be ready within a given amount of time, we begin to regard playing or singing that music as performance-oriented. This position becomes especially true if the amount of available time seems limited, or if there is either an understanding between you and another person or a public announcement as to precisely what time and day this act will take place.
- *Reputed Difficulty:* If we believe that we are attempting to play or sing something generally regarded as difficult or risky, we begin to regard executing the act in a performance light. Our perception is shaped not only by the difficulty or risk inherent in accomplishing the task, but also by having heard about its formidable aspects from others. In competitive situations, the perception may grow out of the awakening realization of the reputed strength of our competitors.
- *Personal Difficulty:* If we believe that we are attempting to play or sing something that is somehow difficult for us as an individual, we begin to regard the performance of this music as an assessment of our achieve-

ment. Perception of how difficult a given piece of music is for you personally is the result of many different factors, such as basic self-esteem, degree of confidence or courage, and, in many cases, even individual aptitude for a required physical coordination.

- *Skill Profile:* The history of the relationship between you and the skills needed to play or sing a given piece of music figures significantly in determining how that task is regarded. Such considerations include how recently you have acquired the necessary skills, how many times those skills have been repeated, how deeply you have analyzed the process involved, and how successful and/or traumatic previous attempts at doing the task have been. Once again, performance becomes the goal that certifies you have mastered the skills that challenged you.

How clearly we perceive all these factors, as well as the intensity of their influence, fluctuates from one set of circumstances to the next, often changing from day to day or even hour to hour.

Our art is so intertwined with performance that we realize that the better we can operate under performance conditions, the more likely we will be to achieve our goals. First, we must prepare for the performance event and later deal with the event itself. Indeed, most of us have come to believe that we will experience at least some stress, nervousness, or excitement at the time of the performance. For some of us such feelings may be merely an underlying awareness. For others such feelings loom ominously, as bugaboos that terrify, confuse, or enervate. These conditions have to be dealt with head-on if one is to perform at all.

To complicate matters, the ability to turn in a successful performance stubbornly resists codification, and to some extent remains a mercurial art. After decades of study and research, the components that make up successful performance remain elusive, differing not only from individual to individual but also from circumstance to circumstance. Even after years of experience, veteran performers cannot and do not take for granted the skills necessary to turn in a first-rate performance. After even hundreds of successful performances, most performers still have to deal with the tension that attends the deed. Furthermore, there often seems little correlation between the amount of nervous tension and the resulting degree of success. Often those who fear performance the most, who suffer agonizing waves of nervous tension before and during a performance, are nevertheless able to achieve an excellent performance even by their own high standards.

In March 1959, when the world-renowned pianist Artur Rubinstein was nearing the end of his long career, *Life* magazine did a photographic spread as a tribute to this artist who had spent more than half a century performing before a worldwide public. One photograph showed Rubinstein, his short stature being underscored by the contrasting length of his formal tail-coat, hunched over a radiator backstage before a concert, warming his hands, and looking fragile and vulnerable. The caption to the photograph quoted the pianist: "Fear before each concert is the price I pay for my superb life." In this epigram Rubinstein captured the quixotic essence of what it means to perform, generously sharing with those less experienced the fact that even he, after years of successful performing, had to deal with the devils of nervous tension and fear.

Notwithstanding such unavoidable and seemingly formidable hazards that attend the act of performing, a body of catalysts exists that can be used to strengthen one's performance ability. These include the following:

- Self-exploration to build esteem and prepare for the rigors of performance, opening up avenues of confidence and creativity.

- Preparation to train and solidify performance skills: organizing content, perfecting techniques, and reinforcing physical responses.

- Psychological exercises to be practiced until they become attitudes that go a long way toward generating the energy and courage needed at the moment of performance. These mind-sets can also effectively aid in maintaining balance during performance, calling into play elements of both control and risk.

- Feedback to improve, correct, and strengthen performance. Such feedback, in the form of both internal evaluation and external criticism, can be invaluable and lead to improvement, but it must be carefully weighed, with the negative reactions of personal hurt sifted out and with the harmful aspects of less than carefully formulated criticism recognized.

- Realizations that come periodically, breakthroughs that help one rethink long-range goals, sometimes even redefining our personal relationships with the world around us.

- And occasionally—not often, but occasionally— spiritual insights that are given to us, flashes offering us a fleeting glimpse into another dimension, the brilliant intensity of inspiration, or the miracle of a wondrous revelation.

All of these beneficial catalysts are available to every individual, but they are not made manifest simply by asking. They must be explored, studied, practiced, and reflected upon with some degree of regularity over a period of time before they begin to take effect. They are similar to lifestyle choices that contribute to good health. We all know that proper rest, sensible nutrition, regular exercise, and restraint from physical abuse contribute positively to good health even in small or intermittent doses. If, however, combined into a regimen over a long period of time, they often produce an optimal state of health, an in-depth well-being that can go a long way toward providing radiant looks, abundant energy, and the ability to ward off illness and disease. Similarly, working intelligently over a long period of time to achieve better performance will result in a high batting average in terms of success.

From childhood Nora cherished the hours she spent at the piano. She loved studying and practicing. She took pride in conquering every technical feat, and she relished the emotional content of the music. When relatives or friends came to visit, Nora's mother urged her to perform. Nora often felt the music was not ready for performance, but mother would insist with the admonition, "It doesn't have to be so perfect. We don't care if you make mistakes." Nora often felt insecure because of these performances. In high school, Nora had no time to spend with her peers because of her practice schedule. She rarely dated, and the boys who did ask her out were the nerdy ones, not those regarded as handsome or athletic. Nora accepted this status gracefully because she had her music. She placed in several local piano competitions, although before each performance she suffered terribly from anxiety. In her senior year she successfully auditioned at a nearby state university to become a music major.

The number of pianists in the university's music school overwhelmed Nora. She felt they all played so much better than she did. She continued to practice very hard, however, and her piano professor seemed satisfied with her progress. At the end of the first semester, Nora got a B minus in piano, partly because she had not played her best at her performance jury. Nora was paralyzed with nervousness, and the night before the exam she had been unable to sleep and vomited twice. At the start of the second semester, Nora went to her advisor and changed her major to journalism. She had always gotten good grades in English in high school, and she felt that if she could not perform music successfully, she could write about it. After a few weeks, however, she was stealing time from her journalism assignments to practice the piano, preparing lessons now for a new teacher, since the previous semester's teacher taught only piano majors. Moreover, she was almost constantly depressed. Boys never asked her out on a second date, because she communicated that she was "down" most of the time.

Late one night Nora saw an ad on television that offered a series of self-help tapes designed to unlock secret inner power. The girls she was with poked fun at the fix-all promises of the promotion. Nora was intrigued by the ad, however, and over the next few weeks saved the money necessary to send off for the tapes. When they arrived, she hid them from her roommates. She began listening to them early in the morning in her practice room, just before she started to play. The tapes contained meditations that concentrated on positive mental feedback, breathing exercises, and a discussion of how these activities helped emotional balance and physical coordination. After several weeks, Nora began to feel more positive, and a trumpet player started asking her out on weekends. At her jury, Nora played well. She was nervous, but in spite of her fear, she controlled her performance. Her old piano teacher talked to her about returning to the music school as a major.

Nora returned to the music school. She began to seek out materials similar to the tapes that had helped her. She saved part of her practice time each day to work on her positive meditations. Three years later, Nora received a standing ovation at the end of her senior recital, and she graduated *summa cum laude* with a major in piano performance.

One cannot eliminate completely fear or anxiety. One cannot guarantee that each and every performance will exhibit the best representation of one's skills or abilities. One cannot escape sometimes feeling let down after a performance, or the sometimes stringing critical assessment of what one has done. Notwithstanding these inescapable hurdles, you can work at performance skills. Your knowledge of how to prepare for a performance does grow. Your ability to deal with the stress of performance will become stronger. You can improve your knack of achieving personal best during the excitement of performance. And finally, you do begin to realize your musical goals as a result of your efforts and a series of successful performances.

Somewhere deep within you is a conceptual image of the living entity you know yourself to be. This inner you is constantly changing, the events of your life and your interaction with them continually transforming who you are. This continuing process molds a new person, little by little, to be sure, but inexorably, as many small changes and influences slowly propel you toward alterations of profound dimensions.

Most of us sometime wish for a comprehensive grasp of this process to understand better who we are and where we are headed. Yet the pressures of daily life offer few opportunities to gain insight into how our routine tasks relate to either the person we are, the person we are becoming, or the vision of the person we wish to become. Not only is it difficult to grasp with clarity the complex dimensions of these highly personal images, but also we find that the barrage of events, emotions, and pressure throw these concepts out of focus. Some of us may try to stop the flow momentarily to forge our self-images into more clearly defined characteristics. More often than not, however, even special efforts to define oneself are met with frustration. We sense that not only does our self-image tend to be fleeting, but also the vision of what we seek is extremely fragile. Direct contemplation of our vision tends to compromise its transcendence, dulling its most alluring, mysterious aspects.

We finally come to the realization that, like falling asleep, visualization of our evolving self is best approached by an indirect process. We learn about ourselves by focusing on alternative but closely related concepts; our perceptions of inner self are a by-product of these efforts. In this context, contemplating performance activities, practicing performance techniques, and perfecting performance goals serve with unusual effectiveness. These processes develop effective tools with which to conceptualize, sense, and gauge long-range personal change and growth. This indirect awareness becomes, in turn, the catalyst in defining who we are and who we hope to become. We experience a paradox that brings us, surprisingly and seemingly miraculously, to a very a clear realization of the dimensions, growth patterns, and attributes of our inner being. In this way performance, properly used, can become a way of life that is personally illuminating as well as fulfilling.

chapter one

Assessing Yourself, the Performer

Achieving a Positive Mind-Set toward Performance

Let us start with the concept of self-perception. When Socrates said *Know Thyself*, he reduced to an epigrammatic command a task that can be difficult, time-consuming, and complex. There are those who, indeed, spend years in psychoanalysis pursuing this goal. Most might agree that such an extended, intricate process would ultimately yield unique benefits, but unless we find ourselves in deep psychological trouble, we will probably not take the time or invest the money for such extended self-examination. Yet we also often realize the need for a more quickly formulated, workable impression of our own being in order to address day-to-day challenges and strive toward personal and professional goals.

In deep analysis, one uncovers and deals with painful or traumatic past experiences. Similarly, to grasp a more pragmatic self-awareness, you may find that in a cursory assessment, the experiences that spring to mind are the painful or traumatic ones. All of us develop strong perceptions of ourselves as a result of having experienced pain, and many of our most deeply ingrained lessons remain in our memory in order to help us avoid such pain again. For many individuals, these lessons are easily triggered the instant self-contemplation begins. These recollections often result in an acute awareness of those personal characteristics that render us vulnerable, frail, or weak.

The opposite could also be cited: that positive past experiences, such as achievement or success, might be associated with our talents and our strong points and they too can be summoned up as powerful components of our personality. Most individuals, however, tend to relegate their strong points to a more subdued role in self-assessment. Some psychologists attribute this tendency to the fact that humans harbor a stronger desire to avoid pain than to experience pleasure.

13

Such theory notwithstanding, we can certainly observe that deeply ingrained in our society is the notion that it is virtuous and attractive to be modest and unassuming, even to the point of self-denigration, and that it is foolhardy and conceited to be assured and self-possessed. After all, haven't we all been taught that "pride goes before a fall"? True, we sometimes pay lip service to revving up confidence and courage in the face of challenge and adversity. However, we usually harbor some degree of reserve when we undertake such self-building, because we suspect that a fine line exists between patterns of positive thinking and attitudes that might be perceived as overbearing or egotistic. As a result, most of us fall considerably short of that dividing line in our attempt to avoid crossing it. Thus the positive components of our personal makeup remain in the background while the negative ones, born of painful experiences or feelings of inadequacy, loom ominously at the top of our consciousness. As a result, the mind calls up the limiting factors when we face any performance challenge: the risks, the insecurity, the lack of skill, and the price of failure. These images, in turn, tend to engender feelings of inadequacy, fear, or avoidance. Thus we often embark on performance challenges with an enormous amount of impeding psychological baggage.

Pulling toward the negative is not entirely of our own doing, for we are conditioned by many daily encounters. The news is filled with misfortune, suffering, and violence. The freeways are reported as problematic, and the weather is causing unhappiness somewhere. Political debates suggest a future fraught with mammoth problems. TV talk shows often focus on aberrant behavior. Entertainment menus are rife with crime, domestic turbulence, sickness, and tragedy. Even comedy is often structured to generate laughs from situations that are, in truth, painful or behavior that is boorish at best and downright cruel at worst.

Much of what we are asked to view, listen to, or read every day is negative. Such fare suggests that human beings have but a limited ability to survive, that we habitually behave like our own worst enemies, and that we live in a malevolent universe. Of course, positive news or entertainment also exists, but usually in smaller, less easily accessible doses. Thus without consciously realizing it, we are subtly conditioned by the preponderance of negativism, so that it requires a conscious effort to feel good about ourselves and what we need to accomplish in any given day.

Trying to be positive may in fact appear downright insipid, a kind of Pollyanna attitude that ignores the truth. Admittedly we need to strike a balance between regarding ourselves positively and the truth of how we can operate in the world around us. Such balance should take into account the logical assessment of our weaknesses or the areas in which we need to grow, but simultaneously should focus on our goals and strengths, so that we consciously attempt to bolster our self-image. As was noted, the negative side of the balance will usually weigh in heavier, so we need to work hard to strengthen those habits that contribute toward more positive attitudes.

Obviously it is highly desirable to reduce deterrents to success as early as possible in our conceptualization of any performance, and we should consciously choose thought patterns that are supportive and impelling rather than discouraging and dilatory. By the same token, we need to maintain a balanced view, so that we do not distort reality to a degree that will render our efforts foolhardy. Attempting, thus, to put a positive spin on one's initial regard for any given performance challenge must be tempered by careful assessment of the degree of the difficulty or risk, as well as the degree of one's readiness to meet such difficulties or risks. Thus you must assess the entity that will be undertaking the performance: you must assess yourself and the potential you bring to the challenge.

In your more rational, thoughtful moments, you probably acknowledge that you are a combination of strengths and weaknesses, a mixture of confidence and faltering, with periods of both high-minded aspiration and self-indulgent lethargy. On one hand, you recognize the need to train yourself to pull toward the most positive, forward-looking, energized aspects of your makeup. On the other, you admit that such an effort is sporadic at best or nonexistent at worst. Indeed, you may decide that such efforts are quite foreign to your habitual way of thinking and that you have deeply rooted thought patterns that gravitate toward negative scenarios. Whatever degree of negativity we find, most of us will probably decide that work needs to be done in order for us to achieve a consistently positive mind-set toward our performance challenges.

The instant we resolve to adopt a more positive attitude, however, we are brought face to face with the fact that establishing such an outlook is quite difficult. Two tasks relating to our thought patterns need to be undertaken.

- First, we must interrupt habitual thought patterns and assess their degree of optimism.
- Second, we need to institute techniques to stimulate alternative thinking in areas where negativism dominates

Interrupting and Assessing Thought Patterns

Each of us participates in an inner dialogue that continues almost without interruption, its clearest babble taking place during our waking hours when we are not concentrating on a given task. The content of this dialogue gives us some indication as to how we regard ourselves. This dialogue flow is so much a part of our consciousness, however, that it is often difficult to gain a sense of perspective on its attitude and tone. As a first step, we need to find out what level we gravitate to as a matter of habit. Use the following exercise to help you assess your present index of optimism.

Exercise for Checking Your Optimism Level

You probably check the hour many times during the day. You may glance at your watch, look at a clock, listen to media announcements of the time, or perhaps even note bells or whistles that mark the start or end of a work period. Whenever you pause to note the time, try to reflect quickly on the general tone and content of both your self-image and the inner dialogue that has been taking place over the last few minutes. At first, just note it without trying to change it. Sense the level of energy you feel, the momentum for moving on with the next item in the day's agenda, and the degree to which you expect to get tasks accomplished efficiently and successfully. (A detailed version of this exercise is at the end of this chapter.)

As you do this exercise, you will probably observe a mixture of positive and negative, but you should also be able to discern an overall tone that is either upbeat, energetic, and enthusiastic, or anxious, burdened, and unmotivated. You should ask yourself if your present state is typical for you, or if it has been triggered by some external factor. For example, the exercise obviously cannot give you an accurate reading of your normal positive/negative index if you are experiencing emotional turbulence caused by some life crisis, such as marriage, divorce, sickness, or death of a loved one. You may choose to wait until life returns to a more even keel before attempting to assess your typical level of optimism.

Still other factors could influence this assessment. For example, time pressure is a powerful catalyst. Some people may react with determination when under extreme pressure, but others will tend to wither, substituting resignation, anger, or feelings of personal inadequacy. Moreover, specific outside stimuli can trigger a conditioned response. Thus we might react with seeming irrational intensity to a certain venue or performance site, or to an individual known to be powerful or critical. Even an inanimate object might engender feelings of inadequacy, such as a camera, microphone, or other media equipment. Sometimes we recognize these influences consciously, but other times they determine the tone of our mind-set without our understanding why we feel the way we do.

Continuing to observe your inner thought patterns will give some indication of how positive you usually are and how frequently you put yourself down, as well as the intensity of your emotional tone. You may find that your attitudes vary, ranging from occasional put-downs triggered by specific stimuli to an almost continuous stream of negative feedback. Some attitudes will be fueled by relatively mild emotional intensity with such observations as "Oh, I'm really not very good at this type of music," or "I'll probably never be able to perform this piece perfectly," or "Dealing with a broken nail is *just* what I needed today." Others will incite stronger feedback, such as "Something must be wrong with me, because I can't learn this piece," or "No matter how hard I try, I cannot sing (play) this music beautifully." A few may be triggered into ballooning to intimidating, illogical dimensions, inciting such reactions as "I'm frightened to death of this performance," or "I'll make a complete fool of myself, or "I'm totally out of control."

After observing your own feedback profile over a period of several days, you will gain some idea of your trouble points and the amount of work you have to do to change the pattern to a more positive one. Make no mistake that forging a balanced, essentially optimistic self-perception is as important to your success as a performer as training, preparation, or experience. It has the potential of becoming the catalyst that will unleash your personal best under pressure.

Stimulating Alternative Thinking

At this point you should move to the second area: instituting techniques designed to stimulate alternative thinking. You are undoubtedly already aware of the fact that the concepts of self-help and positive thinking have been staples in our culture for decades. Thus as you begin to cast about for techniques, you will quickly discover that the marketplace is flooded with affirmations, meditations, books, tapes, videos, and even equipment designed to generate positive thought patterns and self-esteem.

Although choosing a program and embarking on its regimen will undoubtedly prove beneficial, ultimately improving general mental health and impacting many phases of your life, you must also beware of losing perspective. Keep in mind that the final goal is meeting the challenge that lies in some arena of musical performance, and, moreover, that you must invest a considerable amount of time preparing the actual content of that performance. Thus you can't afford to get bogged down in an unduly drawn-out program of improving thought patterns and self-image. At the same time, without a minimum level of positive thinking and self-esteem, performance is rendered much more difficult and even treacherous.

Balance is, of course, the key. On one hand, recognize that you must work to develop positive thought patterns and improve self-esteem. On the other hand, try not to get stuck in excessively time-consuming regimes or get tricked into waiting for some wonderful day in the far-distant future when your thought patterns and self-esteem are deemed positive enough to proceed with the other aspects of developing performance proficiency. In other words, you need to brush your mental teeth thoroughly and regularly, but then you need to get on with the rest of your work.

In selecting the technique for adjusting your mental outlook, recognize that denying the existence of negative thought patterns is neither effective nor positive. Telling yourself *not* to think negatively fails to provide a substantive focus for the constant activity of your mind. It is better to substitute a more positive idea, replacing the negative one with something more optimistic. Recognition of this process has produced a virtual library of positive affirmations, slogans, mantras, credos, litanies, and prayers. Seek out some of these; become acquainted with their content; even select and use several that are personally appealing. This can provide helpful material with which to replace negative thought patterns.

The value of such materials, however, is limited by the fact that the mind quickly tires of repetition and soon begins to disregard the meaning of ideas used over and over again. By the same token, negative ideas, particularly if embedded in emotional reactions—anxiety, fear, nervousness, for example—tend to cling stubbornly to the flow of your thoughts. It is even possible to recite an affirmation on one level of consciousness while simultaneously embracing its negative opposite at another level.

Changing affirmations may provide a temporary antidote. Still, the mind can easily recognize and catalogue an entire repertoire, so keeping the mind from gravitating toward negativism is a constant challenge. One effective technique for maintaining positive mental focus is to create your own feedback dialogue. The very act of thinking up what to affirm usually engages the conscious mind to the extent that the negative fix will be interrupted and thus weakened. Moreover, attempting to create new ideas with a measure of freshness can often lead you to concepts tailored to your individual circumstances and hence be more meaningful.

Such creativity may seem at first to require some effort, but as with any exercise regimen, it is most difficult at the beginning. Once inertia is overcome a few times, creating your own positive thought patterns becomes easier. If you tend to borrow heavily ideas from other sources, especially at the beginning, just accept that reliance as a basic formula to which you can then add your own touches. Originality, especially the first few times, is not to be prized so much as mental activity. On the other hand, it is desirable to provide as much of your own flavor to the thought patterns as possible. The exercise is aimed, after all, at keeping the mind focused on this new pattern, and being creative is the key to engaging the mind. Unless you work constantly at being creative, your mind will find even its own inventions repetitious and become as bored with its own patterns as it was with those of others. Thus maintaining freshness can often be achieved by frequently shifting the focus of your affirmations and moving among several approaches. Some suggestions for starting points are offered at the end of this chapter.

Do not despair if at times your mind resists focusing on the new patterns, if it becomes unruly and rebellious, or if it seems determined to roam about in fields of irrelevant trivia. Achieving some ideal level of concentration is less important than the process itself: that of grappling with the mind to interrupt its usual patterns of thought and instilling new patterns. Like the body, the mind often seems impervious to changing its habits. But persistent effort does make a difference, perhaps small, even imperceptible initially; but eventually powerful enough to forge dramatic new directions.

Sticking with It

Once you have created your own positive vitamin pills, you may experience a euphoric period when the challenge seems mildly amusing, even fun. Enjoy it for as long as it lasts, for the honeymoon will ultimately come to an end, at which time you may hit the doldrums. Whenever this shift occurs, you will need to inject the process with a healthy amount of determination. There will, indeed, be days when you feel neither particularly positive nor inspired, when the time and effort to set a beneficial mental tone seems to require more energy than you have, when the entire process seems pointless or stupid. At these moments, you have to dig in and assume the blind bullheadedness that will pull you out of the rut. Don't evaluate at these times, but rather tell yourself just to do it, whatever it takes.

Using discipline to push yourself past negative moods works if your moodiness is truly caused by boredom, frustration, or fatigue. We all have "those days," or even weeks. There is, however, a deeper negative thought process that does not respond particularly well to will power; this deepdown feeling whispers again and again that your efforts are fundamentally futile. As you work to focus your thought into more positive patterns, you become aware that a dark cloud of basic doubt lurks in your subliminal consciousness, representing a seemingly undeniable conviction that all of this effort won't really make any difference in your performance. Such doubt is far more profound and vague than either boredom or discouragement. Its roots extend deep into the subconscious and are nurtured by the very fact that, in the final analysis, we are all human and must deal with the human condition, part of which is, indeed, having to cope with the inevitability of death.

We live with the knowledge that this condition is inescapable, but unless we are in the throes of a life crisis that forces us to focus on death, most of us do not spend much time contemplating dying as we go about our daily tasks. We simply turn our minds to the demands of the moment and attempt to plan for our "future," that is, the rest of our lives. We keep at bay the fact that at some unidentified point in time, it will be our turn to come to grips with the concept of death and finally to experience it.

Nonetheless, this ultimate fate and our most deeply held perception of its meaning exert some degree of influence on the way we live each moment. If dying is perceived merely as a final destination of extinction, a deeply felt belief that living is futile is inevitably generated. As a result, everything we attempt is colored by an unconscious conviction that we play the game of life because we have no choice. We delude ourselves into thinking our hopes, our goals, our efforts matter, when in fact, the cruel joke of the universe is that we are all headed for the graveyard and our achievements are but fleeting, meaningless fantasies.

This may not be consciously clear to the majority of individuals but rather exists as a disguised, vague feeling. It is potentially corrosive, however, as we attempt to create a more positive mental environment to support successful performance. It whispers that mysterious odds against us are out there somewhere, and that all of our attempts at positive thinking or active preparation will not make a difference at the bottom line. Performing the exercise or task of the day thus becomes wearisome in light of the subliminal conviction that no matter how hard we try, we will ultimately face defeat.

At just this point we must realize that every moment within the process of living our lives is either undermined or supported by our underlying philosophical beliefs. Even the choices we make on seemingly superficial levels connect to our basic convictions about the meaning of life and the organization of the universe. Thus in some measure we cannot escape the consequences of our most fundamental beliefs, even when we have seemingly not given much conscious time or thought to them, and they lie in half-formulated generalities somewhere within our thought processes.

One cannot, of course, expect to meet head-on the great mysteries underlying our very existence every time we begin to prepare a performance. Yet it may be necessary to identify the source of deep-seated feelings of futility in order to exorcise them. We all share the human condition. We have no choice. But we also have no choice in that we partake of life. We are trapped, so we must decide either to feed our life force with our thoughts or to starve it. Precisely at this point, we come to the realization that we might just as well subscribe to a perception of life that defines living as its own reward, capable of generating its own excitement, challenges, achievements, and pleasures.

Striking out in such a direction may require considerable effort at first for some of us, and, like people starting a cold engine, those individuals may have to make several attempts before a new pattern begins to take hold. However, once they are able to rev up this focus and invest in the determination to keep it going, they will sense almost immediately that the newborn life force begins to feed upon itself and ultimately builds a momentum capable of reaching powerful dimensions.

It is important to remember that simple choices that seemingly make no difference at the moment of inception do indeed add up. There can be no place for a "what-difference-does-it-make" philosophy. The difference for each moment is one of direction, and the individual moments eventually add up to a lifetime of purpose. Being able to generate a lifetime of purpose, one that creates, contributes, and serves others, is indeed our destiny as human beings.

Exercises

Here are some exercises to tweak your imagination. Try them for fun if you wish, or, better still, create your own repertoire of challenges. The important thing is to get your mind working in channels that stir you up and point to ways of improving your self-perception.

1. In the morning, while brushing your teeth, identify five time slots in the day's routine during which you will stop to check the positive/negative index of your thoughts. Suggest to yourself that you will remember to observe these pause-and-check points as your day unfolds. Do not be impatient with yourself, however, if you forget some or all of these moments. Rather, persist by repeating the reminder the next day as you brush your teeth. After several days you should begin to remember some of these moments, at least on those days when your routine is not interrupted by the unexpected.

2. When you pause to check your positive/negative index, use a familiar conceptual scale to grade yourself. (1 through 10, for example; or A, B, C, D, and F) Reserve the highest mark for those times when your mind actively embraces the positive aspects of a given situation instead of the negative, not for when you just feel good for unidentified reasons. Use the lowest marks for those times when your thinking seems to dwell on the disappointing, hurtful aspects of any situation, and particularly

when your mind insists on projecting future pain or disaster without factual basis. Score middle-range only when your mind is essentially passive or disinterested.

3. While on hold on the telephone, when you are delayed in traffic, when waiting in a service or checkout line, in any such situation where you tend to be stymied, use the time to make a collection of positive thoughts. Start with trite ones: "All good things come to those who wait"; "Haste makes waste"; "There is no time like the present"; "This is the first day of the rest of my life," etc. Then move on to creative thoughts, observing something positive in your immediate surroundings, or contemplating problems you need to give some thought to but have not yet found the time to do so. At first it will be difficult to focus on these areas, but after repeated tries, you will begin to increase your powers of observation, or to ferret out think-problems, perhaps even keeping a short list of them in a corner of your mind. You might also try to avert feeling frustrated by creating fictitious scenarios in which the schedule readjustment forced upon you results in lucky circumstances that end up being of great benefit. Imagine, for example, that the delay you encounter causes you to cross paths with a person whom you have been wanting to meet, or to confront a crucial situation at exactly the right instant. If your conscious mind deems imagining such scenarios silly or inappropriate, then ask yourself how many times it has embraced the negative opposite, exaggerating consequences or claiming damage that actually never came about. You can train your mind to dwell on the positive, but it takes effort and practice to turn it away from its present thought pattern.

4. Two or three times during both the morning and afternoon, attempt to effect a surge of positive energy by some overt, somewhat exaggerated response. For example, if someone asks how you are, instead of saying "Well, thank you" or "I'm Okay," respond by summoning up an extra measure of enthusiasm and a comment such as "I feel really great today!" or simply "Wonderful!" Or when setting out to perform a task, say aloud "You know, this is really exciting" or "I'm looking forward to this because I bet it's going to be lots of fun." These positive mental sprints are just short, but intense efforts to elevate your levels of energy and positive outlook. They can be effective when undertaken at appropriate times. Even *inappropriate* mental sprinting can be helpful in its potential for creating levity. If, for example, you tell yourself "Boy, this is really going to be fun!" as you scrape dinner plates or deal with the trash, it might evoke a chuckle, and a chuckle over a mundane, odious task is better for your mental health than grumbling.

5. Find some small window of time late in the day when you can focus on the pleasurable or successful aspects of the past twenty-four hours. If the day brought a moment of joy, tenderness, gratification, be it large or small, try to recapture the gut feeling that attended that moment. If your day was red-letter enough to have afforded you measurable success in advancing toward your long-term goals, revel in the sense of efficacy you experienced as you realized this achievement. If your conscious mind objects that such mental preening is self-indulgent, then ask it how many times at the end of a day it has rehashed again and again the slights, the hurt, the pain that it suffered that day. Once again, through effort and persistence you can train your mind to select the upbeat menu of thought patterns.

- Think of aspects of your appearance or personality that you believe are assets.

- See or create humor in your present striving by pretending to be an actor who is attempting to create a funny scene, or a home video buff who manages to capture a funny moment of stress with yourself as the subject; imagine how sometime in the future you might spin a funny yarn about your present situation.

- Make a list of things in your life for which you can be thankful, for which others might envy you, or for which you might consider yourself lucky. Everyone *can* uncover such a list, no matter how dismal appearances are or how much an underdog you think you are. Be both personal and environmental.

  What personal features or traits might you be thankful for? (One of them is the very ambition or dream that drives you to attempt performance.)

  What did you inherit for which you can be thankful? (Health; the physical or mental stamina to live this day; living in an environment, even a country, that offers the freedom to attempt your goals.)

  What relationships do you have with individuals or groups for which you might be grateful? (Significant others; children; parents; teachers; counselors; churches; ministers; social workers; friends.)

  Can you give thanks for the activities or things in life that give you pleasure? (Sports; books; music; nature; animals; food; color.)

  Such concepts might seem simplistic, but remember that the exercise is geared to refocus your thinking away from negative patterns toward more positive ones. Thus the value of the exercise is simply doing it without passing judgment on its level of sophistication.

■ Project vivid images of the events in your life that might take place as a result of your having completed your performance task successfully. Imagine the celebration reception, media or public approval, the feeling of being congratulated, or the luxury of having extra buying power with money generated from your performance. This technique might well seem to conjure up images of vulnerability. "Yeah, but what if it doesn't pan out quite so well. Am I not setting myself up for some horrendous comedown?" Yes, possibly. Consider, however, that left to its own devices, your mind is probably going to toy with images generated by failure, because subliminal visions that suggest the opposite outcome lurk in your consciousness: how you will feel as you watch others celebrate successful performance that you have chosen to eschew, sharing in public approval of performances you were afraid to be a part of, or the feeling of being resigned to modest growth, artistic compromise, or a continuation of managing on your present level of income.

As you work with these or similar exercises, summon up the courage to become aggressive and daring enough to imagine the best possible scenarios. Should disappointing results have to be dealt with later, then just remember that projecting successful images in detail is, after all, a mental technique and, as such. need not lead you to the point of denying reality in everyday terms.

On the other hand, you should be aware that there is a metaphysical bonus that attends positive, detailed visualization. Since the dawn of mankind, seers have insisted that all things are in fact created in our minds. They would have us believe that what manifests itself in our lives as reality is quite simply the product of our own habitual mental activity, and nothing else. In other words, we do, in fact, shape our destinies with our minds, metaphysically creating the circumstances that ultimately determine the success or failure of everything we do as well as the fortune that befalls us. If such wise counsel is to be taken seriously, then our only concern should be the tenor, strength, and clarity of our thoughts. For once our minds are habitually focused on the positive, it inevitably manifests itself in our physical world.

chapter two

Why We Perform

Forging a Performance Philosophy

The desire to spend our life pursuing and giving musical performances is a goal to which many of us aspire. As we begin to assess the dimensions of our pursuit, we gradually come to understand that being a performer has special, perhaps unique, rewards and pitfalls. On the plus side are challenge, growth, achievement, excitement, and, with luck, some degree of satisfaction and recognition. Counterbalancing these attributes, however, are frustration, discouragement, fear, and disappointment, as well as sometimes having to deal with humiliation, criticism, and indifference. Sustaining a career as a performer does, in fact, guarantee a life filled with dreams, surprises, and intense high and low points.

To meet the often extreme demands of our performance goals, we need to think about what motivates us and drives our performance activities, in order to create some sort of philosophical foundation for our performance lives. This foundation can serve as a stabilizing force for long and arduous periods of preparation, as well as an anchor during the storm and stress of performance itself. A well-defined fundamental philosophy, moreover, can act as a conceptual North Star that provides a navigational fix throughout the many directions and various short-term destinations that often attend a performing career.

One of the first things we need to do in forging a performance philosophy is to ask ourselves *why*. What forces motivate us to perform? Four general categories come quickly to mind:

- Response to challenge
- Desire for reward
- Love for our specific field of human endeavor
- Service for an ideal or greater cause

25

Any performer's psyche will combine all of these elements in varying proportions. Moreover, they will intermingle in every individual to form a motivational profile that is both complex and unique. Let us examine each of the motivating factors.

Response to Challenge

Response to challenge is inherent in humans. We see it often and clearly in the very young. Before we become conditioned to regard such activities as wasteful or pointless, we revel in them. How high can you jump? How fast can you run on tiptoes? Can you climb up onto that ledge? Can you walk that fence rail? All of these adventures and thousands more are part of the exploration the young undertake to test their own limits and define the physical realities of the world. Such explorations generate energy, high interest, and performances both successful and unsuccessful. Unfulfilled by their successes and undaunted by their failures, the young pursue these performance goals because the challenge itself is stimulating and fun.

As we grow, we become conditioned by a variety of factors: the responsibility of providing for ourselves and loved ones, the awareness of serious problems in the world around us, our own fear of failure or of appearing to be foolish, dealing with tragic or difficult circumstances in our life. Thus for some, assuming the mantle of adulthood means downgrading response to those performance challenges that are not necessary to achieve adult goals. For others, however, keeping some measure of such challenges in life is vital, even if their pursuit must be relegated to passionate avocation. Indeed, for some, if the mountain exists, the challenge to climb is irresistible, even if doing so serves no other goal. The fact that the mountain is *there* is enough to trigger the desire to climb it. If the puzzle has been proffered, the challenge to solve it must be met, even if the time and effort involved are bootlegged from more serious pursuits. The very fact that the puzzle *exists* means that you *have* to try to solve it.

The spontaneous spirit of adventure implied in this type of response is a desirable attribute. Too often focusing on real or imagined conceptual limitations compromises natural ebullience. Those who admire complex intellectual pursuits, for example, have been known to find this type of activity somewhat naïve and simplistic. Those who value lofty artistic goals have often deemed this mentality as lacking in vision or inspiration. Those who yearn to serve humanistic or social causes often regard doing something just to do it as a waste of energy expended on insignificant ends.

Yet, if we look around us, we see that a natural world is filled with such activity. Every species has patterns of activities not directly associated with survival but inherent in the life form itself. Puppies chase butterflies to see if they can be caught; kittens bat balls of yarn to see them roll; quadrupeds run just for the joy of it; fish dart. As we observe these activities in nature, we sometimes call them "play," but we also recognize them as an integral part of the existence of that entity. All of nature is alive with the challenge of activity.

Accepting this type of motivation as legitimate can lead to energy, high-spiritedness, and pleasure. Such motivation is usually associated with challenges that attract the young, and continuing to embrace such thought patterns helps prolong youthful attitudes. Rigorous engagement in such challenge often generates a sense of efficacy and feeling good about oneself. That feeling comes even without complete success. You may have made it only half way up the mountain, but the adventure and the promise of a better next time generate a sense of well-being. You may not have solved the puzzle completely, but the exercise has left your mind feeling razor sharp and wonderfully flexible.

This kind of panache often benefits other activities of life. The love for adventure results in conceptual innovation. The risk-taking gives edge to daily activities. The determination to succeed becomes persistence that prevails in the face of difficulty. Pushing your limits in playtime activities accustoms you to the feeling of pushing limits when it counts.

Desire for Reward

As one contemplates motivation, the desire for reward probably comes to mind first. And in this context, one thinks of financial reward immediately. If one receives money for a performance, then the prospect of providing for oneself or loved ones offers ample motivation for most people. Our society, however, has a somewhat ambivalent attitude toward financial gain for its own sake. On one hand, it is considered efficacious to earn one's livelihood and cherish the independence affluence permits. One the other hand, unreserved questing for financial gain is easily regarded as greed, especially if it is not supplemented by loftier personal goals or charitable acts.

This duplicitous societal attitude toward making money moves many people to mask this aspect of their motivation by citing other reasons for pursuing performance goals. They can even convince themselves that money is of secondary importance and therefore offer performances at a low or zero market value. They minimize the skill and effort that has gone into preparation, and often the quality of the performance product as well.

Such down-valuing is particularly prevalent among musicians. The amount of preparation usually needed for a high standard of musical performance is often Herculean, much more than that required by many other activities; yet the remuneration is often much less. If you pursue a performance activity largely because of monetary gain, the best mental attitude is simply to recognize that fact and revel in any financial success. Identify clearly the areas in which expecting such gain is appropriate, and go into the marketplace openly bargaining for the best price your performance will command. Realize that such an attitude is born not of greed, but rather of a healthy respect for the investment of time and effort you have made and the level of professionalism you have achieved.

By the same token, most of us do pursue performance activities that we do not regard as part of our working life. In our society a great deal of performance takes place without any monetary remuneration, from music recitals to Little League, from neighborhood teams to community theater, from spelling bees to chess tournaments. These activities may indeed still be linked to personal rewards, but such rewards are more complex and subtle than simply bringing home the bacon. In the environment where these activities take place, many of the participants are unpaid, regardless of their ability or level of achievement. We pursue these activities without the expectation of financial gain, joining in the camaraderie with expectations of other kinds of rewards.

High on the list of such rewards is attracting the attention of our fellow human beings to win approval or admiration. As children, we demand adult spectators for our somersaults, improvised dance steps, or other feats thought to be extraordinary. As we mature, a great part of how we perceive ourselves has to do with how we imagine others perceive us. Thus many of us strive for excellence in the hope of garnering positive or even laudatory reactions. We identify the things we are "good at," and we are painfully aware of any performances deemed inadequate.

This perception shapes to some extent what we choose to emphasize in our lives. If one is good at sports, one relishes going out for sports. With musical talent, the hard work of practicing for musical performance seems like fun. A gift for words makes writing newsletters or being on the debate team viable goals. If academic skills seem to come naturally, then success in school generates a sense of efficacy.

The desire for attention is normal and healthy, and, like all of our appetites, it can be harnessed and put to work as a positive force in our performances. We tend to disdain "showing off," too often calling to mind only the garish aspects of this impulse. Extreme publicity stunts and dubious advertising gimmicks irk us and leave a bad taste for everything that smacks of garnering attention. As a result we risk losing the opportunity to tap into the energy of this motivational force, as well as missing out on the fun of flexing our performance muscles.

Showing off helps define personality and adds color to our lives. Showing off is twirling the ball before you slam-dunk. It's throwing your hands in the air as you finish playing that virtuoso keyboard piece. It's slinking out onto the dance floor because you know you look sexy. It's that extra-long pause in a speech after you've made a killer point. Showing off is the garnish around the entrée, the red sports car, the backless dress, tight jeans, and platform shoes. Unnecessary perhaps, but the world would be a much duller place without the "look Daddy—look at me" moments in our lives.

So when you have a reason to show off, revel in claiming the center of attention. Enjoy your time in the spotlight to the fullest. Just remember to sense limits. Keep your flair within the bounds of what looks effortless and graceful. Sense when everyone has had enough, so that you don't push your showmanship to the point of wearing out its welcome. Remember that your time in the spotlight, like everyone's, is limited, and when someone else claims the attention of the crowd, be among the first to offer applause and accolades. Life is filled with an endless parade of talent, and the best way to keep your own performance vital and upbeat is to be both a great showman and an avid spectator.

Love for Your Field of Endeavor

Love for our specific field of endeavor is an aspect of performance motivation that to some extent permeates our efforts from first activity to the last. In the beginning one becomes involved in any given area simply because that activity is exciting and attractive. As one pursues that interest, the field itself often assumes a greater role of importance in one's consciousness, resulting in intense personal dedication. Thus veterans in many fields express love and devotion for their conceptual ideal. Creative artists, such as musicians, actors, writers, painters, and poets, often speak of an intense love for whatever activity they pursue. Businesspeople love the ritual, lore, and tradition they associate with a particular business. Physicians love the concept of performing the miracles of healing and its humane attributes. Ministers love religion, as well as living and performing in the spirit. Lawyers love the law and performing in the legal system. Athletes love the game.

When a number of individuals profess such love, a bond is forged that generates feelings of being a part of a special society, a community of celebrants that offers understanding and support. Living in this environment and performing in pursuit of a great ideal continue to nourish motivation, often for a lifetime. Many individuals even grow to identify their very being with their passion. In referring to their art, business, profession, or pursuit, they state simply but with metaphysical implications: "This is who I am" or "This is what I do."

Moreover, as the mind associates performance with an ideal, it sees that field of endeavor in the most favorable light possible, even elevating it to the highest realms of human achievement. Thus musicians see their music as human expression of the most exalted kind. Reverence and awe becomes evident as doctors speak of medicine, lawyers of the law, ministers of religion. Businesspeople and sports figures regard what they do more as service than as ways of making money or entertaining fans. Maximizing the virtues of one's endeavors is desirable, for it nourishes efficacy and feeds motivation. Focusing on the idealistic aspects of one's activities, whatever they may be, also brings us to the threshold of the fourth area of motivation.

Service to an Ideal or Greater Cause

The degree to which individuals are motivated to perform service to an ideal or greater cause runs a wide gamut. Most people, however, perform such service at some time in their life. For some it results from adversity that has crossed their paths. Those who have endured disease, or whose loved ones have suffered, often are motivated to work for organizations that help and treat the afflicted or that support research aimed at finding cures. Those who have suffered social or legal injustice found or work for organizations that raise public awareness of such injustice or work to remedy it. For some individuals, just becoming aware of human suffering, wherever it exists in the world, motivates them to do whatever they can to alleviate it.

Only a relatively small percentage of people are motivated to devote more than passing interest to humanitarian causes, however. Most individuals' primary motivation is tied to earning a livelihood, developing a career, and achieving a desired status. Some will not be motivated to help at all, others will offer charitable donations, still others will set aside a little time to volunteer for some benevolent organization.

Observing this gamut is not meant to be an indictment of any kind. Rather it points to the fact that of the four types of performance motivation in the mix, this one is apt to have the greatest degree of variability and, for some individuals, may not apply at all. The needs of mankind are overwhelming, and the fact that no individual can ever do enough discourages some to the point of total inactivity. In our own time the proliferation of (and occasionally fraudulent) solicitation for good works also deters some individuals.

Many, however, combine service with other types of motivation. Thus musicians play benefit concerts. Entertainers appear without receiving their usual fees. Visual artists contribute works to be auctioned to raise money. Other professionals, such as lawyers or doctors, offer free or inexpensive services to those in need.

Each one of us creates an individual recipe of motivational factors, mixing challenge, rewards, love of field, and service in a very personal way. Furthermore, the mix changes constantly throughout life, shaped both by inner changes as we mature and age, and by external circumstances or opportunities. A periodic assessment of performance motivation can be very useful in stimulating activity or in sorting out complexities in times of change.

Too much attention to performance motivation can be enervating, however. Asking oneself "Am I really motivated to perform?" on a regular basis may, in fact, be an indication of something fundamentally amiss. If such is the case, then, indeed, you need to address the issue. On the other hand, many individuals question their performance motivation too often just as a kind of diversionary exercise. This can develop into a bogus activity; stirring the pot constantly wastes energy and often leads to goal confusion. Insecure performance is also a frequent by-product. It is the mental equivalent of shopping for clothes you never intend to buy instead of doing the laundry. It is house hunting and planning the décor of domiciles you have no intention of moving into instead of sprucing up your own home. Such forays can be fun once in a while but should not become a habit.

On the other hand, performers who have latched onto and created performance activities that send positive feedback to their motivational makeup will be able to set up a powerful psychic cycle. The performances they give, although filled with ups and downs, will ultimately nourish their motivational system. They remain motivated to perform, and an unbroken cycle of performance begins to generate a mystical sense of fulfillment. For those so fortunate, debuts are followed by anniversaries, and eventually by farewell appearances.

When these performers are asked what motivated them to sustain their careers, they almost always speak in terms of what they received rather than what they achieved. They often feel a satisfying sense of efficacy in having met various challenges in their careers. They speak of being grateful for having worked in a field that rewards hard work and dedication. They often believe that their work is part of an uplifting aspect of the human spirit. They feel that their accomplishments were a way of offering the best of themselves to their fellow humans beings.

Indeed, they are convinced that following the performance dream has ultimately brought them to a state that is more than the sum of their efforts and achievements, just as each individual is more than a sum of body parts. They have dedicated their life to following their dream of performance perfection, and although they may never admit to having achieved the perfect performance, their pursuit has made it possible to transcend the limitations of their human efforts. They have risen to a performer's Nirvana, and they do not wish it any other way.

Exercises

1. Make a list of ten musical works that represent ultimate challenges for you. Imagine the excitement you will feel one day as you step out on stage to perform each of these pieces.

2. Identify the rewards you hope to achieve as you develop as a musician. Be as specific as you can. If monetary reward is one of your goals, what kind of a fee will your performances be able to command one day? If you crave admiration, identify the form it should take, be it rave reviews or accolades from an individual or group. Imagine three ways in which you might be able to "show off" without being excessive.

3. Can you envision yourself after several decades of successful performance? Can you imagine how you would look back on your career as a performer and what feelings doing so might engender?

4. List two ways in which you might be able to use your present performance level for the benefit of others. Are there opportunities to help raise money for a charitable cause by performing? Can you give pleasure to groups of seniors or those confined to a hospice?

chapter three
Physical Support for Performance

Setting and maintaining overall standards of physical well-being are key to supporting your musical performance. Our focus here, however, will not be skill-specific at this point. Later chapters will deal more directly with assessing and improving physical skills. Nor does this chapter present details of diet, exercise, and rest, important as those considerations are. Such regimes are plentiful, and you can select ones that work well for you. Rather this chapter considers several basic concepts, truths about physical well-being.

First, you can neither ignore nor spurn the health aspect of performance preparation. Such a statement may seem obvious or trite, but many individuals carefully plan for performance preparation in all aspects *except* this one. They identify musical goals, arrange for instruction, practice assiduously, gear up for the stress of actual performance—all this without ever considering how their basic lifestyle supports these efforts. That lifestyle might, in fact, lend positive support, might lie in neutral middle ground, or might even be counterproductive to performance goals.

All of us recognize the long-standing tradition in school athletics that "going out for sports" (football, basketball, track, etc.) means not only engaging in regular periods of vigorous practice but also refraining from patterns that keep players from being in tip-top shape. Regular rest, diet, and exercise are "in," while keeping late hours and partying are "out."

As musicians we need to assess the degree to which we should adopt the same principle. Performance demands and individual propensities toward such discipline will shape our choices. Whatever ultimately emerges, you need clearly to identify and evaluate your lifestyle standards and choices.

For those who like a Spartan lifestyle, imposing demands in order to get in shape for a performance will be easy, perhaps even enjoyable. They will relish positive psychological feedback as their bodies gear up to a higher de-

33

gree of efficiency and energy. Even these seemingly fortunate individuals need to tender some degree of caution, however. In some cases the desire for good outcomes may become so powerful that it sidetracks central performance goals, resulting in excessive involvement in fitness regimens. The most efficient plan is one that identifies the amount of effort needed to achieve a level of fitness that supports long-range performance goals and redirects leftover energy to performance preparation itself.

Curbing the appetite for fitness regimes is a problem only a few must deal with. Most people maintain a love–hate relationship with the demands of an optimum-health lifestyle. They would like to be lean and energized, but they also like to eat foods that are counterproductive to such goals. They would like to be agile and athletic, but exercising is either psychologically or physically difficult, in some cases perhaps even impossible. In all probability they follow some sort of sporadic pattern, alternately engaging in "good" and "bad" behavior.

Such people are probably destined to contend with a constant struggle to keep physically in shape, and it is easy for them to become discouraged. First, these folks need to give themselves some degree of credit. They have focused on the battle and continue to wage it. They know the cycles all too well, but they continue to fight. They put on a few extra pounds because they permitted themselves to indulge. They begin to feel sluggish because they didn't have the time or energy to exercise. They feel exhausted because they haven't been able to take enough time for rest and relaxation. But they also take control and get back on track, at least until the next special occasion or vacation.

This widespread pattern is not as bad as it is sometimes made out to be. Yes, it harbors moments of discouragement, but the cycle also harbors moments of achievement. The pattern actually mirrors cycles in nature. Our pets, for example, do not rationalize in deference to long-term goals, so they often eat too much, sometimes food that is bad for them. They are often alternately lazy and energized, and they can easily become motivated to push themselves to points of exhaustion or overheating. A certain amount of flexibility is part of life's fabric, and maintaining good health involves a continuous process of change rather than arriving at preconceived plateau-like states. Moreover, most performance goals can be supported adequately by a level of health that is somewhat less than optimal. Thus those who continue to strive, albeit imperfectly, to achieve a lifestyle supportive of their performance goals will likely succeed.

Finally, some spurn efforts to manage their physical side. All of us have witnessed examples that seem to contradict conventional wisdom. How many times do we hear stories (best told over calorie-laden dinner menus) of so-and-so dropping dead on the tennis court at the age of forty-five, a person, we are assured, who followed all the rules of good health religiously? How often has it been pointed out by fat and sugar enthusiasts that nutrition guru Adelle Davis passed away at an age early enough to render suspect the efficacy of her work? Our culture is rife with tales of those who broke the rules and got away with it, and those who followed the rules and didn't.

Indeed, every one of us has at some time been able to enjoy our infractions without suffering any immediate negative consequences. You say to yourself, "Yesterday I didn't bother to exercise or get much sleep," or "Yesterday I ate foods that were not supposed to be good for me," or "Yesterday I partied like it was going out of style." And how do I feel today? "Just fine, thank you very much;" or even "Today I feel great and played or sang marvelously." Thus you can trick yourself into thinking that health isn't so important after all and that you can follow whatever lifestyle suits you.

Some part of us knows better. Some part of us knows that notwithstanding the high spirits that attend legends of cavalier escapades, we need to reckon with reality. Some part of us knows that the mind and body store tremendous reserves and often do not show adverse effects of neglect or abuse until much later. The bad news is, of course, that once the mind and body begin to show the symptoms, it is late in the process, and reversing their trend usually takes a considerable amount of time and effort, if, indeed, it can be reversed at all.

Yes, we must reckon with the abundance of evidence that it is wise to adopt a healthy lifestyle, especially if one regularly undertakes the stress of performance. Experimental data supports the contention that the mind and body operate better when they have received optimum rest, nourishment, and exercise. If we show dogs or horses, we subscribe to this theory and take appropriate action. If we expect dependable performance from equipment, we take care of it, checking it over and taking appropriate measures for its maintenance. So when it comes to ourselves, probably the most complex and variable organism we will ever deal with, we cannot get away with neglecting or undermining the basic principles of its well-being.

The lifestyle that results in optimum health varies for every individual. We each need different amounts of rest; we respond differently to given diets; we develop in individual patterns that reflect different amounts and types of exercise, all determined to some extent by our genes, size, age, and present physical condition. In all cases you need to calculate carefully what works best for you. You should evaluate what you are presently doing, determine how you can effect improvement, and institute a sensible and effective pattern.

In shopping for such a pattern, look for a basic core of knowledge about diet, exercise, and rest and adapt it to your particular case. Initiate changes gradually but consistently, and as you do so, sensitize yourself to your physical responses over a reasonable length of time—several days, perhaps a few weeks—and make adjustments. Remember that "miracle" anything—be it cure, weight loss, or level of energy—is likely a commercial venture, pure and simple. Long-term conventional methods in almost all cases offer better templates for achieving results. These methods permit your physical being to tie into nature's rhythms of growth and change with the added benefit of indoctrinating you into a more lasting allegiance to your healthy lifestyle.

Once you have established a personalized set of beneficial lifestyle choices, you need to see how it will benefit your performance goals; seeing the connection will help you stick to this template for optimum health. Longtime investment will result in physical reserves that will enable you to handle the periods of tension and stress attending performance. You may not find any particular conflict here; you may comfortably accept that these patterns not only support what you want to do, but do indeed represent who you are.

Many, however, will react negatively to the prospect of having to live by the rules so much of the time. Popular culture has glamorized rebellion to such an extent that a prudent lifestyle is deemed boring. If you find your motivational philosophy harbors ambivalence in this regard, address the issue. Consciously ask yourself just how comfortable you are with continuing indefinitely the regimen of diet, rest, and exercise that nourishes the mental and physical condition you know you will need for your performance goals. Flesh out mentally the dynamics of long-term allegiance. Realize that you must endure the "in-training" periods during which your regimen will be more demanding. Realize, also, that even when you are "out of training," you probably should not stray too far from healthy patterns.

Focus openly on the insidiousness inherent in the stories of "exceptions." For every such dramatic tale that is publicized, there are dozens of unheralded examples of people integrating their personal lifestyle successfully with what they do. Learn to identify the musicians, models, actors, and rock stars who openly acknowledge an allegiance to healthy habits. Many of them have built careers on years of reliable performance, to the point where their performance excellence is taken for granted. Their achievements are so consistent with their lifestyles that they are generally overlooked in documentation of the newsworthy or dramatic.

Exercises

The exercises that follow can stimulate your own imagination with regard to managing your body and creating a healthier lifestyle. Grappling with the exercises is paramount, because doing them even imperfectly will result in both physical improvement and a level of well-being sufficient to support your performance goals. Also these exercises address only moderate degrees of weakness or addiction, patterns that most of us feel we can do something about without professional help. For deeply rooted physical addictions and destructive psychological patterns, such help should, of course, be sought without delay. Finally, use the exercises as springboards. Resist the impulse to dismiss the ideas behind them merely because the details don't fit your situation. Extrapolate underlying principles and create details that work in your particular case.

1. Take stock of where you are in regard to the patterns of living that impact your physical well-being. Do not stop at a simple, "Oh, I smoke," or "I drink," or "I'm overweight," or "I stay up too late," or "I'm out of shape." Rather, keep a record over a three-day period that brings you face to face with the extent of your weakness. How much alcohol do you consume? How many cigarettes do you smoke? How many calories do you take in every 24 hours? How many hours of rest do you get? How much activity have you engaged in that contributes toward building you up physically? At the end of the three days, set aside some time to examine what you found. Ask yourself at what points you could have made alternative choices, identify the specific moment in which such choices could have been made. Some such moments may remain elusive, but others may be tied to patterns that are habitual. Look for examples like the following:

   - You usually take a rehearsal break midmorning, when you drink coffee or soda and smoke.

   - You usually fix a cocktail for yourself the moment you get home.

   - You usually stop to buy a bag of sweet or salty snacks to keep in your practice area.

   - You usually watch at least an hour of TV, sitting in an easy chair.

   - You usually start watching a television movie that keeps you up past a sensible bedtime.

   Begin to plan how you can interrupt your patterns by substituting something you have wanted to experience but just haven't found the time to get done. Applied to the preceding examples:

   - Use your rehearsal break to go someplace nearby to get a greeting card that will give pleasure to someone you like. Leave your caffeine drink and smokes behind.

   - Use your cocktail hour to be creative in your living space: plant something; straighten out a closet or a drawer, looking for things you no longer need or use that might be given to someone who does and can. Skip cocktails and go directly to dinner.

- Explore new food or drink snack menus: what do you know about seeds (pumpkin, sunflower, sesame), dried fruits (raisins, figs, apricots), juices (fruit and vegetable), or teas (spice, herbal, ginseng)?
- During the TV commercials stand and do stretching exercises.
- Instead of watching a TV movie, opt for a good book, one that you find entertaining or informative but without a story line so intense that it will keep you from turning out the light when you begin to feel sleepy.

2. Try to find five areas in your life in which you can increase your physical activity, such as the following:

- Force yourself to take regular breaks from your practice schedule. Plan when the breaks are to occur and militantly follow your plan.
- Whenever you break from your practice schedule, stand tall, stretching your shoulders and back and forward for a few seconds. Stretch your neck and move your head from side to side for a few seconds.
- Park your car further from your destination so that you walk more.
- Get off the elevator at the wrong floor and walk up a flight or two.
- Get off the bus one stop before yours and walk the difference.
- Trot to the doorbell or the telephone whenever they ring.
- Bend and balance to don your footwear rather than sitting in a chair.
- When you greet people, wave by bringing your elbow as high as your ear lobe.
- Stand on tiptoe a few seconds every time you pause to fix your hair or face or to wash your hands.
- Contract your abdomen for the duration of every traffic light you wait through.

3. Program yourself to regard all encounters pertaining to diet, exercise, or physical well-being as worthy of your attention. When others start talking about these subjects, pay attention and draw them out. When you make small talk, bring up subjects such as working out, watching weight, or controlling cholesterol. Watch for media items that deal with health and exercise. You may or may not obtain substantive information from these encounters, but the purpose is not to get data, but rather to raise your level of awareness to build motivation for taking action in your own life.

4. Set up your own personal diet improvement plan and see if you can stick with it for 24 hours. Do not set your goals unreasonably high, for it is important for you to succeed . Know you *can* meet them, and resolve that, come what may, you will. Goals must be simple if they are to work. Here are some examples. You will recognize those that challenge you personally:

- I will eat only fruits and vegetables for 24 hours.
- I will substitute water and juice for caffeine and alcohol for 24 hours.
- I will refrain from second helpings of food for 24 hours.
- I will eat nothing between meals for 24 hours.
- I will limit myself to one cocktail for 24 hours.
- I will eat no sweets for 24 hours.
- I will eat no salty snacks for 24 hours.
- For 24 hours I will try to distinguish between the feeling of being no longer hungry and that of being full, and I will stop eating after the former has been achieved.

Do not extend this exercise for more than 24 hours. Otherwise your psyche might rebel and the game will be lost. If you are successful the first time, then wait a few days and do it again. Gradually you can decrease the in-between periods, provided you begin to get some positive feedback from the exercise in the form of weight loss, increased energy levels, or just an unexpected feeling of general well-being.

chapter four
Conceptualizing and Scheduling Goals

Conceptualizing musical performance goals and planning a procedure to achieve them are often hard to institute. Novices often feel that it is much easier just to wade in and start working. Even those experienced in performance find that their lives are geared to a repetitive cycle of activities designed to prepare and produce performance events. Such a cycle is almost always tied to a timetable of some sort, so that getting ready to perform and meeting the challenge of the next deadline tend to be all-consuming activities often attended by pressure. As a result, these individuals feel they have no time to stop for some vaguely beneficial reorientation.

Yet conceptualization and planning are fundamental to performance success. The energy needed to undertake and sustain any performance is generated by our ability to glimpse an overall picture, to conceive a mega-goal, a larger plan, with as much clarity as possible. Moreover, focusing on a goal and direction renews motivation by helping to pinpoint what it is we are attempting to achieve and by what route we plan to get there. In addition, we garner an understanding of the connections between our immediate tasks and the achievements we hope to forge over the long haul.

Let us deal first with the conceptualization of goals. Later we will examine techniques with which to chart our course, planning the intermediate steps to get where we want to go. Right now let us start by dividing our goals into two categories: long-range and short-term.

Long-Range Goals

For many of us long-term goals are often hard to articulate with any degree of detail. We may have a general sense of what we would like to achieve, but specifics remain elusive. One technique you can use to clarify long-term goals is to ask yourself what you hope to be doing on a Monday morning ten years from now.

Exercise

Visualize getting up and preparing for the day's activities at the beginning of a typical workweek ten years down the pike. Ask yourself a series of questions to help the visualization come alive:

- What will be level of the performance I am involved in? Do I expect to have developed greater technical skill? More effective communication? A greater degree of satisfaction in my quests? More sharply defined expressiveness, beauty, or spirituality?

- How will the characteristics of the audience have grown? Do I plan to be performing, teaching, or interacting with essentially the same group I presently address?

- Do I plan to have acquired outer symbols of my rise as a performer? A larger audience through major media exposure? An academic appointment? An award, prize, or grant that symbolizes distinguished performance?

- Will my vision include a significant service component to my profession, my colleagues, my students, or my public?

- Can I sense how the ten-year snapshot fits into the rise of my career? Am I still at an early stage? A midpoint? Or close to the apex I have set for my life's work?

Having sensed the scenario ten years hence, follow through with a day or two of activity in your imagination. Fill in as much detail as you can imagine in order to sense the degree of excitement and creativity you will experience. Make up specific detail. Since live performance will likely be part of what you do, create an imaginary performance, filling in the location, the venue, the size of the audience, the repertoire, the challenges. If teaching is part of your picture, fill in the type of institution, the level of student, the repertoire, the results you will be striving to achieve. If learning new music is part of the scene, ask yourself what you are working on, for whom. If public service is important to you, ask yourself whom you will be helping, why, and to what extent.

As you perform this exercise, you will probably emerge with renewed energy for pursuing the career you always knew you were born to follow. If your goals ring true right down to the conceptual details, you will experience a rekindling of the fire in your belly. It does not matter that some of the details were of your own fabrication, for what counts in this exercise is *who* you imagine you are and *what* you imagine you are doing. If you experienced a rush with your vision, your goal will have been sufficiently conceptualized, and you are ready to proceed to the consideration of the next steps.

What if, however, your psyche began to squirm? Could it be feeding back to you the mental equivalent of that message often encountered in computer programs after a command has been executed: *Are you sure?*

You attempted to project ahead ten years. Ten years—a decade—can be construed as a significant amount of time. It becomes especially so if you reflect that a lot of famous individuals did not have much more than a decade of adult life in which to make their mark on history: Jesus of Nazareth, Mozart, Joan of Arc. Therefore it is important to be sensitive and open to the possibility of revising your vision if, indeed, something within you suggests uncertainty. Moreover, the number of men and women whose careers have taken right-angle turns, sometimes more than once, is legion. There are those who would, in fact, advise that you continue to do your highly focused musical performance work now but also that you keep an eye out for any fresh opportunities that might be cast your way, in or out of your present specialization. We might ask ourselves how many conductors started out as instrumentalists? Or how many writers, critics, managers, and teachers as practitioners? The probable answer is "most of them."

Thus, if you begin to lose singleness of purpose in the course of this exercise, do not despair. You are, after all, learning something about elements that live somewhere within you. Moreover, this diversity of purpose can actually be turned to good use when detected early and applied to your professional planning. Many experienced professionals would even advise searching for alternative strengths and interests at the earliest possible stage of career development, identifying them, and developing them concurrently with your primary thrust in order to give your profile diversity as you attempt to climb the professional ladder. This concept is explored in more detail in chapter 14.

Short-Term Goals

Let us now consider conceptualizing more immediate goals.

Exercise

Imagine a performance that you might plan to give in the foreseeable future, a few weeks, several months, or a year away. Stimulate your imagination into conceptualizing a highly successful performance, incorporating accurate physical response, emotional intensity, and effective communication. Concentrate on this vision for several seconds. Once it takes definite shape, connect it with your concept of yourself, incorporating your perception of your present level of ability and achievement. As you connect these two concepts, you will begin to sense whatever distance exists between the imagined *you* and your imagined effective performance. The distance you sense, even if imperfectly realized, offers an initial perception around which you can begin to forge a sensible plan of action.

As you set this exercise up in your mind, you need to take into account a number of factors. Some rational voice in the back of your mind may insist on reminding you that in actuality people are seldom able to reach the level of achievement they might hope for. Indeed, that voice may try to instill a vague feeling of insecurity. Just answer the voice by remembering that less-than-perfect realizations of our hopes is a frequently encountered fact of life. We learn to regard such shortfalls as part of being human and learn not to let frustration deter us from staying the course.

Also, visualizing your present level of readiness may be a tough call. It becomes especially difficult because physical response plays an important role in musical performance. If you plan to play or sing music that requires technical skills you have not yet mastered, you may not be able to visualize how much practice you will need. Thus pianists, for example, might have a hard time sensing at what point a Rachmaninoff concerto will be ready to be rehearsed with an orchestra. Similarly, singers learning a leading role in a Verdi opera may find difficulty in projecting when it can be presented as part of a staged production.

Thus it often seems next to impossible to imagine some future point at which executing that task at performance level is facile and confident, much less near-perfect. Moreover what we hope to perform must be projected and adjusted during performance to achieve some abstract or aesthetic goal. Indeed, we may never admit even to being "ready," for we feel there is always room to improve expression or to garner a more deeply rooted feeling of security. Two courses of action will assist in this challenge.

First, study in some detail the performances and careers of role models. Such study encompasses not only appreciation of the performances these role models achieve, but also the training they endured, the setbacks, the triumphs and failures they experienced on the road to their present level. Virtually any career reveals that results were achieved through sustaining goal-directed efforts through many difficult times. Analysis of performance techniques, of strengths and weaknesses, can also build acute observation of detail and sensitivity to effective expressiveness.

It is vital to temper research of this type with the constant reminder that you cannot become a clone of any of your idols, nor should you wish to be. Being influenced by great performers may be beneficial; but aping relegates your own efforts to that of a carbon copy and stifles your individual creative energy. Study, analyze, criticize, admire, but stop short of forging a literal copy.

A second way of helping you to conceptualize your goals is to rely on the advice of those who have experience in achieving such goals, having traveled the route themselves and/or coached others who have done so successfully. You probably have a teacher or coach who helps you on a regular basis. An occasional inquiry on your part as to where you are on the road to your goals can be helpful. But remember, teachers or coaches are not always unbiased in their assessment. Part of their job is to keep you upbeat about your progress. Moreover, those who have watched and helped you grow may tend to emphasize the improvement and downplay the length and/or difficulty of the road ahead.

Thus you should occasionally move outside your immediate circle of training and seek counsel from an outside expert. Many celebrated performers turn to teaching late in their careers. Search for them on the faculties of universities and professional schools. Performers on tour in your area are often willing to take time to hear and advise young musicians. If music competitions are staged nearby, learn who the adjudicators are and contact them. Overcome your shyness in approaching these experts, for most experienced professionals welcome auditioning and advising young musicians.

Seeking such counsel should be a part of your planning process, just as you might seek the opinions of several physicians in making important choices about your health. In fact, you might even prepare for such consultation by regarding the process as similar to a physical examination. Plan to demonstrate your present level of achievement for your consultant, be prepared to reveal your history of training with regard to a given skill, and be as clear as possible about your immediate and long-range goals. Your advisor should be able to assess your present level, formulate a fairly clear picture of your aptitude, and project that picture onto the goals you outline. The result should yield a picture of the level you need to achieve to give the type of successful performance that will serve your goal, as well as an estimate of how much time it will take you to get the job accomplished.

In seeking such advice, keep in mind that there are good gurus and less-than-good gurus. Your advisor, like your physician, can offer only a carefully considered opinion. Most of those in a position to offer such advice will be quick to qualify their impressions, for they know the myriad of influences that shape performance goals. If you do receive a report that seems discouraging, you may want to remind yourself that such is only one person's opinion, and many such assessments have been proven wrong in the face of the determination and subsequent success of the aspirant. If, however, two or three professionals of good repute begin to say approximately the same things, then it seems the better part of wisdom to listen and plan accordingly.

Establish a Game Plan

Once you have conceptualized your long- and short-term goals and made an attempt to sense what has to take place for you to feel ready to perform, you now need to construct a more detailed game plan. Perhaps these goals were so lofty that you are daunted by what you have set out to do, or you don't know quite where to begin. It is at just this point that the next step should enter the picture.

Outline

Outline the various stages involved in preparing for your goal. An outline will help to break down into segments the process you are about to undertake. First, set up a series of interim goals, markers along the way. These psychological breathers provide points where you can pause to appreciate the distance you have come, check your bearings, and, if necessary, make adjustments before you begin the next segment.

Setting up these interim goals often reveals what must be completed first to lay a solid foundation and also shows the logical sequence of steps you need to follow. Such organization may save you from some awful moment when it dawns on you that you should have done one task before you undertook some other task and now you have to double back and fill in gaps.

Several guidelines may help you in setting up these interim goals before we turn to some useful examples.

- Set up *all* of the segments that lead to the completion of the project and your final performance. Avoid the tendency to stop after you have set the first one, two, or three steps to be taken. If you fall short of total organization, you may fail to uncover logical sequences that make doing some tasks before others beneficial. You also court the danger of dimming the vision of the final goal and getting stuck on interim activities that have become comfortable.

- Set beginning goals that fall within your present skill capabilities, so that you feel confident in being able to accomplish the first steps. Doing this gives you the benefit of positive feedback early in the process, and the feeling that you have at least accomplished something in preparing for your ultimate performance.

- As you set up these goals, ask if some should precede others, which skills might be regarded as basic to your entire undertaking, and which skills learned early in the process might make achieving later goals easier or quicker.

- Create interim goals, small and large, so it will be easy for you to sense where you are at any time. These provide you with an ongoing fix, giving up-to-date readings of both accomplishment and direction, very useful psychological tools.

For those who initially find this structuring somehow limiting, consider that most people organize their everyday lives along these lines. Think, for example, of a commute you make frequently. You have probably already divided it into segments, noting some point as being about halfway, others as marking the completion of the first significant segment, still others that signal that you are close to your destination. We unitize such divisions when we think of an hour of time, marking the half hour, the quarter hour, and the smaller units. Similarly, we mark off the twenty-four-hour day into two segments of twelve hours each, and provide markers in the form of various kinds of breaks for lunch, coffee, classes, appointments, or other scheduled activities.

Different kinds of performance goals lend themselves in varying degrees to the kind of structuring you need to do. Performance based on musical techniques you already possess simply requires assembling and organization. Performances that require new intellectual or technical skills, such as playing music by composers whose style is unfamiliar, are tougher to nail down, but even they can be facilitated through these exercises.

Let us examine an example. A singer has been invited to fill a vacancy in a local vocal quartet that specializes in vintage musical theater. Although this quartet is homegrown, it has achieved a widespread reputation as an outstanding group at community functions, and the quartet has decided to enter a national competition in two months. The vacancy occurred when one of the members moved out of the area to take a new job. The new singer was chosen because she had been singing locally for two years and had garnered a small circle of admirers. Moreover, as a close friend of one of the group's members, she had on occasion helped with transporting props and costumes.

In accepting this new challenge, the singer realizes that her physical stamina will have to be increased to meet the demands of the singing and stage movement. Her current exercise routine of an occasional leisurely stroll will have to be escalated. She outlines a training program leading up to the performance by conceptualizing the following:

■ Take a short, brisk walk once a day, increasing both distance and speed methodically. During the walks, engage in breathing exercises.

■ In addition, start a period of more focused exercise three times per week, starting with an easy stretching program and after a week working into entry-level videotape aerobics or exercise programs.

■ Spend two hours a day practicing the music, setting aside an extra thirty minutes a day to memorize the lyrics.

■ Begin private vocal coaching sessions twice a week and movement sessions once a week. In the first week learn or review basic vocal techniques of warming up, tone production, text articulation, as well as the songs to be sung. Work also on stage movement exercises designed to build grace and flexibility. Begin work on the movement specific to numbers.

■ In the second week of lessons, begin performing segments of the song texts from memory, as well as the choreography, putting these elements together by increments.
First rehearsal with the group at the beginning of the third week.

■ Continue individual exercise, practice routines, and group rehearsals until performance time.

Here is another example. A university graduate student decides to enter an international piano competition, for he believes that winning or placing will enhance recognition as a rising concert pianist. As he reviews the rules of the competition, he realizes that he has studied music that will fulfill about two-thirds of the required repertoire but that he will have to learn several new works to advance through the various stages of the event. He has five months in which to prepare. He outlines the following:

■ Select repertoire immediately, enlisting your piano teacher's advice.

■ Plan what you will bring to each lesson scheduled before the competition, setting aside the last three lessons for performances of large segments of the required repertoire.

■ Boost practice time to five hours per day by meeting with an academic advisor to plan a light course load for the upcoming semester.

■ Make a daily practice schedule that allots a specific amount of time for technical exercises, reviewing old pieces, and learning new ones. Break down the new material into segments and set timelines for being able to play each, first with music, then without. Leave three hours per week unscheduled, as a cushion to address problems that were not solved in the allotted time.

- Integrate your daily practice schedule into a weekly cycle, planning time for schoolwork, rest, recreation, meditation, and life's necessities.

- Set deadlines by which each piece must be synthesized, memorized, and ready for performance, earlier dates for review music and later ones for new music. Deadlines should be approximately one month before trial performance dates to allow for stabilization.

- Arrange and set dates for as many trial performances as possible (informally for classmates, in your piano teacher's weekly recital class, in local assisted living facilities, for a gathering of family and friends).

- Explore the campus gym and set up a program of an hour of vigorous exercise three times a week.

- Revise your diet to emphasize high-energy, low-carb, low-fat foods.

- Break your schedule every two weeks by planning a day away from your usual environment (hiking, beach, museum).

In these two examples the performers had already garnered a measure of achievement in their music-making, and their tasks were structured with timetables. The less prior experience you have, obviously, the more difficult it will be to create a realistic timetable. If your experience is minimal, a realistic outline can be tricky and may require some guesswork. Such a limitation does not, however, negate the efficacy of the process, so you should attempt to forge a plan understanding that you may be estimating many of its components..

Within the limits of a deadline, should it be part of the picture, it is better to allow too much time to complete a segment rather than not enough. If you reach a point where you feel "ready" before your schedule suggests moving to the next phase, then you can congratulate yourself on being ahead of schedule and adjust accordingly. If, on the other hand, you find yourself regularly falling behind, try to avoid negative psychological consequences, such as feelings of pressure or futility, by making the necessary adjustments quickly. Adopt a tough-mindedness that does not allow you to exaggerate the meaning of such adjustments, to assign self-blame, or to distort your delay into a failure forecast. Accept the situation, make the adjustments, and continue working with a new timeline in place.

Note that the foregoing examples included time for general conditioning. Be sure not to bypass important initial steps in your eagerness to tear into the meat of the challenge. You have to exercise a degree of discipline in order to include all the necessary preparatory stages. Some part of you may feel that it is better just to go for it. If you take that route, remember that you court the very real possibility that your progress will be delayed later if you have to go back and "fix" problems engendered by your haste. If the performers in the two examples did not take the time to get in shape physically through exercise, they might have ended up being incapacitated later as a result of intensive rehearsals. Or if they did not set aside time to memorize their music early in the preparation, they might ultimately have had to assimilate so much so rapidly that they became overwhelmed and confused.

If at all possible, you should try to incorporate into your timetable an extra measure of time for performance preparation and drill in the few days just before the performance. If the performance is added to other responsibilities such as going to school, tending to family needs, or earning a living, you may not be able to encroach upon your workday schedule to any greater extent that you already have. If, however, you can invest extra time, make the upcoming performance the focal point of your day for several days; the result is often beneficial. During this time of intense focus, the mind will gradually relegate other concerns of living to ancillary spots in your consciousness and will elevate this performance to a position of prime importance. Such temporary prioritization is useful, for when performance pressure, nervousness, or stage fright enter the picture, the mind is able to hang on with more tenacity to its recently adopted focus, and concentration during the actual performance is often rendered stronger.

Until you gain experience in setting up timetables, seek advice from several sources. There may be written documentation or professional lore as to the amount of time a given musical project usually takes. Ask others who have undertaken similar projects, keeping in mind that rates of development vary for different individuals. Such differences are usually not indicative of probable success or quality of work. (The quality issue will be taken up later in chapter 8. Although haste sometimes contributes to slipshod work, quality control is a far more complex matter involving several components in addition to time, as will be seen.)

Once again, seek advice from teachers or coaches who have observed many patterns of growth, both the accelerated and the deliberate, for they will more often than not be able to offer sound advice with regard to projecting a reasonable schedule. Finally, if you have engaged in similar undertakings in the past, ask yourself how much time they took previously, taking into account that you may be a quicker study now. In addition, compare the dimensions of the projects, as well as the amount of time you were able to invest earlier with the amount you now plan.

Structure Your Time

After you have constructed an overall plan with a timetable, it is usually wise to ask yourself just where in your daily routine this block of time is going to fit. Schedule it there, and then try to be as specific as possible about what you hope to achieve each time you work. Single-session goals are appropriate in varying degrees depending on what you are attempting to prepare. If, for example, you are at the note-learning stage, set up daily segments based on what you are able to cover in the first few practice sessions. If, however, you are attempting to synthesize a long, arduous work, your daily goals may have to be tempered by the physical stamina the work demands. To support this growth of stamina, you may be working to improve your physical condition, and your routine in that effort probably will have its own increasingly challenging aspects already programmed. If your preparation involves conceptualizing the emotional content of the music, you may, indeed, not be able to determine how far toward realizing your final goal you will travel in a given session.

Similarly, if you are trying to stabilize your performance of music that is almost ready but is subject to mishap as you perform it, then the amount of drill may be hard to calculate and the process seemingly endless. In fact, one often has to invest more time than seems reasonable to achieve this stability. The famous Spanish pianist Alicia de Larrocha once described the frustration of this investment amusingly in a lecture given at a summer piano festival. She likened the process to dealing with an erratic soft drink machine. She described "putting the money in" and "waiting for the Coca-cola." Nothing. Putting the money in again and waiting for the Coca-cola. Nothing. Again and again and again. "I must wait patiently days and days and days," she said sadly. "Then one day." she cried happily, her face lighting up. "At last! The Coca-cola!"

These working sessions can often benefit if you attempt to formulate exactly what you wish to accomplish. Keeping track of even minuscule progress and quantifying the time invested can bring a sense of progress to such work, provided you can do so with an upbeat mind-set, resisting frustration.

The absence of such a focus often encourages open-ended practice. At first this open-ended work may be attended by a vaguely defined conviction that benefits will result somewhere down the road. Later, that conviction may evolve into frustration over the fact that improvement cannot be clearly recognized. General, open-ended work is analogous to resolving to eat wisely and exercise a little more as a means of getting yourself ready for the Olympics. Such activities may be beneficial, but they are neither sharply enough focused nor intense enough to get the job done.

No matter what the component of the preparation process, determine what you expect to accomplish in the hour or hours ahead. If you can, come up with a plan in light of the type of activity you are undertaking; then the exercise will have served its purpose. If you find that some phase of your work seems impossible to structure in this way, you will at least have identified special difficulties in this phase. And probably too you will have logged in the back of your mind some approximation of how much time it will take to get through this segment of the work.

Structuring in the way described here offers several advantages, but it also contains pitfalls. The advantages have already been observed or implied:

- Encouraging an awareness of where you are in your developmental process.
- Frequently clarifying which segments should come before which other segments.
- Helping you to form a realistic expectation with regard to the investment of time it will take to get ready for your performance.
- Helping you to keep focus and momentum in each session you undertake.
- Providing psychological perks by enabling you to note the completion of small work segments.

The downside of structuring, however, needs to be considered as well. Excessive attention to structuring can lead to obsessive rigidity in maintaining a schedule or to overconcern for results. Remember that you created the schedule, so it is not carved in stone. Realize that you may need to revise it from time to time for a variety of reasons:

- Some unexpected problem surfaces that delays your progress.
- You find you have allotted too little or too much time for a given phase of your work.
- You discover a new technique or expressive device that you deem so valuable that you wish to delay pursuit of your main agenda in order to practice and integrate this new device.
- You experience some kind of breakthrough or sudden inspiration that you need to follow through with before the light dims, thereby altering your previously planned agenda.

The last concept is particularly important. As we work, we develop a psychological affinity to a multitude of aspects our project. The mind has a wonderful way of making connections, realizing relationships, racing down new avenues of creativity, often unannounced and unexpectedly. We call these breakthroughs, inspirations, visions, or realizations. We need to develop a residual sensitivity to this aspect of our consciousness and adopt an expectant attitude, one that awaits the next such illumination. You need to agree with yourself in advance that the instant you sense this wonderful phenomenon is about to take place, you will without hesitation set aside any other structuring or planning and clear the field for this windfall. We revel in glorious moments, and they must be embraced without the least recalcitrance, lest the creative juices dry up before we can capture their essence.

※

Hopefully you will now feel that you need to spend some time conceptualizing and setting goals, developing a plan, and scheduling your time. Perhaps the answers you initially come up with will be neither definitive nor permanent, but attempting to forge them will give you a clearer picture of the goals you seek, the journey you must take to achieve them, and the configuration of the road itself. Such knowledge both defines purpose and stimulates motivation.

chapter five
Keeping Preparation Fresh and Focused

New performance projects usually inspire excitement. The challenges inherent in the project, the initiation of a fresh practice routine, and the prospect of a rewarding performance down the road all combine to generate excitement and anticipation. You may even feel a period of euphoria.

Earmarks of this honeymoon will be an eagerness to start practicing each day, an attitude that relishes the tasks and anticipates the progress you expect. As your preparation continues over days or weeks, however, you will probably find that the energy and freshness of this initial attitude wanes. Diminishing momentum is likely because preparation is usually full of repetitive patterns and the frustrations that go along with the acquisition of new skills or physical responses. After a while, daily execution of the same or similar patterns often results in a sense of weariness and perhaps even downright revulsion. Such feelings give rise to boredom or feelings of "going stale."

Thus it is impossible to bask indefinitely in the glow of initial euphoric enthusiasm. The end of the honeymoon period is, after all, inevitable in life. On the other hand, there are several ways to stimulate energy and freshness. Some of these methods have already been mentioned. Pausing to appreciate the distance you have traveled, learning to sense improvement, and taking pride in short-term achievements, for example, all contribute to the maintenance of a high energy level.

This chapter will explore other techniques for stimulating energy and focus. These are the following:

- Changing your physical state
- Warm-up exercises
- Changing the order of work patterns

55

- Changing your work environment
- Pep talks
- Analysis
- Shifting your learning pattern

Changing Your Physical State

Changing your physical state is the simplest of the techniques, and it works best as an antidote for short-term feelings of sagging interest. We see this in operation when breaks or intermissions are inserted into programs of some length. Such breaks relieve the lethargy borne of inactivity or sitting for long periods of time. We get up out of our seats, move around a little, get the blood flowing, take a drink of water, and we then feel ready to settle back for another period of time.

Such breaks are just as beneficial during work sessions, but we often forget to include them. Because such intervals interrupt our concentration and progress, we often resist them, continuing to work past the point of maximum effectiveness. Eventually the mind and body complain, and we develop a headache, visual blurring, muscular aches and pains, or a general feeling of fuzziness. Not until these symptoms of strain present themselves do we break off our activity. By this time, however, we may have temporarily damaged our ability to focus at maximum effectiveness, and longer periods of recuperation are required. A far better procedure is to plan changes of physical state before symptoms become noticeable, for most people every hour or so. Taking such breaks will extend considerably both your ability to concentrate and your feeling of well-being.

- Use the break time to maximize your change in physical state. Engage in light exercise-like movement: walking around, stretching, rolling your head, swinging your arms, and bending.

- Deep breathing is one of the most long-standing, effective techniques for revitalization, and it is often overlooked. Sound physiological reasons support this activity, for forcing oxygen into your bloodstream initiates a process that eliminates the poisonous by-produces of physical and mental activity. Few of us in the West have practiced deep breathing to the extent that we are good at the technique, and as a result when we try it in passing our breaths tend to be too few, too rapid, and too shallow. Study the proper method of deep breathing and add it to your arsenal of tension-relieving devices. It is time well invested.

- Chapter 1 discussed the fact that according to many philosophical systems, mental states determine reality. Belief in this tenet gives rise to the technique of pretending to feel the way you would like to feel. On the surface this appears to be Pollyanna-like nonsense. We generally accept the fact that if we feel weary, out of focus, frustrated, or even depressed, then that is, indeed, how we are, and simply telling ourselves not to be that way stands a poor chance of changing reality. Yet those who have experimented with the technique of *pretending*, both psychologists and laypersons, report surprisingly beneficial results.

The key to the technique lies in your ability to adopt the external symbols of the mood you want to institute. To replace a weary, downbeat mood with one that is upbeat and energized, assume a posture of attention, hold your head high, and place an artificial smile on your face. While holding these external symbols in place, remember a specific time whenyou felt absolutely wonderful and highly energized, bursting with enthusiasm and happiness. Project yourself mentally into that time and place while holding on to all of those external, physical signs. Use your will power to hold that package in place for several minutes. When you release it, you will find that you will not, in fact, return to your former state but will be able to keep in place some, and perhaps most, of the feelings you pretended to experience. The long-term effectiveness of this exercise may be somewhat limited by overall physical tiredness or mental anxiety, but it can almost always offer temporary relief, and if you are not totally exhausted or excessively worried, it can improve both your outlook and your energy level.

Warm-Up Exercises

Warm-up exercises are an integral part of many physical activities. Athletes, dancers, and musicians all warm up as a part of their regular routine, by jogging, stretching, or running scales, respectively. We even warm up some types of machinery before we put it to work. An activity that demands movement benefits from a period of general or simple movement before more highly complex, job-specific demands.

Warm-up exercises are often repetitive and relatively easy to execute. As a result, they can quickly become routine. This is not all bad, because, after all, their purpose is to prepare you for more focused activity. On the other hand, they need to be imbued with enough energy to serve their purpose. It is a good idea to vary the patterns of warm-up routines, and also to shift mental focus from day to day. If you are using scales, change the musical focus from day to day to tease your mind into listening more closely; for example, concentrate on legato one day, on tone production the next, on rhythmic precision the third, on dynamic control the next, and so on. This procedure will not only help you stay interested in your warm-up period but will provide short periods of time when your complete concentration is on refining your musicality in some way. The result is that you improve your basic musicianship and technique for later, more focused demands.

Changing the Order of Work Patterns

Thinking about such variations in your warm-up routine forms a prelude to the next technique, changing the order of your work patterns to maintain a high energy level and sharp concentration. When first establishing work habits, it is often helpful to create a program of activities that you run through at every practice session. For example, your plan might consist of warm-up exercises, technique-building material (etudes, vocalizes, or working on problem passages from repertoire), working on new repertoire, and reviewing old repertoire. Such a routine can help build consistent work habits and ensure that you don't neglect some important segment of your work. It also helps you conceptualize an overall plan of what it is you are working toward, giving you a sense of where you are in your daily task, how much you are accomplishing, and in what kind of time frame. All of this suggests good organization and clear-headed focus—up to a point.

The moment this menu begins to become predictable and dull is the moment its benefits are reduced, perhaps even to the point of becoming counterproductive. As your mind registers ever increasing boredom, your enthusiasm and energy wane, and your tedium becomes an open invitation to sloppiness or mistakes. It behooves you to trick your mind into staying engaged. One way of doing this is to set up a series of program variants, so that the activity appears to be new and fresh. Vary the order in which you do your work, if at all possible, putting first today what you did last yesterday. Even trading places of adjacent activities can be helpful.

We vary the patterns of our everyday life all the time. How often do we make a conscious effort to vary our meals? We try new recipes. We eat Chinese tonight, choose Mex-Tex the next, and feel like having prime rib the next. We thus constantly tempt our appetites and often discover new, tasty foods in the process. Some of us make changes in our wardrobe to inject variety into the day. We amuse ourselves with color coordination or wearing things appropriate to a holiday season. If we get bored walking around the block one way, we reverse the route, changing our perspective and sometimes seeing things we hadn't noticed before. Sometimes we even add flourishes to routine activity. For example, the cook who turns the omelet by flipping it into the air has perfected this flourish as a fun diversion from the routine task of preparing food.

Applied to a rehearsal or practice schedule, such variation might result in changing the order of the pieces or segments you rehearse on a daily basis. If you started with Bach yesterday, start with Beethoven today. If you started practicing at the beginning of the piece yesterday, work on the coda first today. Rehearse the finale rather than the opening number. If yesterday you engaged in a period of repetitive drill, change something about it today, be it tempo, organization of sections, or type of expression. If you were very involved in the physical aspect of a performance yesterday, start by thinking quietly about interpretative goals today, conceptualizing your completed performance from another perspective.

If you are at the point of playing or singing from memory, return to your score to cultivate a new set of questions about its demands or implications. Why did its creator indicate these directions, those dynamics, that accent, this crescendo, that harmonic change? Did the creator ponder other possible choices but come up with the documented one instead? Play or sing a phrase with a different emphasis to stimulate a fresh interpretation. Examine your reaction to the music by trying to discover a different response from the first one that came to mind. Are you really projecting the essence of the music you now seem to know so well? How do the composer's directions fit in with what went before and what comes after? You may or may not experience daily breakthroughs or revelations with such exercises, but thinking up such questions keeps your mind active, keeps your creative juices flowing, and banishes boredom.

Knowing that this kind of effort and imagination reaps multiple benefits, we still sometimes forget to institute these variants. We may feel we don't have time for anything but pure drill, or a misguided seriousness of purpose may deter us from experimenting with changing patterns or whimsical speculation. Perhaps you have not used variation enough to experience fully its value, but such exercises do serve a purpose. Rightly used, they can stimulate renewed interest in the music that needs to be practiced, be a source of passing pleasure, and even act as a catalyst to significant insights.

Changing Your Work Environment

Similarly your mind can be refreshed by a change of your work environment. We see this phenomenon all around us. Holding classes outside on the lawn occasionally provides a welcome change, as does eating in a new restaurant or even eating in a new location at home. Seek out new areas in which to practice, if possible. In a music school you may be able to switch practice rooms. Sometimes singers and instrumentalists do not require a piano, so it becomes easy to choose a fresh practice area.. Even if your practice area must be more or less permanent, it is sometimes possible to add personal items that suggest something different from standard issue and humanize the area. These personal touches may seem insignificant, even frivolous. Yet the fact that such items are seen so frequently in workplaces outside music is testimony to both their efficacy and the respite they offer through momentary pauses to acknowledge the beauty of a flower, the face of a loved one, or the humor of a cartoon.

Changes should be used occasionally or in moderation if they are to remain effective for stimulation. If you hold class on the lawn or shift your dining area too frequently, the change no longer remains a perk. If you decorate your studio with too many personal items, it begins to look overdone or junky, and the respite from the momentary contemplation of your personal treasure diminishes as a result of the clutter.

Pep Talks

The value and effectiveness of self-generated pep talks probably gets mixed reviews in the minds of many. On one hand, it seems obvious that devoting the time and effort to creating pep pills for yourself would be helpful. You review how important it is to continue working efficiently at a given task. You tell yourself how much fun it is, what great benefits will accrue, how much has already been accomplished toward your performance goal, the improvement you have made in your skills, and the original motivation behind the desire to gear up for performance. It stands to reason that this kind of thinking ought to provide ongoing energy and focus.

The fact is, however, that these pep talks often lose their effectiveness when the serious doldrums hit. At such points we often express sentiments such as "I keep trying to talk myself into practicing," or "I just don't seem to be able to make any progress on this piece." For such times, pep talks might be supplemented with the aforementioned changes in physical state. When such talks are part of a package that includes effective posture control, breathing, movement, or exercise, their value increases. Even if self-generated pep talks don't seem to be eroding your feelings of lethargy, they may be preventing you fromsinking even deeper into your funk. Moreover, you may be sure that if you abandon efforts toward positive motivation altogether, the negative opposite is very apt to rush into the vacuum, and with considerably more power.

Group pep talks, interestingly enough, enjoy a firmly rooted reputation for effectiveness. What team sport would be complete without the coach's pep talk before the game? The corporate world invests heavily in seminars, professionally planned pep talks designed to increase productivity. Belief in the effectiveness of such activities is so strong and demand so great that an entire industry flourishes around such programs. One might, therefore, pose the following question: if individual self-generated pep talks often seem benign, why do group pep talks seem to work so much better?

Part of the answer lies in the fact that individuals generate negative feedback even while attempting to administer pep talks to themselves, whereas in group environments such feedback can be virtually expurgated amid group momentum and interaction. Another part of the answer is, of course, the expertise and motivation of those who lead the group. Coaches and corporate seminar leaders are trained, and, if they are good, they produce results. After all, their professional success depends on demonstrating effectiveness. This activity is *their* performance. When you generate your own pep talks, you are put in the position of being both the physician and the patient. You don't have the desired drive or the motivation to begin with, or otherwise you wouldn't need the pep talk.

We can tap these experts through one-on-one assistance, group classes, or published material. Many people hire experts privately for short periods of time. We take music lessons, play in master classes, or hire coaches to help us polish the details of our work. However, the expense of such one-on-one assistance limits its availability to only very small amounts of time, at least for the majority of people. During these sessions we can pick up information and procedures that will help us when we work alone, but we must still shoulder the responsibility of maintaining momentum for most of our work time, especially if we work on a daily basis.

Self-help and motivational books, manuals, or tapes were touched upon earlier in our assessment of basic self-image. These aids can be helpful for short periods of time, and investing in them may prove to be worthwhile. Their disadvantages are twofold, however: since they are prepared for a general audience, they may not address your specific problem, and, as was noted earlier, with repeated consultation these materials eventually become so familiar that their effectiveness declines.

Even so, with all of the pitfalls and redundancy, pep talks remain a valuable tool that you should use regularly. As with many other repetitive patterns, we tend to be lulled into doubting the impact of an activity until we stop doing it. Moreover, cajoling yourself into being upbeat and energetic feeds into the continuing process of building your self-image. That process dovetails with the fundamental concept that was discussed in chapter 1, and it will return again in the final mental preparation of the eve of your performance (chapter 9).

Analysis

Let us now consider the role of analysis as a way of maintaining momentum in performance preparation. To some extent analysis is inherent in concentration, so it operates at some level in everything we focus on. We often analyze on several levels at once, scrutinizing the content of the music we are mastering, the dynamics of our ongoing relationship with it, and the quality of the product being amassed as a result of our efforts. During this process, analysis operates like the zoom lens of a camera; it can operate at extremely close range, magnifying details for organization or assimilation, or it can encompass larger segments, even the whole of the performance, garnering comprehensive information.

Analysis connotes something intellectually or research oriented, suggesting a process, an efficacious, useful, and supportive process. When we take the time to analyze, we presumably learn more about the music we want to present, and we assume that that knowledge will translate into the ability to perform it more powerfully. All of this seems so obvious, in fact, that we seldom stop to debate the issue. In reality, however, for analysis to function as the support tool we assume it is, we should pause at the outset to ask several questions about the process:

- What it is we want to glean out of the analytical process?
- Why do we want it?
- How much time is involved in making this analysis?
- To what extent might this analysis inhibit our imaginative, creative input?

If you are conducting the analysis out of your personal curiosity, the question of what you want to get out of it is probably fairly clear. You determine that certain information would be useful, and you zoom in on the material, digging until you uncover whatever it is you seek. For example, if the earliest sources of the music you are learning present conflicting interpretative indications, then scrutinizing the editorial history of such discrepancies might help you decide which set of directions to follow.

Isolating what you really want, however, can become problematic.

Present-day research, supplemented by references available on the Internet, may offer so much data that you find it difficult to maintain focus on the desired information. You may seek the proverbial needle in a haystack, and you now have the resources to find it rapidly. By the same token you do not need to know the number of haystacks in the world, or the dollar amount of revenue earned last year by the needle manufacturing industry. You may be presented with all of this information and more in your quest and may become sidetracked. "Wow! Look at how many haystacks there are in Kansas as opposed to New Mexico," or "I never realized that the manufacturing of needles was so important to the Swiss economy." You need to stop yourself, remember what it is you really want, and sort it out promptly.

It may be useful at some point to read C. P. E. Bach's entire *Essay on the True Art of Keyboard Playing,* but you do not need to do that in order to learn how to execute an eighteenth-century ornament. It may indeed enhance your performance of all Richard Strauss's music to delve into the underlying psychology of the persona in his operas, but you do not need that information to understand the meaning of the text in one of his art songs. Many pianists give effective performances of Liszt's "Vallée d'Obermann" without ever having read the Senancour novel on which it is based, notwithstanding the increasing understanding such reading might engender.

Closely related to keeping focus on what you want out of your analysis is the question of why you want it. To some extent the answer must have been obvious as you thought of what you were going to search for or analyze. On the other hand, pausing to focus directly on why you undertook this analysis may suggest other helpful questions or observations:

- What is the relationship between the knowledge you will gain from this analysis and your final performance goal? If you are analyzing musical structure to learn how to pace a lengthy work, the relationship is direct and obvious. If, on the other hand, you are studying the anatomy of the body to help you understand how to sing or play an instrument, the relationship seems less direct. Although such knowledge may lead to an awareness of how to care for and handle your body in performance, not undertaking such analysis will not necessarily prevent you from effective, even outstanding performance.

- To what extent will the information from the analysis have to be integrated or digested before it becomes useful? Analysis of musical structure leads to awareness that rests beneath the center of the consciousness as you play or sing. It resides in a secondary position to make room for the more immediate concern of producing the music. Similarly, when you play or sing, you need to think about the musical result rather than how your body is operating.

- Are there by-products of the analysis that might be counterproductive? Just mentioned was the fact that analysis might lead to a misplaced focus that would inhibit throwing yourself into the act itself when the time came. Even if you manage to subdue focus on the analytical product at the appropriate moment, an intellectual residue may color the tone of the performance. The casual observer might assess such a performance as being "cool and calculated" rather than "wild and passionate," or the performer as taking "an intellectual approach" rather than an "emotional" one. You must ask yourself what effect you really want and work to erase any counteracting residue the analytical process might have left behind.

You also need to assess how much time analysis will take and whether the time invested is worth the benefit you expect to reap. You must sort out irrelevant data, consider how desired data bear on the final performance, and relegate analysis to an appropriate level of your consciousness during performance. If you begin to sense that this process might consume so much time that progress toward your final performance bogs down or gets hopelessly behind schedule, you have to consider limiting the analysis in some way.

Common sense will usually combine with pragmatism to guide you in setting those limits. For example, you might stop once you have an understanding of sonata-allegro structure in a classical sonata, but never go so far as to learn how that structure evolved. You might consult a simplified sketch and gain a general understanding of the anatomical support system you use in your performance, but you may never be able to name the small muscles involved. Often limited analysis will provide just as good support as detailed analysis, and setting appropriate limitations can save valuable time.

Finally you need to assess the extent that an analytical process might inhibit imaginative creative input. It has already been mentioned that analytical fallout might color the ultimate effect of a performance. You also have to beware that you do not bask in the analytical process to the extent that you do not give free reign to your imagination. You need to construct flights of fantasy that are not supported by analysis and sometimes need to improvise without fearing mistakes. In fact, your goal will become focusing on expressing the music to such a degree that you are conscious only of the immediate involvement.

Thus during the preparation process, you need windows of time in which your primary purpose is to test how far you can go in creating what is generally regarded as impossible. Dare to seek out relationships that seem remote on the surface, or to establish connections that heretofore have not been conceived. Such windows of time should be scheduled and regarded as refreshing opportunities to let your mind run free. Such periods may, indeed, be the catalysts that trigger your most individual and valuable ideas.

Shifting Your Learning Patterns

Having looked at the advantages and disadvantages of analyzing, let us now turn our attention to shifting learning patterns. We have already explored techniques to combat tedium and loss of concentration when we must repeat material to master it. The creation of new learning patterns does not refer to these techniques, but rather is a conscious attempt to improve our ability to assimilate or respond to new material. To do this, we must begin by taking a look at the way we each learn, discover where our individual tendencies lie, and then experiment with enough boldness to improve and expand those patterns.

What are some of these patterns? For some of us, the learning process begins with an overview of the whole picture, or as much of it as we can hold in our minds. Continuing work then consists of filling in and perfecting details, much as you might decorate a Christmas tree or build a house. For others, the process is more a sequential filling in of details as you go along, continuing to perfect them daily. Those who learn this way tend not to move on to the next segment until the present level of ability has reached some minimum standard, then they assemble or synthesize the segments as a final step, much as you might bake a cake or make a movie.

To some extent the nature of the task itself dictates the basic approach, and both approaches must be used to some degree. Over and above this, however, is your own predilection for how you approach your work. Some of us are more comfortable getting an idea of the whole and then filling in the fine details; others like a piecemeal approach and pull it all together near the end. These two approaches have been elevated to the status of learning theories, and psychologists have touted the virtues of one over the other. You need to use both to some extent. In some cases, the overall approach (one psychologists often refer to as *Gestalt*) works best where some kind of framework is needed in order to accommodate the details. In other cases, the overall framework may not be possible. For example, acquiring physical patterns or learning new technical skills must often proceed by stages, because simple responses may have to be established before more rapid or complex ones can be executed.

Thus the approach to a task may be directed by the inherent nature of the task itself. On the other hand, you need to take a look at your own tendencies, determine to what extent you depend on one approach or the other, and assess if you can improve your preparation by working against the grain. Let 's look at these two tendencies at close range to consider their strengths and weaknesses.

If we tend to work piecemeal, we wade into a long preparation process, often determined to perfect each detail as we go along. We linger and repeat, practice and perfect. We may invoke imagination and discipline to create a high level of performance for each segment before permitting ourselves to move on to the next. Thus we may experience positive feedback as we assess the quality of the first completed segment. So what could be wrong with creating a string of highly polished gems?

Well, for one thing, you may find that dedication to the perfect segment may cost an extra measure of time. Some things will grow even after we leave them and move on. It is possible to plant the seed, return to water and tend it from time to time, and find that it grows up and bears fruit by itself. Tending it beyond these minimal needs is an unwise investment of time and robs us of energy that could be used for other plantings. You may also find that after you have taken the time to perfect many segments, a sense of disunity begins to form. The material seems fragmented, and when you try to bring continuity to your presentation, you experience roughness in moving from one segment to the next. Even when you manage to improve the flow of the material, the performance still leaves the impression of a series of vignettes; it fails to gather an overall momentum or to deliver an impact born of singleness of purpose.

Many will feel nevertheless that having to synthesize at a later stage is worthwhile in order to preserve the order and security that comes from working in small segments The shortcomings can be remedied. You must simply take the time to step back from your work and envision the overall effect you want to create. Alter details in ways that contribute more clearly to that overall concept. Conceptualize longer segments. Perfect transitions from one segment to the next. Plan pacing that takes into account the total impression. Working piecemeal has its virtues, but you may have to synthesize the work before your performance presentation can realize its maximum potential..

Working from the perspective of the whole offers a different set of strengths and pitfalls. Here, right from the start you push through from the beginning to the end of your performance to sense the dimensions of its entirety and to capture its overall effect. If details fall by the wayside, if there are blank spots, you temporarily ignore them and forge ahead. You thus garner some sense of the totality near the beginning of your work and often experience a sense of excitement and adventure as you simulate the performance you will eventually give. At some point, however, you must go back and perfect the details or fill in the blank spots. This work may seem unusually tedious after the headiness of simulating the whole, and so it may take an extra measure of discipline. Moreover, in your attempt to keep moving at early stages, you may even have picked up some patterns that have to be corrected. Mistakes and oversights in a score may have been imprinted on you, or physical responses may have been bootlegged in inefficient or harmful ways. Making the necessary corrections may require extensive drill and cost extra time.

Instituting a pattern of change back and forth between these approaches can bring valuable benefits. For example, you might leaf through a work, hearing it inwardly but not actually making any music. In this way you simulate a brilliant, expressive performance, sensing its overall intent as well as its musical and technical components. Then you might work in segments, perfecting technical details and noting every mark of expression in the score. At some later point you might attempt a run-through of the music to experience the feel and excitement of it. The inaccuracies that will likely occur need to be curtailed without delay, so you return to working with small segments, often more slowly and deliberately, correcting and perfecting.

Changing your learning patterns in this way offers variety that dispels boredom or tedium. Whenever you feel you are getting bogged down with detail, lift your sights and do a trial run. Whenever you feel frustrated that your simulated performances lack precision and completeness, return to perfecting a segment. On one hand you can enjoy the security and satisfaction of doing small segments of detailed work. On the other, you can sense the excitement and adventure of the performance you aspire to achieve. Training yourself to use the best of both patterns, regardless of which is more comfortable, can refresh your efforts, stimulate your creativity, and ultimately strengthen your final performance.

✦

In dealing with the rigors of preparing for your performance, remember that virtually every performer comes to the point of having to use plain old-fashioned discipline to keep the process going. All the tricks and techniques may have delayed the ennui and stalled off the mental balking, but eventually you will come face to face with the realization that you just don't feel like going on with the work. This point may, indeed, come in the final intense hours of preparation before the performance, at a time when you cannot afford to slack off. At that point, give yourself a short break, move around a bit, then tell yourself to quit stalling and get the work done. Tell that nagging little voice to shut up because you *will* see the preparation through.

Such militant self-driving can obviously spawn a lot of unwanted side effects: tension, feeling lousy, and even depression. Therefore, forcing yourself should be used sparingly, employed only for that last sprint. But it still needs to be there as a part of your arsenal. Know that every successful performer has had to call upon mental teeth-gritting at some point. Moreover, getting tough with yourself at the right moment often leaves you feeling good about yourself because you rose to the challenge when the going was rough.

chapter six
Dealing with Repetition and Drill

Let us turn now to a more detailed examination of repetition and drill. Chaper 5 discussed ways of maintaining energy and freshness despite hours and daily cycles of repeated routines. Often, however, a movement or pattern needs to be repeated over and over within the time span of a few minutes to impress the detail on your consciousness and work toward an automatic physical response. Such repetition can be a means of grasping complex concepts, lies at the heart of all memorization, and is the foundation of preparation for all musical performance.

Unfortunately, we tire of repeated patterns very quickly, both mentally and physically, sometimes after only a few repetitions. If we persist, the tiredness mushrooms to the point where we have no choice but to stop. The most obvious example occurs in muscular activity. Our muscles begin to ache, and if we do not stop to relieve the pain, the muscles simply will not respond. Usually pushing our bodies even close to this point will result in soreness at best and permanent damage at worst. The mind tires of repetition almost as quickly. Mental tiredness is characterized in its early stages by lack of concentration, and in later stages by physical symptoms: headaches, tension in the neck and shoulders, or blurred vision.

Thus we are caught on the horns of a dilemma. We really *do* need to repeat certain patterns many times just to understand them or to organize them in our thinking and movements. We really *do* need to master the physical responses we must call upon in our performance. In certain cases we might need to devise and repeat preparatory exercises. Finally, we need to assess how much repetition will achieve the clarity and security we desire.

However, we must constantly work around the fact that our minds and bodies seem to be in a constant state of rebellion. They signal us to stop the very repetition that is necessary to achieve our goals and to move on to more creative aspects of our preparation. To deal with this dilemma, you must finesse your drill in ways that circumvent the limitations of your mind and body, learn to be creative with repetition, and figure out how much repetition is appropriate. Several techniques make it possible to do this:

- Varying speed of repetition
- Varying repetition patterns
- Practicing intermittent repetition
- Creating easier versions
- Assessing security

Varying Speed of Repetition

Varying the speed of your repetitions is perhaps the most significant variable in any practice routine. As we learn new material or acquire new physical responses, we most often must do so at a slower speed. The territory is unfamiliar, and we must feel our way, moving carefully in order to cover the ground with an acceptable degree of precision. The hallmark of progress in early stages is being able to increase the speed. We gradually develop fluency, move ahead as expeditiously as possible, and eventually may achieve virtuoso-like rapidity. If we begin to make mistakes or move with less precision, we slow down to a the point where we can once again have some measure of control, then speed up again once we feel that control return. This speed fluctuation is a lot like driving safely in traffic. When the way is clear, we move ahead as rapidly as possible; but when we encounter barriers, we slow down.

We often repeat at a slower, more deliberate pace in order to increase the index of security. To be effective, however, this technique must be attended by a moderate degree of concentration. The theory behind it is that it gives the mind additional time to focus clearly on the details of the pattern, and that additional time permits the mind to lock in on those details with more clarity. Our resulting physical responses become stronger, faster, and more secure as the mind clarifies and intensifies the neural signals it sends to the muscles. In cases where understanding is sought, insight can be achieved; if memorizing is the goal, later recall is improved.

How much extremely slow repetition is required to trigger a rise in performance level? The results are often almost immediate, after perhaps only two or three careful, slowed down repetitions. This quick improvement often causes us to stop short. We observe the marked improvement, become satisfied that the treatment has worked, and move on. Yet staying the course somewhat longer and investing in a few more slow, careful repetitions will often yield even more marked benefits or, perhaps more important, will help ensure that the improvement will be long-term.

The fact is, the improvement often erodes. We feel secure and comfortable in our knowledge and our physical response for a while, but eventually some measure of insecurity or fuzziness returns, especially in difficult areas. Thus we return again to the slow drill to restore the clarity and security. Periodically returning to slow repetition can become a way of life over time, providing a mental house cleaning that sharpens and clarifies our thinking and responses for a while.

Some music presents challenges so complex that they always require hours of slow practice. Musicians know this pattern intimately and accept as a matter of course that performance on a virtuoso level entails a considerable amount of slowed down, repetitious practice. Some experienced, gifted professionals build a technique that transcends the need for this type of work, but such a level of competence generally is achieved only after many years of hard work and successful performance. Even so, this freedom is comfortable for only some professionals; others, equally gifted, prefer the efficacy of slow practice routines.

Varying Repetition Patterns

No matter how much we are motivated to reap the benefits of slow repetition, it tends to deaden our interest and erode our concentration. On the one hand, we crave the security familiar patterns, while on the hand we desire constant variety to enlist our continuing interest.

During drills, the impulse to push on to the next activity begins to form once we are past the initial stages of perceiving information and executing a physical response. The impulse becomes stronger, and after only a few more repetitions, the mind may simply turn off, sending the message that if we persist in this tedious activity, we will do so without focus. Concentration returns only when we move on to something else.

One school of thought suggests that it is still helpful to continue the drill even without a high degree of focus. Let your mind wander, or engage it in something else, but continue to practice your drills. This division of focus is usually recommended with physical conditioning, like running for exercise while listening to a portable radio. Moritz Rosenthal, the well-known concert pianist from the turn of the twentieth century, is supposed to have recommended reading while going through a daily regime of finger exercises.

Most experts, however, insist that results from repetition come only with some degree of focus. We have all experienced rereading a difficult passage of text, perhaps several times, without concentrating on its meaning. The result is that next to nothing is accomplished. Moreover, those who coach physical development remind us to consciously concentrate on perfecting the movement and the muscles we wish to tone. Studies show that such concentration actually contributes substantially to muscle growth and development.

Thus we need to find a way to keep our concentration while repeating the patterns. In other words, the mind needs to be tricked into staying in focus. In the last chapter we considered varying the order of the daily practice routine to stay fresh. Expanding on this concept, you can use your imagination to vary the pattern of your repetition so that your mind perceives the repetition as a new learning experience. In this process, you actually do, in fact, explore the activity or material from new or different aspects, a procedure that often results in deeper understanding of its content and structure.

Exercise in Varying Patterns

Begin by organizing your score into small segments. Use as a basis two-, four-, or eight-measure units, perhaps phrases, perhaps text, perhaps a physical movement. Label those segments (for example: segment one, segment two, three, four, five; or A, B, C, D, and E). Now learn to perform each segment separately. Doing this may be more difficult than you expect, for remembering any given segment of the material often depends upon cues from the preceding segment. When you interrupt the flow and attempt to remember some middle segment without having the cues to trigger its beginning, you may find yourself stopped in your tracks. If so, deal with it. Simply regard having to perform each segment from scratch as a new learning experience, instituting new cues starting from zero momentum. The final flourish is to scramble the order in which you perform the segments: begin with segment five; skip to three; then to one; to four; then to two. Or perform it "backwards" (five, four, three, two, one). Once you can do this easily, you will have strengthened your ability to execute the individual segments, but you may be unprepared for the ease with which the segments follow one another in their proper order. You will likely experience a "magical" flow and new security as you perform the entire section.

This exercise works well for music over which you have some technical control. If, however, the coordination is strange or complex, it may take quite a bit of time before the initial faltering stage is behind you. For example, if you are just learning to play the piano, you are called upon to execute a very complex pattern of control even at the beginning stages. You have to perceive signals that tell you what musical sounds you want to produce, translate that information into which keys to select, and refine the control of the arms, hands, and fingers to the point of being able to push the proper keys. In addition, you are often seeking to incorporate goals such as which finger to use or how long the note should be held. Moreover, you may be trying to control how fast to push the key down (which determines the loudness or softness of the tone), or how hard to aim for the bottom of the key descent (which determines the degree of accent). More than one key may be involved in any given musical pattern and perhaps both hands must be used, demands that require even more unfamiliar coordination.

It thus becomes apparent that, given the amount of complexity in meeting even the simplest demands of playing music at the piano, you may have to use a full measure of concentration for some time in order to get the activity accomplished in any form. Trying to hurry the process or add further challenges is apt to be confusing rather than helpful.

If, on the other hand, you are trying to tailor an existing technique to new music, you may be focused entirely on basic execution for a short while, but you should be able to adapt fairly quickly. For example, if you are a pianist addressing a formidable octave passage in a new work, you may initially have to figure out the patterns involved and work slowly. If, however, you possess a solid octave technique, you do not have to deal with maintaining a firm hand position or a flexible wrist. Although you may have to repeat the new passage several times or even several days, your underlying technique should allow you to play the new passage in an acceptable manner after investing a relatively small amount of time.

Practicing Intermittent Repetition

Even in the initial stages of organizing the coordination required for new physical response, intermittent repetition can be beneficial. This means nothing more than taking enough time between repetitions to release tension and organize your mental signals, so that the next repetition is executed with as much care as possible physically and as much meaning as possible mentally. Each subsequent repetition is thus executed at its most beneficial level, that is, with enough conceptual purpose to be as accurate and as smoothly flowing as possible. Even after fluency is achieved, it is beneficial to take the time to conceptualize clearly what you are about to repeat. In fact you may have progressed to the point of rapid execution, so the image of what you do is represented by only a fleeting cue, but that small instant when the cue flashes through your consciousness will bring purpose to your moves.

Pausing long enough between repetitions is a principle we use constantly in speech. Although we may at times converse freely, we nevertheless do pause long enough to organize speech into recognizable words, phrases, and sometimes sentences. If we are speaking in our native tongue, those pauses may be very small, but they are present, nonetheless, and form an important part of keeping us intelligible, even to ourselves. Conscious awareness of the value of these small pauses will maximize their effectiveness.

Creating Easier Versions

Sometimes the physical skill you are trying to execute may be so difficult for you that at first you cannot do it at all. If this skill is fundamental to your performance, then you will need to find a way to deal with the impasse. One possible technique is to ask yourself if there is some easier version you can use as a preparatory exercise. Accepting the easier version may seem like a detour and offer reduced benefits, but it can also keep you in the game.

Easier versions of technical challenges have the advantage of keeping you from injuring yourself by attempting movements you are not yet in condition for. For example, you may not have the vocal range demanded by the aria you want to sing. But you can use vocal exercises to explore your present range, increase the ease of your production, and push toward the range you want without straining. If you are a pianist with hands that barely reach an octave, you can do exercises that increase the flexibility of the hand and strengthen the arch. Cécile Genhart, for many years a well-known piano professor at the Eastman School of Music, insisted that several of her students expanded their "reach" by a note or two after engaging in daily Yoga-like hand-stretching exercises away from the keyboard for two or three months.

In some cases, easier versions are not available. An example is music with large intervallic skips. In these cases there is no alternative but to repeat your attempts, missing and adjusting until you are successful. This awkward stage is uncomfortable, not only because of the frustration of not being able to accomplish the task, but often also because of the embarrassment. Several reminders, some of which have been mentioned in other contexts, can serve as facilitators during this process:

- Keep goal oriented. Focusing on your inability will prolong your period of trial and error. Focus on the goal, not where you are. Conceptualize the sound you wish to play or sing, not the distance you have to travel to reach that sound, not your fingers or your vocal chords.

- Make adjustments. Listen to your coaches or observers. They offer advice because they want you to succeed, not because they wish to put you down or to be critical for the sake of being critical. If the adjustments are self-generated, try to observe what changed with each attempt and whether you came closer to successful execution. Remember that it's common to compensate for mistakes too much and sometimes in the wrong ways. Only careful observations of cause and effect will reveal what is an appropriate amount and direction of adjustment.

- Dissolve embarrassment. If embarrassment tries to come between you and your focus, call to mind some old saws: everyone fell down when they learned to walk; even Babe Ruth had to learn to hit the ball at some point; birds do not sing at birth—they cheep. Finding some humor in your predicament can introduce healthy joviality; however, avoid the temptation to regard your failed attempts as fool's play.

- Dispel tension. Shake yourself loose between tries. Walk around in a circle. Roll your head around to loosen your neck muscles. Swing your arms. Bend at the waist. Big movements tend to clear out tangled physical responses. Take a few deep breaths inhaling and holding the air for several seconds before you exhale. Deep breathing removes the toxins that are formed in your system by heavy effort and stress.

- Keep the faith. Should you make little or no progress in any given practice session, remember that the subconscious has a remarkable ability to direct physical response during periods when the conscious mind is otherwise occupied or even sleeping. Send a conscious message to the subconscious, setting forth the goal you want to achieve; combine it with a positive thought, release it, and go about your business. At the next practice session you may be surprised at how much your physical responses have improved, seemingly without your having practiced.

Assessing Security

Ultimately you will reach the stage where your new physical skills are fundamentally in place but you need a lot of repeating to garner more fluency. Moreover, you will need to establish a deeply rooted security that will enable you to perform the skill under the pressure of performance. The role of mental focus during this phase begins to shift. As you get more fluent, the natural tendency is to gradually withdraw your full attention simply because it is no longer required. You will find you can execute the activity without devoting very much mind-power to it, and, as was noted before, your mind will always gravitate toward newer and more interesting thought patterns. In some cases this automatic response is exactly what you hope for. In others, you still need to engage your concentration.

Automatic response might be desirable where the skill exists simply to enable you to perform a more complex operation. For example, for instrumentalists, the sooner fingering or bowing becomes automatic, the sooner one will be able to focus on musical values. If you are singing a role in an opera, the sooner movement about the stage and handling the props becomes automatic, the sooner you will be able to focus on the music you must make or on the qualities of the character you are playing. If you are playing a concerto with an orchestra, the sooner you can garner the freedom to focus on the conductor and the orchestral soloists rather than on playing your own instrument, the sooner you will be able to solve ensemble problems and project concerted music-making.

There is a paradox here, however, because often achieving that automatic response requires repeating the activity a number of times. To some degree repetition is a by-product of daily practice. If you repeat a passage day after day with the same fingering, the patterns will soon become automatic. If stage directions remain unchanged for the most part during rehearsals, you will quickly be able to relegate moving about the stage to a lower level of your consciousness. If you think about imaginary conductors and orchestral soloists as you prepare, you will be able to adjust quickly to distance-focus when you experience the real thing.

New technical skills and new music often take time to become firmly rooted in the performer's system, both physically and mentally. For a considerable period of time, an underlying insecurity may be hidden somewhere in your consciousness even after you are able to execute your new challenges at will. This insecurity may, indeed, show itself the instant any environmental factor is altered, your ability is placed under scrutiny, or you know there is something at stake.

The need to focus on establishing a deeply rooted sense of security leads to two questions.

- How do you enlist the focus and attention of your mind in an activity that is already semi-automatic and has already lost its claim on full concentration?
- How much repetition is enough to establish a sense security that is strong enough to withstand the vicissitudes of performance?

Part of the answer to the first question lies along lines similar to those discussed under maintaining focus during repetition. You must use your imagination to create continuing variation and, if possible, challenge your mind during the repetitions. One possible way is to alter speed by small increments.. Use a metronome, setting it considerably slower than your optimum. By small increments, increase the settings up to your optimum. Then decrease its settings by the same increments until you return to your original speed.

Play or sing the piece you are drilling by moving ahead three measures and dropping back two, starting from that point and repeating the pattern. If the music is written in such a way that using this technique with measures is cumbersome or unmusical, then use it with phrases.

How much repetition will establish enough security to support your performance? This second question is sometimes difficult to answer. Until you experience what happens when you are under pressure, you may be somewhat naïve with regard to the actual strength of your preparation, especially if you are not a veteran of many performances. It may surprise you how poorly your preparation shows when it is put to even seemingly innocuous tests.

Let's create a hypothetical scenario. You have busied yourself with your preparation. Gradually you come to believe that your playing will withstand the scrutiny of disinterested or critical parties, that the memorization you have completed will flow easily in all situations, and that technique you need can be called up at will. Then by chance a friend stops by and asks you about your progress. The request has no far-reaching consequences, for it is the product of passing curiosity. You oblige your friend's curiosity by talking about the music and illustrating various segments of it. As you do so, you are surprised by the fact that you suddenly experience an unexpected degree of insecurity. Your physical responses are awkward or break down. You feel uncomfortable during your demonstration and annoyed or embarrassed at the overall impression you seem to be making.

On balance, the presentation was probably not as bad as your subjective reaction might lead to you believe. The very insecurity you experienced when put to the test may convince you that the result was worse than it probably was. Nevertheless, you have had a taste of the pressure you will have to deal with as the real performance approaches.

Other seemingly innocuous changes can also trigger these patterns of sudden insecurity. Environmental factors are frequently cited culprits. The temperature in an unfamiliar location is either too hot or too cold. Vision is impaired because the light isn't right. Concentration is disturbed because a strange place carries an ambiance that seems too imposing, too formal, or too aloof. Unfamiliar acoustics make it is difficult to hear what you are doing. Peripheral noise or movement becomes distracting. Pianists frequently complain about not being able to control an unfamiliar instrument. Seasoned performers learn to expect these disturbances, even to the point of joking about them. Such in-house sayings as "It went better at home" or "It was just fine this morning" elicit smiles of recognition from the experienced.

To some extent early trial "performances" or demonstrations will always be plagued by some measure of insecurity. Use the discomfort of that insecurity as motivation to invest more heavily in preparation and practice. Above all, guard against letting that insecurity loom so large in early performances that you lose control altogether, give up, and permit the demonstration to end in shambles. Learning to fight to do the best you can in the face of insecurity is an important part of the training itself. Besides, giving up could have far-reaching consequences. Even when nothing of importance is at stake, an experience that defeats your spirit may invite such extreme discomfort and embarrassment that you become traumatized and begin to dread any further attempt to display your work. You do not want that to happen, for overcoming the feelings generated by such a trauma, although possible, will add an extra burden to your performance preparation.

The feelings of security you build during your daily practicing may not in fact be indicative of the security you will need when you take your work out of an accustomed environment and show it. This realization rightfully leads you to the conclusion that you had better invest an extra measure of time in double-checking your musical intent, memorizing the necessary material, and practicing your physical responses. How much is enough?

A musical score can be studied so thoroughly that you know every mark of expression and articulation and every hint the composer left as to how the music should sound. When text is a part of your music, it can be digested and reflected upon in such depth that every word and phrase carry meaning. Memorization can be drilled to the point where you feel that nothing will deter your ability to recall the music. Physical skills can be ingrained so that, on balance, they seem impervious to outside distractions.

Notwithstanding these determined efforts, professionals bemoan the fact that that there is *never* enough practice time to build the degree of security needed to feel totally confident and free. Therefore practice and drill become an ongoing training program. Indeed, such programs may become a way of life. A famous saying among musicians, attributed to several pianists including Hans von Bülow and the Polish pianist Ignacy Jan Paderewski, is reported as: "If I miss a day of practice, I know it; two days—the critics know it; three days—the audience knows it."

Even so, you can learn to sense an index of security. Armed with the knowledge that pressure may erode your efficiency, use your imagination to simulate performance conditions and garner feedback. This technique will be discussed later in detail under the heading of "dress rehearsals." You can set up test runs and performances for observers that have no far-reaching consequences. You should also seek out the expertise of those more experienced than you. Teachers, coaches, and peers can often offer valuable advice from their own experience.

Stuck in Repetition

You've seen that you may need more performance preparation than you originally planned in order to establish security. Let us now look at the opposite, when repetitious preparation becomes an end in itself, acting as a deterrent to your taking the next steps along the preparation journey. This wasteful pattern may develop as an established work routine has proven effective and becomes very comfortable. The very fact that the pattern is beneficial offers an excuse never to check bearings, never to put what is being practiced to any kind of test, procrastinating with regard to moving on to the next logical step in the name of not being "ready." This pattern results in your getting stuck in practice activities that support your main goals but that do not generate direct progress toward them.

For example, suppose a would-be author collects voluminous amounts of data for a book but cannot summon up the focus to do any writing. A would-be linguist habitually memorizes vocabulary and studies word usage in a foreign language but never has the courage to get out in the real world and attempt a conversation in that language. An athlete trains incessantly but never plays a game. An entertainer assembles material (songs, dances, jokes, props, costumes) for an act but never puts the act together. Applied to the musician, the pattern becomes the person who practices exercises and musical fragments but never plays a piece, especially for anybody else.

Those caught up in this strange pattern are often very dedicated to their goal, and they are willing to expend time and effort. However, the fact that they linger for indefinite periods in the comfort of a routine robs them of the performance aspect of their dream. In cases where no external schedule makes demands upon them, they may get caught up in this no-man's-land for so long that they eventually lose all motivation to realize their performance.

If an external schedule does not demand performance, it will likely never take place. Moreover, if circumstances *do* force a performance on the victims of this pattern, they will probably experience a last-minute sense of panic. They are especially scared, for since they have lingered so long in an intermediate stage of the preparation process, this performance seems to loom up abruptly, and they will have to scramble on the eve of their deadline to pull together some kind of presentation.

Correcting the tendency toward overpreparation is much like that for addressing underpreparation. You first have to be sensitive to the possibility of developing an aberrant pattern. In most cases, you can give yourself a kick in the pants when it becomes apparent that it is time to move on to the next stage. There are times when you simply have to force yourself: "I will make myself try to play or sing a piece from beginning to end today [perhaps for a friend] even if I have to stop sometimes." Using your imagination to simulate performance conditions will often provide the needed challenge. Finally, once again, seeking guidance from an expert or more experienced peer can be extremely helpful, especially if such guidance forces you into some kind of action.

chapter seven
Techniques to Develop Secure Memorization

Memorization is an integral part of most performance. If you are a musician, you may be expected to perform music, and possibly text, from memory. If you are an actor/musician, you must memorize dialogue and movement.

Not only must you know what to play, sing, or do, but also you must recall what you need at a prescribed time. Performance does not allow the luxury of time to search your mind for musical details or to reconstruct patterns of movement. Thus memorization means preparing your mind not only to give you exactly what you want, but also to give it precisely when you want it.

We memorize constantly in our daily lives, and most of us store a large amount of detailed information: addresses, telephone numbers, birthdays, anniversaries, how to get around, how to operate equipment, even bits of poetry, song lyrics, and (sometimes to our annoyance) advertising slogans. Our memories thus work constantly and effectively without generating concern or anxiety. Yet the more formal "memorizing" aspect of performance preparation often inspires fear and insecurity.

There are four characteristics that do not appear in the memorization we undertake in our daily lives but that are usually present in memorizing for performance.

- Complexity of material
- Anticipated level of precision
- Time issues
- Anxiety

Let us addresses each in turn, looking at techniques that will help overcome the difficulties they seem to impose.

81

Complexity of Material

The level of complexity of the material is one of the first impressions we form, and often we conclude that the material to be memorized is "difficult" or "complex." These perceptions are, of course, relative and subjective, and they will change. First-time learning is always more difficult. Thus if the kind of material you are undertaking to memorize seems foreign to you, its details will impress you as being complex.

For example, you may not remember how much of a challenge learning the alphabet was, but when you were at that stage of development, memorizing a string of twenty-six letters in their proper order was indeed tough. Suppose now you are faced with a similar task, that of learning the Cyrillic alphabet in your study of Russian. For someone experienced in the Western alphabet, learning another string of letters would not be as challenging. You understand the concept of the alphabet, comprehend its relationship and usage in language, and can even create references to the alphabet you know that will assist you in learning the new one.

Our fear of complex material can be dispelled through the use of specific techniques. Let us look at a few of them.

- First, attempt to analyze whatever structural organization may exist within the material itself. For example, your music may have an introduction and then proceed according to often encountered phrase groups and sections. Repetition, even with small variations, can be observed in much music. Before you launch into memorizing from the beginning, take time to look at the complete work, forging a conceptual overview of its organization, even sketching an outline of what you must memorize. Figure out the overall pattern the composer used, noting areas that reuse the same harmonic or rhythmic material. Some musical works, however, lack the more frequently encountered patterns, being organized on very complex relationships that are not obvious. In these cases you may wish to enlist other techniques.

- Second, take the time to think about the conceptual meaning behind the material. For all textual material, you ask yourself "What is this saying?" and then put it in your own words, as if you were explaining the content to someone else. For music, make your own version of the musical essence of what you are memorizing, breaking down the components of harmony, rhythm, and melody to the simplest form, noting interval relationships and the interplay of meter.

- Third, disarm complexity by breaking the material down into small units that seem easy. Identify the simplest, shortest, most fundamental element, one that will trigger your inner voice to respond, "Well, of course, I can memorize *that*. Anyone can." Some inner nay-sayer may then offer something like, "But if I try to memorize this project by dealing with such easy, short units, I will *never* get it done." This is wrong. You will be able to get the job done, for the mind has a remarkable ability to compress material as it memorizes over a period of time. Fragments that seem to take a lot of attention when they are being memorized undergo a shrinking process as new material is added, and they can be recalled intact with minimal cues. The advantage of dealing with small units is that from the outset the mind regards the task at hand as a piece of cake, an attitude that results in both accuracy and security.

- Fourth, construct your own mnemonic references as you memorize. This technique is particularly useful where the material seems to have no structure. At first glance, it would seem that creating such references is a lot of extra work, but in fact the exercise provides associations that your mind can gravitate to as it recalls the information you want. This universally accepted technique is an important component in all courses designed to develop your memorizing abilities. (Remember "Every Good Boy Does Fine," in which the first letters of each word spells out the notes on the lines of the treble clef?) Notwithstanding the beneficial reputation of such frames of reference, we often fail to use them, because creating them takes time and effort.

Let's look at a couple of nonmusical examples of mnemonics first.

If you have to memorize a list of vocabulary words in a foreign language, divide the list into groups of four words. Figure out the acronym formed by the first letters of the four words. Make up a slogan that these letters might stand for. (Have a little fun here by making up something funny, silly, or naughty.) Then backtrack from the slogan to the acronym, to the first letters of the words, to the words themselves, adding their meanings in the new language. Run the process forward and backward two or three times. When the first group seems secure, move forward and do the next group of four words. This exercise will formulate a reference process substantial enough to deliver the necessary information later on. As the mind becomes familiar with the words themselves through continued usage, the reference structure will drop away naturally. (Or it may continue to provide a chuckle if you have been clever.)

Here is another, more difficult example.

Suppose you have to memorize a sequence of numbers that represent settings on a piece of equipment you must learn to operate, each number consisting of four digits. Take the first set and think about the numbers to see if they form some kind of pattern. Some numbers flow easily, others do not. Many people choose telephone numbers, for example, for patterns that are easy to remember. Numbers with double anything, 1511 or 2255, usually fit this description, especially double zeros, 0200, 0030. Numbers that run consecutively either up or down fit the bill as well, although these flow a little less well: 2345, 3234, 6545, 9898. Odd–even patterns can be helpful: 2468, 9753, 2464, 7535. You can look for internal relationships such as multiples or divisions. The number 1248, for example, is easy to remember if you realize that one doubled is two, two doubled is four, and four doubled is eight. The number 9327 might be thought of as nine divided by three is three and multiplied by three is twenty-seven. Relating numeric combinations to other meanings is also useful. The number 5197, for example, might seem hard until you realize that it could mean May Day of the year 1997. Where were you then? Is it on or near someone's birthday? Does that day or month have a personal meaning for you? Did anyone you know turn 51 in the year 1997? Someone I know remembered a house number because it was the same year he was inducted into the army.

We musicians have a useful tool for remembering numbers. We can equate the numbers one through eight as degrees of a major scale, adding even nine and ten if they extend over an octave. Number combinations can then be converted into melodic fragments, patterns of sounds that musicians often have the ability to recall swiftly and accurately. The number 16545, for example, converts to the first five notes of "My Bonnie Lies Over the Ocean" (fixed *do*). So remembering that combination is as easy as remembering the first few notes of a well-known tune. And even if the tune the numbers convert to does not resemble anything one already knows, it is sometimes easier for us to remember the tune rather than the numerical sequence.

Now let us turn to a musical example.

It is often difficult to remember harmonic structures in contemporary music if they do not conform to those used in eighteenth- and nineteenth-century common practice. But we can begin to nail down more contemporary sounds if we can relate them in some way to the older material that we know so well. Thus study your music for such relationships. Take, for example, a chord that is spelled C, D, F, F-sharp, B-flat, and D-flat at the interval of a ninth from the C. You can relate it to familiar territory in several ways: F-sharp (G-flat), B-flat, and D-flat forms a familiar triad and you add to it the first, second, and fourth degrees of the C major scale. A second way: C, F, and B-flat form a trio of fourths; add to it the root, third, and seventh of a D major major-seventh chord. A third way: D, F, F-sharp, B-flat is a D augmented triad with both the major and minor thirds; it is girded by a minor ninth interval on C (C–D-flat).

Examples of such invention could go on and on. The point is that memorizing material is rendered easier if you make up associative relationships and remember the entire package rather than the details. It really doesn't matter much how crazy the association is, and, indeed, screwball associations often work better simply because they are so off-the-wall. Once the mind becomes skilled at creating such associations, it can not only invent something for almost any memory challenge, but also have fun doing it.

Level of Precision

From the outset you will have a concept of the level of precision that will be needed in your performance, and this expectation will have a bearing on how you perceive the memorization process. At the high end of the precision scale are musical performances that continue an established tradition. Musicians preparing a work by Mozart, for example, will probably try for a note-perfect performance that satisfies established expressive parameters. Actors creating roles in the standard operatic repertoire may have a bit more leeway, but they too must deliver a precise musical performance, as well as a character steeped in tradition.

When precision expectations are high, memorization becomes more difficult because there is little margin for variation. Although one may understand the underlying musical or poetic idea behind the expression, that is not enough, because the goal is to recreate the idea *exactly* as it is notated by its creator. This expectation results in more intensive examination of details during memorization, more repetitive drill to solidify the process of re-creating the material, and a great degree of psychological pressure during the actual performance.

There are areas of music where memorization is less precise, but here there are other demands. Musicians whose music calls for substantial improvisation may not have to deal so carefully with preset detail, but they face the challenge of exhibiting a high degree of creativity during the performance. Chamber and orchestral musicians may, indeed, have the music in front of them, but they cannot be tied to the score to the extent of reading it; their attention must be focused not just on the sound, but also on ensemble precision and balance, and in some cases on responding to a conductor or listening for intonation.

Recognizing such demands should trigger a rigorous program of memorization training, similar to training for some taxing physical feat. Often it does not. Often memorization is put off until just before the performance, resulting in a high degree of insecurity because the memorizing process is rusty and the material is still relatively new. One of the oldest homilies around is "memory is like a muscle." The implications are obvious: the memory has to be exercised and developed on a regular basis to function at a high level during performance.

Musicians who plan to play without the score should memorize some segment of music in every daily practice session, setting aside time specifically to this process. Those who must memorize words should also set time aside daily for doing so. Organize this daily segment of time along lines already indicated. Set up a specific memorization project. Break it up into segments, right down to daily memorization goals. Allow time each day for reviewing earlier material, since freshly memorized material will fade, even in twenty-four hours. After the mind has reviewed memorized material several times, the material will begin to "stick" and recall will become increasingly facile and secure. After reviewing memorized material each day, always try to add new material, the next small segment, pushing forward as a daily exercise.

Some segments will be easy to set in the memory. Others will resist, sometimes to a point of exasperation. There are segments that you will think you have memorized, only to be confronted with blocks or confusion in recall the following day. Be patient with yourself, for everyone encounters these obstacles. Just keep reviewing, analyzing, setting the mind back on course, until that day when recall flows without error. Such a day will come without fail if you persist. The memory process can be compared to boiling an egg: after enough heat has been applied, it solidifies, and what seemed hopelessly unstable congeals remarkably into a well-defined entity. Once this transformation has taken place, the amount of time and effort needed to maintain recall diminishes significantly, freeing the mind to focus on new material.

Time Issues

How much time you should set aside to memorize each day is a matter to weigh carefully. You will sense the point at which your mind has absorbed all it can take. It will balk at memorizing more detail, or it will start confusing what it is trying to memorize with what it has just memorized. When you reach this point, review what you memorized one last time, put it away, and wait until the next memory session. If your memory is out of shape, then a small amount of time—perhaps only ten or fifteen minutes—may be the best you can manage. As your memory process becomes stronger, you can extend the time of the memorizing exercise by increments until enough time is invested each day to make measurable progress.

Continue to combine memorizing new material and reviewing old material until a given project is completed. Just after this completion stage, , you may encounter an awkward point, at which the performance is now memorized but your mind is so focused on recall that other aspects of your performance may suffer. Physical aspects may not flow quite as comfortably. Interpretative and expressive aspects, even those already rehearsed, may be minimal or temporarily nonexistent.

However, as your mind becomes increasingly comfortable with the material you have memorized, it exhibits a remarkable ability to compress that material so that recall seems psychologically less daunting. Thus with repetition, the impairment of other aspects of the performance lessens as your mind is once again freed up to concentrate on the those aspects. At this point, however, it is often good to review consciously those other aspects, emphasizing once more the goals associated with them as part of the recall process.

While a daily memorizing regimen can shape up the memorizing process, it's important to determine ways to handle the time requirements inherent in every memorized performance project. Performance is usually scheduled for a specific day and time, so a target date is more than likely on the docket. You will need to plan your work to be ready ahead of the deadline. How much ahead of the performance time is a question that needs to be addressed.

At first glance, the sooner the better seems like a good approach. There is wisdom in this idea; it's never good to slide into home base if one can arrive in a less risky manner. You should certainly plan to complete the memorizing days ahead of the deadline, perhaps weeks for extremely challenging performances, even months. Certainly a long-term incubation period is desirable if, for example, you are playing a difficult concerto with a well-known symphony orchestra, or you are making your debut in a starring role with a world-famous opera company.

But life doesn't always work that way. Many successful debuts have been made as a substitute for an indisposed soloist. Intense last-minute work, including memorizing large amounts of material, does take place and often with notable success.

Knowing that this alternative exists, however, does not mean it is recommended. You should be ready to summon the determination and energy for last-minute cramming if it is absolutely necessary but should also do everything possible to keep it from becoming the last-ditch stand between success and failure. Such monumental effort at the last minute might leave you exhausted at the time of performance. It might also leave a wake of confusion about the details of the hastily memorized material. And since physical response is an important part of successful musical performance, an additional measure of danger is courted: that the physical aspect, already under strain from nervousness, will simply jam and falter.

Both your mental and physical preparation will undergo cycles. After memorization is completed, you will experience an upward swing, a period in which you feel the performance is pulling together and the memory work has become more secure. Try to go with the flow. Don't force your mind to review with prolonged focus memory work that has already been completed, but don't let your mind off the hook entirely. A period of gentle daily review in which you check and observe memorized details will probably suffice to keep the material clearly in your mind. If your mind feels tired or bored, then after a reasonable period of focus, let it go until the next day. You might even skip a day, provided the performance date is not looming. Sense when that performance date is, however, and try to restart the upward cycle so that you can time its peak at performance time.

Anxiety

All of the foregoing techniques and plans may seem to fly out the window the moment the adrenaline begins to flow and you feel anxiety just before and during the performance. Memorization seems particularly vulnerable when the mind is flooded with worry, because it has difficulty focusing clearly and recalling the patterns it needs. Moreover, the stimulation of adrenaline causes many to short-circuit mentally, unable to tap the lineup of cues to keep the memorization process flowing.

Chapter 10 deals in detail with performance nerves, and chapter 6 presented repetitive drills that strengthen security of both physical performance and memory. One technique touched upon in the context of repetitive drill works particularly well for the recall process: setting up periodic points in your presentation that act as stabilizers. In the music these points may be every few measures. In song or operatic text they may be every few lines. In stage movement patterns they may be every few seconds, a point at which a new sequence of movement begins.

These points act as restart stations should anxiety cause you to short-circuit or blank out. You should actually mark these places in your music or stage directions, so that your entire blueprint is marked off into segments. Give each a number. These represent points at which you must learn to start securely and proceed. Memorize the sections and their numbers in your preparation, and train yourself to start cold at any one of them. Begin your day of preparation by ordering yourself to "Start at number 5," "Start at line number 3," "Start where I move upstage and mingle with the crowd: number 11."

In the beginning this exercise may disturb your ability to remember the material, but after a few prompts, you should be able to latch on to the memorization you have done at these different starting points. Play games with yourself by starting at all the odd sections in turn, all the odd sections backwards, all the even sections in turn, all the even sections backwards. Make slips of paper with each section number on them, throw the slips in a bowl and draw out starting points at random.

This may seem like an arduous, mechanical process. You may want to give up as you discover you have to relearn a lot of material to be able to start the flow at these arbitrary points. If you persevere, however, you will accomplish two important feats. First you will have built a safety net, so that if something *does* happen to your recall during your performance, you have a means of recovering your flow without flailing about in a panic. Remember that handling a memory slip without prolong upset minimizes the effect of that slip. Remember also to go to the *next* start-up point rather than the one you just passed, to avoid traveling once again past the point where you forgot. Many performers drop back to regain their equilibrium, only to lose it again at the same place they lost it the first time. This second failure only exacerbates the problem.

Second, and more important, this safety net sends a message to your brain that no matter what happens, you are prepared to deal with it, to recover, and to continue with the performance. After all, with all these start-up spots in place, there is no reason for concern. This knowledge does not relieve you of all anxiety but will likely convince you at some level to stop worrying about "What if I forget!" When your mind begins to fret, simply feed back the answer: "If I forget, I just go to the next start-up place and pick up the performance." Having that simple answer in place will often relieve the mind to an extent that will permit it to function without memory failure.

❧

No one is ever completely free of the fear of memory slips. Every performer, no matter how accomplished or how experienced, has had to deal with a memory slip at some point. On balance, however, getting the memory in shape and keeping it there, in addition to using the well-known techniques discussed in this chapter, will go a long way toward letting you give securely memorized performances regularly.

chapter eight
Ensuring Quality

Up to this point we have been addressing mostly the issue of the quantity of your ongoing work, exploring techniques that help keep you forging ahead in your preparation process. Let us turn now to the question of the *quality* of your work. The quality guideline you adopt is related to a standard that will firmly support your ultimate performance. You should understand what that level needs to be and form a symbolic concept of it, one that hovers subliminally in your consciousness as you work.

If the quality standard is not in place, your performance may falter. There is nothing more disheartening than amassing work that falls short of providing the necessary support when the pressure of performance begins to mount. You suddenly feel like you are stranded at the very moment you need the security born of solid preparation. You are in danger of being victimized in this way if you misread the musical score. Or if your study does not focus on interpretative details you need to know. Or if your physical training does not result in precise response. Or if the directions you follow are executed sloppily. Or if the problems you encounter along the way are never quite solved. Or if the memorization is neither clear nor sure.

Remember to distinguish between quality control and honest error. There is always the possibility that some misconception on your part will lead to an error somewhere down the road. If you learn a wrong rhythm in a concerto, the error will likely surface when you begin to work with your conductor or the orchestra. It has been reported that composer Robert Schumann scored the horn parts in the wrong key in his first symphony, a fact that became painfully obvious when Felix Mendelssohn rehearsed it for performance on March 28, 1841. We all make such mistakes, and we learn to live with them, adjusting and correcting whenever such errors present themselves. This occasional mistake or misconception is *not* the same as basic quality control, although high-quality preparation tends to minimize the occurrence of even these mistakes.

Rather, the quality control we seek is born of the level of work that permeates our preparation. It needs to be established at the outset, and working habits need to be instituted from the beginning that ensure this level is being met. As you consider conceptualizing and establishing this quality control, you might find it useful to ask yourself the following questions:

- Does my rate of work permit me to be thorough and accurate?
- Do I follow through and complete each segment of my task as I go along?
- Do I ever mentally step back from my task and ask myself if I am missing anything?
- Do I sense some measure of security in what I am doing?
- Do I have some sense of overview, the ability to look back along the road I have traveled and see a building pattern?

Rate of Work

We have already considered techniques to help you organize data, as well as to sustain your rate of work when problematic areas invite stalling. We need also to consider speed in the context of quality control. The old adage "Haste makes waste" comes to mind, yet we live in a society that values saving time. The drive is to get everything done as fast as possible. To measure the degree to which we subscribe to this philosophy, simply observe the amount of irritation that attends the small delays of living: waiting in line, telephone busy signals, computer screens that don't pop up immediately, traffic signals that have just turned red. This frustration is understandable if we are actually running late, but the desire to save time is so deeply rooted that often annoyance is triggered even when we have time to spare.

Most of us want to achieve our performance goals as soon as possible. In many instances, moreover, we have a performance deadline. You have logged in the day and time of the performance and taken this into account when you set up your working schedule. You understand that you need to cover a certain amount of ground each day to meet the performance deadline. But even with this time pressure, you have to strike a balance with regard to the speed of preparation.

At any point in your preparation, apply a test for precision. If excessive speed impairs precision, then you'd better slow down. If you try to ingest the notes and rhythm of the score so quickly that you misread many values, you have established patterns that need to be broken. If you overlook details of expression, you are perfecting musical ideas that are not those of the composer. If you practice any physical response with so much speed that the mental signals to your muscles are not established clearly, then you will build into your response a sense of insecurity that will increase the normal level of stage fright.

Following Through

Closely connected to the lack of precision caused by going too fast is the problem of not always following through or completing each segment of a task. This habit is usually triggered by time pressure. As you approach the end of a segment, you are eager to get on with the next part, thereby marking progress. So you jump ahead to the new beginning before entirely finishing the previous one. Eagerness to get ahead is joined by the assumption that since you already know the final details of your present task, you can omit them, move ahead, and save some time with impunity.

We see haste manifest itself myriad ways in our personal lives. Sometimes people don't finish sentences (often substituting for endings catch-all phrases like "you know"). Sometimes we don't pick up our clothes after getting dressed; or don't put away tools or cleaning materials around the house. We may encounter stray telephone numbers without names or appointment reminders without the place or time.

You may assume that some sections of music are exact repetitions and therefore don't examine them for variants. Or, you may not take the time to read editorial notes that may point to performance practice problems or offer assistance. You may not take the time to look up an unfamiliar word in the score, but instead guess at its meaning. Or you may not make note of practice exercises given by your coach at your last session that now aren't too clear in your mind.

Haste is, indeed, often behind these glitches. Equally at fault, however, is the perception that inasmuch as the main body of the task is finished, the completion of the task is either so obvious or routine that it is not necessary to follow through. Everyone knows how the sentence is going to end, so why end it? You're dressed, so why pick up? You've made the repair or cleaned up, so it's boring to put away. You'll remember whose number that is or when and where you're supposed to be. The fact of the matter is, it doesn't always turn out that way. Sooner or later you must either correct or adjust your elision, so it makes sense to establish the habit of following through as you proceed.

On the other hand, life does not always cooperate. Sometimes events unfold in unexpected ways or at an accelerated pace, and you may be faced with moving on without the preferable follow through or cleanup. You might find that as you complete one task, you are pressured to get another done immediately, and it is better to leave the routine for another time. In an emergency you give concise orders, taking time to explain why later. You are dressed and need to leave immediately to be on time for an appointment, so you leave your dressing area in shambles. You fixed the household problem but need to get to work, so there is no time to put away your tools. Your only pen runs dry, so you will be forced to remember the significance of the telephone number or the details of the appointment you are making. You are handed a score and asked to collaborate in a performance within the hour, so you are forced to play or sing without examining many details. Whenever these situations occur, you simply have to maintain the awareness that you have left an important part of the task undone: its completion. That awareness itself represents good working habits, and it will motivate you to backtrack to complete details at the first available opportunity.

Stepping Back

Taking the time to step back mentally from your work from time to time to study the quality of what you have been doing offers several benefits born of temporarily shifting perspective. You probably remember the adage that we can't see the forest because of the trees. The fact is, when dealing with immediate details, we lose sight of the overall picture. The antidote to this shortsightedness is to set aside a time to look at the overall picture and try to determine if you are missing something important. To do this, you usually must take a break from your normal working pattern, stopping long enough to conceptualize, observe, and think.

In this intermission from activity, consider both quantity and quality. Check your schedule to see how you are doing and assess the value of your work. Much of this reflection can be self-generated. Ask yourself if there is information you need or an important component of training you are forgetting. Look at what you are doing in large chunks, looking for any helpful connections. Consciously reflect on the degree of creativity or inspiration you are enlisting, or the extent of expressiveness, emotional intensity, or communicative power. Ask if there are ways these elusive qualities might be strengthened.

Sometimes it is helpful to get an outsider's perception. Frequently a person remotely connected to our arena of concentration can offer telling insights. Since such a person is not concerned with the details, his or her view is not cluttered with so many trees, and the forest appears in bold relief. Bring such a person into your working world by explaining your activities in a conversational summary—describe what you are attempting to do and what challenges you face. Perhaps even an early-stage performance or demonstration is appropriate. Such an exercise can expose overlooked weak spots. Playing or singing your music at its present level of development brings you face-to-face with your weaknesses. You are apt to recognize them instantly as you perform and sense what ways you need to return to the drawing board.

Moreover, an offhand comment from your observer sometimes zeros in on some aspect of your performance that comes as a complete surprise. For example, the remark "Gee, that's heavy stuff" might trigger you to realize that your intense concentration has caused you to project a seriousness, a pedantry, even a glumness in your performance that was not your original intention. Casual observers often pick up on unwanted body movements: a questionable posture, a facial expression, a nervous gesture. An amateur might ask a question so basic that it appears naïve or simple, but when you try to answer it, you become aware of some fundamental premise you have overlooked. The comment "I can't understand many of the words you're singing" might reveal that what is obvious and clear to you through familiarity is less so to your audience. Or you might find yourself adjusting the pacing of your performance as a result of casual comments about being "awfully fast" or "kind of draggy."

While your observer's comment may reflect lack of expertise or sophistication in the area of your work, always ask yourself how it came about that, out of all the rejoinders your observer could have made, this one came to mind. Often you will need to interpret what this nonexpert is trying to ask or tell you. To be sure, sometimes responding to such comments is, indeed, not particularly helpful to your work or your goals, but more often than you might expect, this exercise will reveal some aspect of your performance that you should think about, or will point to some flaw in your preparation you need to address.

Measure of Security

In assessing the ongoing quality of your efforts, ask yourself if you feel a measure of security with regard to the efficacy of your preparation. This sense of security suggests work well done, and having it in place will serve as effective support for your performance. Such a sense does not preclude your continuing attempts to improve on the quality of the work, nor does it guarantee faultless or inspired preparation. All of the preparation techniques still need to continue. Still, the sense of security should be present as you reflect on the quality of your work, and its presence should provide confidence as you build your performance preparation. Occasional reflection to acknowledge its growth, as well as to nurture a subliminal, continuous awareness of it, often results in a good feeling about what you are doing.

Sense of Overview

Closely related to this sense of security is a sense of overview, an awareness of the progress that has already taken place in building toward your performance goal. As you climb the mountain, there are spots to pause momentarily to look back into the valley, taking in the beauty of the view with the knowledge that your perspective comes from your successful efforts. As you survey the vista, you experience a sense of power and satisfaction in the knowledge that you have come this far, and that feeling, in turn, energizes you for the next step in your journey. Enjoy such moments psychologically in your preparation progress.

❧

Your allegiance to quality should not escalate into a fetish for perfection. As human beings, we will always be subject to error, and our performances subject to variability. This is not necessarily a completely bad thing; nature is constantly engaged in creating beauty but seldom produces the symmetrical perfection we humans strive for. If we think about performance effectiveness, we realize that while it may be related to, it is not absolutely dependent upon executing every detail perfectly. Thus quality control is an ongoing, important issue during performance preparation, but as the performance itself nears, concern with quality per se probably should be supplanted by efforts that deal more directly with nervousness and the dynamics of the performance itself.

chapter nine
Self-Regard at the Time of Performance

We have now examined many of the things you can do to prepare for performance. You have conceptualized your goal, set up your preparation schedule, practiced, drilled, mastered the necessary technique, incorporated expressive aspects, engaged in rehearsals, synthesized the entire process, and attempted to add a measure of security to your playing or singing. In this section we need to consider how to deal with the actual performance.

Individual attitudes toward the performance vary widely, running the gamut from being relatively calm to fighting hard to remain in control. Individuals who can undertake performance with but little trauma are rare. In those cases, the performance may be executed as just another run-through, perhaps attended by a pleasant but controlled edge of excitement. We can sometimes observe this rare pattern in children who perform. Children are often motivated to give a satisfactory performance simply to garner approval from the adult world. Thus the child doesn't attached significant or far-reaching consequences to degrees of success. The ice cream and cake at the reception following the event may generate more interest than the challenge of the performance. This naïveté often permits the child simply to get up and do whatever has been prepared without much self-consciousness. The performance then reflects the preparation to a high degree and, given the fact that society is conditioned to expect tension-laden performance in an adult world, conveys a kind of artless freshness that is often beguiling.

The ability to perform with this kind of aplomb almost never attends adult performance. Somewhere along life's journey, the adult performer has almost always been conditioned to the pain of failure, the frustration of disappointment, and his or her motivation to perform has usually become intertwined with significant and far-reaching goals. In addition, a few other

97

ingredients are in the adult performer's mix: basic temperament of the individual; physical well-being at the time of performance; environmental factors; in competitive situations the degree of challenge posed by others; and even a mysterious psychological X factor that sometimes works to support a performance and at other times seems to undermine it. Thus performance success varies widely from individual to individual and may vary for the same individual from performance to performance.

This state of affairs must not, however, intimidate you. Rather you need to understand how to take all possible measures to stabilize your performance, to ensure that you can present your best possible version, and even occasionally to use the pressure of performance as leverage to overreach yourself. So we have traveled full circle and now once again must consider self-image.

We addressed the conceptualization of who we think we are in chapter 1. We return to it here, because doing so reflects what often happens as we approach the moment of performance. During preparation, our mind is usually occupied with the many steps involved, so there is generally not much predilection for asking ourselves who we think we are and what we think we are doing by attempting to meet this performance challenge. As we emerge from the preparation stage, begin to synthesize our performance, and step back to view the totality, we once again invite the kind of rapid self-assessment that gives a telling glimpse of our basic self-esteem.

As when you first began to conceptualize your relationship to this performance, you have to manage your present psychological state. Your performance cannot be put off until you realize the benefits of long-term analysis or treatment, helpful as such procedures may be. You may decide to work on self-image as a project apart from the performance in order to improve your overall mind-set, much in the same way one might improve one's diet in order to have as healthy a body as possible for supporting performance. In a few cases, low self-esteem may be so deeply rooted that quickly instituted techniques applied at the last moment are too superficial to do much good. Most performers, however, will find self-help techniques beneficial, notwithstanding the performance anxiety. So summon exercises from your repertoire of positive thinking: prayers, slogans, mantras, whatever you are accustomed to using.

Even so, the tension and fear leading up to performance may be powerful enough to shake your self-esteem to the core and convince you for the moment that you have extremely low self-esteem. In reality, this will probably not be a valid assessment. Rather, the impression is born of performance nerves. The antidote becomes, then, to summon the courage and energy to move ahead, applying techniques to put a positive spin on self-esteem.

Delaying Confrontation

One technique is to agree with yourself to delay improving your basic self-esteem until later, sometime after the performance. Logic says that this puts the cart before the horse, because self-esteem supports performance and should be firmly entrenched before you perfor. At this particular point, however, if you are to give the performance at all, you need to be as focused and purposeful as possible. You do not need the free association, retrospection, and (sometimes) temporary confusion that attend self-reflection and evaluation. Therefore momentarily defy the logical cause-and-effect relationship and simply say "Not now, I'm busy."

As was noted earlier, some individuals who perform regularly and brilliantly and build strong and vibrant performing careers exhibit many symptoms of extremely low self-esteem outside the performance arena. Their successes should nurture a self-esteem that, in turn, would strengthen subsequent performances, all resulting in a powerful upward spiral. In actuality, many brilliant performers gear up to their performance by focusing on the challenge of the moment, setting aside deeper perceptions of their self. As long as such individuals are in the throes of the performance itself, they function brilliantly. Once they return to a more normal mode, they have to deal once more with their low self-esteem, notwithstanding the fact that successful performance not only was possible for them, but, in fact, took place at a high level. Just because bifurcation works in some cases is not an endorsement. On the other hand, knowing that it is possible to perform effectively without having solved all of your self-esteem problems can be a solace when you are poised on the brink of a performance.

Replacing Unwelcome Thought with Positive Patterns

Side-stepping this fundamental consideration of who you are and what you are doing means that you eschew several old saws probably buried somewhere in your mind. These may suggest a fundamental weakness that keeps you from successful performance or may imply that you are singled out by cosmic forces as a special target for disaster. The "weakness" pattern usually takes the form of an inner dialogue centered on the concept of "never could." "I never could do my best in front of an audience . . . ," "I never could get my hands to stop shaking . . . ," "I never could feel secure about that high note (run, skip, passage). . . ." The "cosmic forces" pattern is often expressed by sentiments that include the phrase "with my luck." "With my luck, I'll probably blank out . . . ," "With my luck, I'll probably pull a muscle . . . ," "With my luck, it'll probably rain that day and I'll catch a cold. . . ."

Such thinking is rife in our culture, so you probably can't completely avoid the tendency to fall into similar patterns. Denial is not a very powerful tool for dealing with unwelcome thought patterns. The very fact that you command yourself not to think in a certain way brings the unwelcome thoughts into focus. Substituting other patterns provides a more effective antidote. You can, for example, substitute the expectation of a cosmic payoff for the work you have invested. "I've paid my dues now; so it's time I got the break." Or recall past instances of success. If this performance is a new endeavor for you, recall a very successful rehearsal, or even areas of activity in which you know you are good, adding the postscript that if you were so successful at that activity, then the current one ought to be similarly blessed.

By definition you have no control over the luck factor, so you might just as well chose to imagine that you are the beneficiary of good luck as bad luck. If, indeed, you have no influence over your luck, then you're no worse off playing the fool and expecting the best. Doing so will at least relieve you of torturing yourself with imagined bad luck. Moreover, many people contend that indulging in fantasies of bad luck sends out vibrations that, in fact, attract such luck. If you fantasize that your luck will involve you in some kind of accident, then you invite becoming "accident prone." This school of thought also endorses the converse: imagine good luck, and you will attract good luck. Although the cause-and-effect relationship here is seldom clear-cut and often not traceable, it nevertheless exists.

Understanding Your Basic Temperament

Take care to distinguish carefully between your self-esteem, something you can improve or choose to ignore on occasion, and your basic temperament, something you cannot change. Temperament here is defined as one's natural disposition, and it is for the most part determined by heredity and early environmental influences. Medieval physiology identified four basic types: sanguine (warm, passionate, cheerful); phlegmatic (calm, cool, stolid); choleric (quick to anger, irascible, irritable); and melancholic (sad, gloomy, depressed). It was believed that the amount of blood, phlegm, and yellow or black bile, respectively, one's body retained determined the tendency toward one or another of these states.

A mix of complex and often inscrutable ingredients determine our temperament. We have elements in our makeup that we may need to take into account whenever we address the rigors of performing. For example, if you become excited easily to the point of losing control, you need to know about that tendency and institute techniques to help keep calm enough to stay on track. If you tend to withdraw into yourself under duress, you need to recognize that fact and work to project an outgoing demeanor in performance. If you tend to be overly precise at the expense of the dramatic, you may need to goad yourself into making a few grand gestures at performance time. If you tend to focus on perfect form and accurate detail to the exclusion of emotional intensity, you may need to inject a more obvious display of your feelings at performance time.

Using Internal Imagery

Use your imagination to create the self you desire, one that embodies all of the attributes you long for, and project yourself into that image, much as an actor might project him or herself into a role. This exercise is most successful when you can set aside a short period of uninterrupted time and focus your entire being on it. During the exercise, imagine yourself as possessing the qualities you want, see yourself in specific circumstances or situations in which you exhibit these qualities, internalize the picture, and generate mental impulses that are appropriate to the physical response you desire.

Exercises

For example, you may worry that the physical coordination you practiced so much will fail you when you perform your music. Deep down you believe that you are a person who inadvertently stumbles at important moments in your life. To clear this pattern, become quiet in a relaxed position, focusing on concepts such as perfect physical response, beautifully coordinated movement, effortlessly efficient motion, graceful gestures, and muscular power. As you contemplate these concepts, you see yourself moving in ways that exhibit these attributes. At first, see yourself moving in fantasy-like settings, such as gliding through space, entering a roomful of people, dancing, performing physical feats that require a high degree of coordination or athleticism. Gradually fill in details, making the settings increasingly more detailed. Transform the space into a familiar workplace, and make the people in the room those who make you self-consciousness. The dancing is now with a partner with whom you are romantically involved; the feats become the ones that challenge you in your music.

Now is the time to internalize these detailed images and generate commands to execute them. First, shift the focus of your imagination so that the images are no longer outside your being, as observed concepts, but rather are pulled into your being. Then generate mental impulses that would initiate this wonderfully coordinated motion, even while you remain immobile. You may even detect slight sensations in your body, as if your muscles were about to respond to these impulses. You may perceive these sensations as a tingling or warmth.

This final stage might seem bizarre or difficult to achieve. Actually, it's both familiar and easy. Try sitting down, relaxing, and then, without actually moving a muscle, generate the mental impulses for something you do frequently, like washing your hands, cutting your food with a knife and fork, or driving an automobile. You will sense that you almost respond by going into action. The final stage of the exercise is thus simply a way to generate your new set commands to trigger the coordination you will need to perform the way you want to.

To take another example, perhaps physical clumsiness doesn't bother you, but rather the inability to express yourself. You sound uncharacteristically stilted or halting when you talk to an authority figure, such as your boss or someone for whom you have a strong attraction. This tendency inhibits the expressive aspect of your music-making. Here use your quiet time first to imagine concepts of flowing speech, eloquence, and wit. See yourself possessing these qualities in fantasy-like situations: speaking brilliantly in front of some audience; causing friends to laugh at your clever remarks; explaining clearly to students some complicated concept; making your case eloquently to some supervisor. Finally see yourself making music that communicates its emotional content so powerfully that your audiences are visibly affected. Then fill in the details with specific places, persons, and concerts. Finally, project yourself into that situation, bringing yourself to the threshold of actually verbalizing the words and experiencing inwardly the sensations of expressive communication.

The simple act of doing the exercises sends messages to the subconscious, the most powerful force within us for directing deep-seated motivation, emotional tenor, and reliability of physical response. The subconscious is a level of our brains we cannot reach easily, for it seems unresponsive to the babble of our consciousness. For the most part, it formulates truth from the pain and pleasure we experience and observe rather than what it is told. At some point, however, you can convince your subconscious of the veracity of the beliefs fed to it by your conscious mind, especially when the conscious mind is insistent by repeating something over and over again.

The value of conceptualizing your ideal world and concentrating on it becomes apparent when you recognize that, unlike the conscious, the subconscious makes no distinction between fantasy and reality. Thus if your subconscious mind is told often enough that you have in fact achieved your goals, and you imagine those accomplishments are real (in our examples, that you move gracefully or that you make music eloquently), it will eventually begin to believe such precepts and to direct responses within you that support such a belief. When the subconscious starts to deliver that support, you experience an often dramatic change in the ease with which you accomplish your goals, and the conscious mind is amazed that somehow you have begun to overcome your inhibitions, now performing securely and expressively.

If you were to explore various systems of metaphysical speculation, you would quickly encounter the belief that the subconscious mind has the mystical power to manifest reality in the face of all odds; once the subconscious mind is completely convinced of a given set of parameters, it will transcend the boundaries of the physical world and forge ahead to produce a reality that conforms to the circumstances it has become convinced of. This belief is a component part of virtually every philosophical or religious system in the world. For example, it was this tenet that Jesus Christ referred to in the Bible when he said that faith could move mountains or commanded his followers to produce the miracles he was noted for.

Tapping into this seemingly supernatural power, of course, requires a belief system powerful enough for the subconscious to buy into. Since we cannot communicate directly with the subconscious mind, we are directed to address it through meditation while creating and living in the fantasy of the reality we hope for. We are, furthermore, given complete assurance that persistent use of this method will create whatever miracles are needed to change our lives and that, in fact, the occurrence of these miracles is absolutely guaranteed if we will but stay the course long enough with intensity of purpose and thought.

Those who are not practiced mystics react to such claims with varying degrees of credulity. Some dismiss the matter as "pie in the sky." Others claim to have tried it and found it to work. For example, we constantly encounter reports of miracle healing brought about as a result of prayer. Still others use it as a means of seeking guidance they deem valuable without necessarily claiming to have crossed over into the world of the miraculous. For example, many successful individuals tell of imagining conferences with guides or famous people from past eras. In the classic self-help book *Think and Grow Rich* by Napoleon Hill, the author describes his technique of holding imaginary meetings with great fortune builders of the past, such as Carnegie, Mellon, and Vanderbilt.

Whatever the individual variance, the concept of possessing such unlimited power fascinates and entices most of us. As if trying the traveling medicine man's cure-all tonic, many of us are willing to give it a shot with the attitude that nothing ventured is nothing gained. Prior belief by the conscious mind is not a necessary condition for instilling the same belief in the subconscious. Indeed, our conscious mind can even hold considerable doubt as to the effectiveness of the visualization. None of this matters, for the subconscious will eventually respond to whatever it is repeatedly told without checking to see if its counterpart, the conscious mind, believes it or not.

Thus the effectiveness of the process is not impaired even if the conscious mind insists on regarding the entire procedure as a waste of time. To reap the benefits of these exercises, we simply must do them carefully and regularly without regard to how our conscious mind might evaluate their usefulness. Such an arrangement opens the door to being able to try out the process with a simple investment of time and effort, but without having to accept a metaphysical phenomenon that the conscious mind may find questionable. There are, however, legions of experimenters who will tell you that you will be surprised at the results and that you will eventually come around to being a believer in the effectiveness of this technique.

Self-regard sets the tone for undertaking a performance project. It may seem to recede from our consciousness during periods of intense preparation, but it becomes paramount again as performance time nears. Even so, improving self-regard should be an ongoing process, and musicians should practice self-regard exercises with the same regularity and rigor they use to improve technique and musicianship. Adherence to such a regime will absolutely increase performance success.

chapter ten
Managing Stage Fright

This chapter addresses head on the excitement, tension, nervousness, stage fright, or trauma—whatever name it goes by, the state that to some degree envelopes everyone who attempts a performance. Some performers seem to enjoy this feeling, claiming they actually get turned on by its stimulation. Most, however, do not look forward to experiencing the symptoms of this condition. The symptoms vary from person to person but almost always include both physical and psychological elements. The physical signs might include an increased heartbeat, breathing irregularity, tiredness, headache, blurred vision, tension in the abdomen, upset stomach, dryness in the mouth, and the sensation of weak or impaired muscular control. The psychological manifestations almost always have to do with a strong desire to escape or retreat from the discomfort of the challenge at hand. Like a bird caught in a room, the mind seems to race from window to window in its attempt to free itself, often ignoring logical connections and gravitating toward various unfocused states by indulging fleetingly in such moods as being depressed, bored, silly, cavalier, sleepy, sleepless, annoyed, or angry.

Residual Tension

This state of tension does not always present itself with the same level of urgency. True, just before a performance, nervousness is usually at a fairly high level, but even at this time some moments are more intense than others. By the same token, the first symptoms may occur days, perhaps even weeks, before the performance. One generally experiences an anxiety attack of relatively short duration, subsiding whenever the mind is able to focus once more. But

105

it is sure to return with increased regularity as the performance time nears. Like an uninvited physical disorder, it seems to lurk within you, and it makes sneak attacks on your consciousness. This low-grade tension comes and goes and periodically rises to engulf you in what might be called *residual tension.*

The first appearance of residual tension, then, may be well in advance of the actual performance. Frequently it starts in the middle of the night. You awake from sleep to find that on some level you are thinking about the performance, the consequences of its outcome, or some aspect of preparation that needs work, or you might just repeat over and over the patterns associated with the performance. You direct your mind to dismiss these concerns for the moment so you can go back to sleep, but your mind seems tenacious in its focus and impervious to your wishes. You toss and turn or do something (like read or watch TV) until your mind gets weary and releases its focus, at which point you may be able to drift back to sleep. At other times you may be fully awake and engaged in some other activity when your mind sets off an alarm and tension wells up. You must go about your daily business, but you feel some physical symptom of this tension, and your mind seems torn between focusing on the task at hand and the future performance.

As performance time nears, the individual attacks of residual tension may coalesce into a constant state. You sleep, eat, go about your daily activities, including your practicing, with the sense that you are no longer quite your normal self, or that something hovers over you stalking you night and day. Of course you know that this specter is the prospect of the upcoming performance, but even with that knowledge, you wish you could be free of the residual tension, even if only for a short period of time.

Residual tension is widespread among performers. Because of its discomfort, you may feel singled out for a special version of torture, either by virtue of your inexperience, lack of ability, or unlucky fate. In fact, this is not true. You are experiencing some version of the same affliction that almost all performers must endure. Testimony to this fact comes from all sides, even from those with years of performing experience. Having to handle the tension simply goes with the territory. Very few individuals actually enjoy this tension, but very few are so traumatized that they forgo the challenges and benefits of performing rather than face its effects. Knowing you are just part of the human race does not remove this burden but at least offers the comfort that many others have endured it and dealt with it successfully.

Also, most people deal with residual tension without incurring ill effects. Indeed, it's rather amazing that something capable of causing so much discomfort for so many days, as well as escalating just before the performance to the point of seeming to take over one's entire being, can vanish so quickly without a trace the instant a performance ends. One may experience other feelings after the performance (addressed in chapter 12): relief, elation, satisfaction, perhaps even disappointment or depression. But almost always that feeling of having to suffer a day with inner tension will have disappeared. Furthermore, although you may feel exhausted after a performance, in all likelihood you will observe no lasting side effects, no permanent physical damage. Therefore take consolation in the knowledge that residual tension will become benign once the performance is behind you.

Diversion

There are many techniques that provide momentary release from the pressure of residual tension, creating temporary distraction or diversion. You will have to experiment to discover which work best for you. For some, periods of meditation wherein you attempt to blank out your mind and enter into a deep trance-like state will help you forget the urgency of the performance challenge. For others, some form of entertainment (a movie, book, or concert) will provide temporary escape. For still others, some form of hobby-like activity does the trick, perhaps cooking a meal, playing with pets, working in the garden. Whatever activity you choose, it should appeal to you personally, offer short-term satisfaction, and be easy and pleasant to engage in.

You may tend to deny yourself such diversions, reasoning that you could invest that time improving your performance. You may, in fact, become compulsive about spending every possible moment getting ready. We do reach points of no return in our performance preparation, however, particularly when the performance is imminent and residual tension is running high. You have reached such a point when you begin to experience one or more of these symptoms.

- Your concentration becomes fuzzy and forced.
- You are prone to making mistakes that you don't usually make.
- You become irritable or temperamental.
- You feel physical pain as a result of tension (headaches, neck or back pain).
- You are consistently getting results that you know are below par for your present level of ability.

Taking the time to indulge occasionally in some pleasant diversions thus becomes a helpful and even necessary form of therapy. Like a child who has been unusually good, the mind and body demand a reward from time to time. Moreover, if we can't enjoy life a little along the road to success, what is the point of traveling it? In fact, if we do not adopt this balanced approach, we are apt to find ourselves exhibiting uncharacteristic personality traits. For example, we might put on a display of how busy we are and how important our task is. Or we may feel that we are being neglected or victimized by others' lack of interest or support, or even by God or cosmic forces.

Cécile Genhart, the celebrated teacher who was on the faculty of the Eastman School of Music for many years, reported that her father, Gottfried, a professor at the Zurich Conservatory, forbade his children to speak at the dinner table two or three weeks before every piano recital. If she or her sister broke the silence, their mother would shush them with the admonition: "Have you forgotten? Your father must play a recital soon!"

Such aberrations are simply indications that we need to put a little fun in our lives. As a human being, you need to take time out to do something you enjoy, even if it seems to have no connection with the upcoming performance. Such an excursion often acts as an antidote for surliness and will bring the necessary relief to get back on track emotionally.

Dress Rehearsal

As the time for the performance draws near, you will likely begin to sense the totality of what you have committed yourself to. Even if you have developed a good conceptual grasp of your overall performance, set aside special times to run your performance from beginning to end, simulating as closely as possible all of the conditions of the performance itself. Having several such "dress rehearsals" provides one of the best antidotes to excessive nervousness when the real performance rolls around.

Several rules of thumb are important to observe if these trial runs are to serve their purpose:

- Set a specific time for your dress rehearsal in advance.
- Simulate as closely as possible all the conditions of the performance.
- Once you start the performance, do not allow yourself to back up and redo portions.
- Play it to the hilt.
- Seek outside observation and evaluation, if possible.

As you approach the time of the actual performance, nervous tension may cause you to avoid the reckoning of a dress rehearsal. Under the guise of not being quite ready, you may delay it until the last minute. Even a late dress rehearsal can be of some benefit, though. Remember, however, that part of the benefit is being able to assess and strengthen weak spots and correct mistakes. If the dress rehearsal is scheduled very close to the performance, you may not have enough time to work in the changes you need.

Schedule Your Dress Rehearsal

Therefore schedule your dress rehearsal in advance, perhaps as part of your original scheduling operation, allowing enough time between the dress rehearsal and the performance for changes. Scheduling it at a given time and place endows it with the parameters that attend most performances, and so you will likely see the need to rise to the occasion. Although a part of you will cling to the reality that it is "not for keeps," having to run your show at an appointed day and time will go a long way toward making the dress rehearsal an effective testing exercise.

Simulate the Actual Performance

Simulating as many conditions of the actual performance as possible also contributes to the verisimilitude of the dress rehearsal. Consider the environment in which you will perform, the clothes you will wear, the instrument you will use, and the unexpected challenges you may be called upon to meet during the performance. The degree to which you can create all of these conditions in advance may vary.

For example, if you have no advance access to the performance venue, you may have to forgo experiencing the exact environmental conditions you will have to deal with at performance time. You can, however, garner helpful information about the performance site, such as the size of the space, how it will be lit, acoustical properties, and possible distractions. At this point you might want to turn to the technique of using your imagination to create images that suggest the conditions you cannot simulate in reality.

Exercise

As you prepare for a run-through of your presentation, take a moment to become quiet. Imagine the environment in which you will perform. Imagine the setting in as much detail as possible. Will there be an audience? A panel of adjudicators? A watchful teacher or coach? Press? Special guests? Will you be in a different sized space than you are used to? A concert hall? A theater? A stadium or amphitheater? Will you have unusual lighting? Spotlights? Floodlights? Unusual darkness? Will you be able to hear? Crowd noises? Reverberation? Earphones? Or will you have to project your music in order to enhance presence? Will there be unexpected challenges that may distract you? Competitors? Stage prompters? Applause? Interruptions?

Your imagination may be inaccurate or imperfect in simulating these conditions, and the reality of encountering them will undoubtedly carry more impact than these mental images. On the other hand, the exercise can at least engender an inner attentiveness, even excitement, as you go into your run-through, thus lifting the dress rehearsal above the level of the routine. This added ingredient will give you a foretaste of the performance itself and, even in a watered-down form, will help prepare you for its rigors.

Resist Starting Over

Once you have begun, resist the temptation to start over. You might get off to a rocky start. The fact that you intend to run the entire performance, that, indeed, this is a dress rehearsal, may result in some foolish error just after you've begun, or at least the feeling that you could effect a better beginning. The temptation will be strong to start over. You formulate a quick agreement with yourself that this dress rehearsal didn't really "count," and you stop and start over. Although yielding to this frequently encountered temptation is not of monumental import, resist it. During the actual performance you will not have the luxury of starting over. Even if you are permitted to do so, as perhaps in an audition, you may leave the impression of being less in command than you would like.

If you do permit yourself to start over during a dress rehearsal, limit your indulgence. Starting over or doubling back to redo something that didn't quite suit you can easily become habitual. Before you know it, you will find yourself starting over a third or fourth time or making constant corrections as you go along. Jumping back is likely to become frequent and almost automatic. In its epidemic form, a pattern of doubling back to repeat may appear so frequently that it begins to resemble stuttering. Once such a habit gets entrenched, it is extremely difficult to break. Thus, if you do permit yourself another start, do so with full awareness and place strict limits on the number of times you allow yourself this luxury.

Moreover, if you do permit yourself another start because of a technical mishap, try not break the continuity of your performance until you have it squarely back on track. Being able to stabilize a rocky performance helps prevent you from getting into a habit of breaking the continuity when the actual performance is less than smooth or not to your liking. Learning how to get back on track while forging ahead is a good skill to develop.

Running several nonstop dress rehearsals often results in the additional benefit of a psychological readjustment. As you conceptualize the total performance, a process that may have seemed long, complex, or ominous begins to shrink in your mind and running it in its entirety seems a less formidable task. This conceptual shrinkage happens every day. For instance, the first time we have to find a new place, we follow directions. The distance to our destination often seems sizable, and the process of getting there complex. Later, after we have made the trip several times, the distance seems not as great as we originally thought, and the place becomes quite easy to find. A similar readjustment will probably take place after a few nonstop rehearsals. Happily, increased confidence and command almost always accompany this psychological shrinkage.

Play It to the Hilt

At least some of your final run-throughs should be played to the hilt. During the actual performance, the knowledge that this one is "for keeps" will set off an adrenaline flow that will motivate you to give it everything you've got. Learning to handle the effects of adrenaline is a challenge in itself and is considered more thoroughly in the next chapter. In the best-case scenario, that increased burst of energy will cause you to overreach yourself, and you will turn in a performance of such power and excellence that even you will be astonished. At its worst, adrenaline can dispel your concentration or stimulate erratic physical responses. Thus gaining some experience in dealing with that adrenaline rush is of great value. It cannot be simulated completely in rehearsal, simply because it is, indeed, born of the awareness that the performance is the real thing. But use your imagination. Conjure up sharp images of a given time and place, of the audience or the other people you will encounter. You can often garner enough tension to get a foretaste of the real event. Then remind yourself to make it a nonstop, full-throttle performance, and you should be able to create synthetically a challenge that, if not quite the real thing, at least rises above the usual run-through.

Enlist Observers

You might go a step further in this simulation by setting up a dress rehearsal with observers. Enlist family or friends to watch. Often social groups, hospitals, or retirement centers welcome such diversions and will eagerly schedule you for a trial run. In audition-type performances, find someone to act out the role of the adjudicator, someone who will choose when to stop you and ask you to go on to another section or piece.

You will be able to assess yourself to a great extent in these run-throughs, but do not overlook the value of openly soliciting critical evaluation from those who observe or challenge you. In most cases, they will not offer such evaluation unless you urge them to share their impressions. Casual observers may not be qualified to offer sophisticated observations, and to some extent the attention you pay to reactions may be tempered by your own evaluation of the source. By the same token, as was noted earlier, you can sometimes glean valuable information even from general offhand comments made by unsophisticated or disinterested parties. Remember to ask yourself why, out of all the comments this person could have made, did he or she choose to communicate this particular thing?

Response from more experienced sources, of course, might be examined more closely. You may be able to zero in on a number of small changes that will polish up your performance. Tender even these changes with caution, however. Remember that you are the best judge of how much you can afford to change at this particular time, for if you are in a dress rehearsal mode, you are probably also in the eleventh hour before the real event. Of course, small mistakes should be addressed; insecure moments need to be drilled; expressive misfires need to be rethought; you can add a flourish here or smooth a rough edge there. Realize, however, that you are limited in how much you can change successfully at the last minute. Initiating new physical responses take time to integrate into the flow of your performance, and last-minute changes can become stumbling blocks under the pressure of the real thing. Therefore take into account the comments and suggestions you collect, and do what you can to improve your performance, but leave yourself a small but important segment of time to pull yourself together before you step up to the real event.

Just before the Performance

The hours before a performance can be a problematic window of time for many performers. This "dead time" may come between the final dress rehearsal and the performance. In a few cases the preparation time may be so tight that you are working right up to the moment of performance. In most cases, however, the "dead time" window consists of a few hours so close to actual performance that energy needs to be conserved for the real thing. Furthermore, it is too late to work productively at the performance, bcause doing so can result in your getting hung up on fussy details when you need to be approaching the performance with a sense of the whole. Moreover, you may feel restless because by now adrenaline has kicked in.

The best use of this window of time is to focus on some engaging but inconsequential activity. The exact nature of such a pursuit depends, of course, upon personal taste. We noted some of these activities earlier in this chapter: light reading, watching television or a movie, indulging in a hobby such as gardening or cooking, playing with your pet, or tinkering with a car or piece of equipment. Whatever it is, it should require enough concentration or physical involvement to give you partial respite from the anxiety of your imminent performance, but it should be light enough in its demands not to drain you of your main reserve of mental or physical energy. Some experienced performers like simply to lounge about, indulging in culinary delicacies, bathing, or massages. During this time you will not escape entirely the awareness that a time of testing approaches, but you may ease the pressure enough to achieve a degree of flexibility and perspective that will actually enhance the performance.

Tension of a new type escalates in the moments just before the performance: stage fright, performance nerves, or simply being scared. It grows out of residual tension, and the symptoms of residual tension are all present, but usually in a much more intense form. And like residual tension, it is universal. Even the most experienced performers must deal with performance nerves. One might imagine that years of experience would provide a track record of success so formidable that performance nerves would eventually become a thing of the past. Such is simply not the case for most performers. The issues may change slightly with experience, but the anxiety remains.

When a musician attempts a particular type of performance for the first time, the main worry may be just getting through it from beginning to end under pressure. Thus anxiety centers on continuity, remembering, and staying in balance while realizing expressive goals. To some extent this concern never vanishes. Many seasoned performers have experienced the shock of an upset in a well-oiled performance simply because their high confidence permitted their concentration to stray. Thus, as many seasoned performers know, beware of regarding any performance as "easy." Wise performers regard every new performance as a new challenge.

Still, after many successful performances, the focus of your anxiety may shift to new issues. These might include remaining fresh and energized, maintaining or improving quality, or being required to perform when tired or sick. In competitive situations, there is the anxiety of knowing your performance is being compared to those of others. For those with a strong reputation, living up to the high expectations generated by earlier successes can sometimes cause concern. And for those who have performed for many years, the psychological and physiological changes of aging bring a special set of worrisome adjustments.

While residual tension and performance fear are universal, they do differ in other ways. While residual tension does not usually result in permanent damage to either our minds or bodies—it vanishes once the performance is over—but the intensity and all-encompassing power of stage fright have the potential to forge deeply ingrained psychological patterns. That intensity and power can combine with various kinds of evaluation during or after the performance to cause withdrawal or depression. Chapters 11 and 12 deal with these manifestations of performance fear. For now, let us simply note them in the context of residual tension escalating to performance anxiety.

When you recognize a full-blown case of stage fright, remember that you have been handling these same symptoms over the past several days as residual tension. To be sure, the symptoms may have been less intense, but garner confidence from the knowledge that you have functioned in performance rehearsals even with the devitalizing effects of tension. This knowledge leads to the realization that you will be able to function at performance time, even if you feel that stage fright might immobilize you. Hang onto this thought even in the roughest moments of preperformance jitters. You have prepared, and you know you have the foundation to give a creditable performance. Focus on these facts and cling to the belief that you can do it no matter what kind of storm stage fright may have unleashed upon you. At the moment it may seem like whistling in the dark, but your choice as you step up to perform is either to whistle and summon up your courage or be silent and fearful.

It is important at this point to establish a pattern of fighting back. The feeling of insecurity is likely not going to go away. As performance time rolls around, use your full arsenal of firepower again and again to demolish negative thought patterns and maximize your will to do your best. At this point intrepid bullheadedness is useful. Remind yourself over and over again of your high level of preparation, of successful dress rehearsals, of the communication you want to establish, and of the results you know you can achieve. Envision yourself as calm, strong, unbeatable, focused, and successful. Repeat these thoughts and images, hurling them in the face of your nervous symptoms. Keep firing away, even though some part of your mind reasons that the positive bullets are doing no good.

Force yourself to change your physical state with the techniques you have practiced. Move. Swing your arms. Roll your head around to loosen your neck. Stretch your back. Breathe deeply. A good chuckle over the predicament you've gotten yourself into can be healthy at this point. And even at the last possible moment, in the instant just before you step up to give your performance, shove the anxiety aside with an additional chuckle, whistle, smile, deep breath, lifting of the chin, straightening of the spine, and a final upbeat thought. The moment has indeed finally arrived. This is the point you've been waiting for . . . you're on!

chapter eleven
Dynamics during Performance

In an ideal world, self-awareness during performance would be non-existent. Yet we are forced to deal with it. Imagine for a moment giving a perfect performance, one that flowed without a hitch, where you surmounted all challenges and overcame all adversaries effortlessly. If such a performance were to take place, you would be completely focused, submerging yourself without any reflection or self-consciousness. You would fall into this state quickly and easily, stay under its spell until completion, and return to your normal state with the knowledge that your entire being was immersed for the duration of the performance.

In reality, we are almost never able to achieve the perfection just described and lose ourselves completely in the performance. Most performers find that they experience a variable state during the performance, fluctuating between focused immersion in its best moments and sensitized self-consciousness in its worst. A number of factors contribute to this imperfect realization.

First and foremost, adrenaline makes us unusually sensitive to outside stimuli. Thus environmental factors we might ordinarily take in stride, such as temperature, lighting, acoustical properties, or getting used to strange venues or instruments, often become distractions. Second, this high degree of sensitivity will probably affect physical processes, so as we start the physical activity of the performance, we feel a sense of strangeness or newness, as if we were doing it for the first time and were unsure if we would be able to get started or keep going.

Moreover, as we wade into the performance, we are likely to become painfully aware of every flaw, either real or imagined. Sometimes, indeed, small glitches occur near the beginning of a performance, a momentary adjustment in which we find our sea legs. Sometimes such an adjustment does

117

not take place, but instead we receive a stream of doubt-filled feedback on the general quality of the performance. Eschewing specifics, a voice warns that this "just isn't going very well" or "needs to be better." Often this voice of dissent will attach itself to some icon of insecurity and dangle it before our consciousness like a malevolent amulet: the difficulty of what it is we are trying to do; the embarrassment or other consequences of failure; someone we spot in an audience who we believe will be critical.

In fact our imagination may get so sensitized that it begins to create threatening images out of perfectly normal or innocuous observations: a look on an adjudicator's face, a chance comment by a well-wisher, or a gesture by someone in attendance. Later we may see such aberrations in their proper perspective, even amusingly so, but at the time our mind may imbue them with great import, often attributing to them some symbolic meaning as to how the performance is going. It is as if someone said to you, "Have a nice day," and your reaction was "What secret knowledge of my destiny do you possess that results in your wishing me a nice day?" "Do you know something I don't about my day?" "Why should you care if I have a nice day?" "What business is it of yours, anyway?" "Things were going just fine until you told me to have a nice day," and on and on.

All of these symptoms represent nothing more than yet another facet of performance tension. Yet they become particularly annoying because they flit in and out of your consciousness when you are trying to give your best performance. You must deal with this aspect of self-awareness decisively, strongly, quickly, and persistently:

- Recognize such aberrations as tension manifestations.
- Stand up to them mentally rather than cowering at their appearance.
- Repudiate them, perhaps many times.
- Continually turn you efforts toward immersing yourself in the performance.

Even so, all of your efforts to banish periods of self-awareness in the heat of performance will probably not be entirely successful. On one hand, you will try to shove it out of your consciousness. On the other, you must acknowledge it with the belief that you can keep your performance on track and preserve enough of your preparation under fire by consistently overriding it. In other words, exorcise it repeatedly, but learn that you can live with its persistent returning and still manage a fine performance.

Up to this point self-awareness has been characterized as a distracting influence during performance. There is another side to this coin, however, for you can also use it in a beneficial way. To do this, you still have to keep it some distance from the focal point of your concentration. This awareness, when resting somewhere beneath the surface of your attention and carefully controlled, can give an added thrust to your performance. The impulse to "give it all you've got" during the performance, when utilized successfully, can add an edge that will make your performance extraordinary in the true sense of the word. At such times, you have the sense that the performance is, indeed, going well, you are truly representing what you prepared to do, and you have a good feeling about the performance.

This feeling of riding high during a performance is extremely treacherous, however, so work with it cautiously. Remember that the excitement of just giving the performance may have already put enough spice in it. Furthermore, the awareness that "you are giving them hell" can turn on you in a heartbeat. It can throw the delicate balance of performing out of kilter, causing you to make foolish mistakes (the kind where you knew better), or of creating overblown proportions or effects. In retrospect many a performer has bewailed becoming overly confident during a performance just before a significant upset.

Experience in performing often builds a sense of knowing just how far to go in enlisting self-awareness to give the performance an extra kick. Some performers handle this volatile ingredient with expertness, opening the throttle wide during a performance and overreaching themselves. Other, equally fine performers prefer more caution, never giving full reign to impulse and opting for a greater measure of control. Moreover, a given individual's predilection for one mode or the other may vary from situation to situation, feeling at times comfortable in being freely creative and less cautious during a performance, and at other times less so.

Indeed, no two performances have identical conditions. The physical, mental, and emotional state of the performer, the performance environment, new adversaries, unfamiliar acoustics, instruments, or props—all contribute to making each performance a unique experience for the performer. Thus, an x factor attends every performance. It may be comprised of the influences just noted as well as less obvious ones. This "unknown" element renders some performances better than others, even when external circumstances appear constant. Seasoned performers speak of being "on" for some performances and "off" for others. The "off" performances are not necessarily failures. Often a performer feels that a performance is "off" even when those in attendance deem it perfectly fine or results seem totally satisfactory. Much of the performer's "on/off" perception has to do with the degree to which self-awareness was handled or utilized. We learn to use self-awareness beneficially to the extent we can, but it remains an uncontrollable power, a live wire with the potential of both generating an extra measure of energy and causing considerable havoc.

For less seasoned performers, simply maintaining balance in the face of nervousness and self-consciousness will be an all-consuming challenge. Several tips can be of use in this effort:

- Pace yourself during the performance
- Refreshing your physical state during the performance
- Keeping withdrawal impulses in check
- Regarding competitive challenges without emotional baggage
- Being creative under pressure
- Assessing the risk factor

Learning to Pace Yourself

Adrenaline almost always distorts a sense of tempo. Most performers react to increased adrenaline by feeling an urgency that incites forward motion. Thought processes and the movements they direct are speeded up. If adrenaline release were limited to its original purpose, to help us defend ourselves, we would be able to fight harder and run faster with increased adrenaline. Our needs during performances, however, are of course much more complex, both mentally and physically, so harder or faster are not necessarily what serve us best. In fact, letting such effects run freely may result in careless mistakes or loss of control over physical response.

You should be aware of the effect of adrenaline and think before you jump in at a faster than normal pace. Wade into your performance deliberately, taking care to keep the pace similar to that in your rehearsals. At points during the performance where you can pause and take stock, reset the pace, especially if you note there was marked acceleration during the preceding segment. Mentally cling to enough detail, such as phrasing, articulation, or dynamic changes, to hold in check your impulse to rush forward. Resist the temptation to gulp segments so large that weak rhythmic beats are rushed or articulation in passagework is scrambled. By the same token, ride the flow gracefully. Imagine yourself surfing, Rollerblading, or bicycling.

Also be careful not to control the flow with too much insistence. Sense how much pulling back you can get away with without inciting jerkiness or moving in erratic directions. Indeed, too much resistance can throw off your timing and result in breaks or breeches in the forward flow. To make matters harder, becoming expert at pacing the flow of performance requires a special skill you can learn only under fire, when the adrenaline factor is actually present. Take heart, however, in the fact that learning is quick under pressure and that you have conceptualized a strategy in advance. You can see that dress rehearsals before an audience take on new importance as a training aid for developing this knack.

Refreshing Your Physical State

During a performance remember to breathe deeply and to consciously release muscle tension with a shake or a shrug. Such techniques can often be instituted in the throes of forward motion. Typically, your performance will be moving forward smoothly, then suddenly a sense of insecurity begins to overtake you. Such a feeling may be triggered by a tough challenge looming in front of you, a distraction, or simply a subconscious message of doubt that bubbles up to bedevil you. When such a feeling of insecurity begins to take root, try the following:

- Breathe more deeply, even as your continue your performance. (Your breathing has likely become shallow.)
- Readjust your posture. (You have likely become rigid.)
- Loosen your shoulders and back. (You are probably quite tense.)

These simple, on-the-fly techniques can be helpful for all activities but are particularly effective for physical response. Simple as such actions are, they often have the power instantaneously to clear the head, straighten out tangled mental signals, avert breakdown, and restore balance as insecurity recedes.

Keeping Withdrawal Impulses in Check

Withdrawal impulses may tempt you during a performance as you receive signals that tell you to retreat. This "flight impulse" is part of the primal function of adrenaline. Appropriate though it may be in some instances, it is not an option during musical performances. Resorting to flight translates into quitting the performance, walking out mentally, cowering as you approach a challenge, rushing off stage, or in some measure giving up.

The impulse to retreat may also manifest itself in less obvious ways, such as an intense desire to escape the pressure or unpleasant feedback that exaggerates mistakes or flaws. You might feel overwhelmed by difficulties that lie ahead or make a negative projection about the performance outcome. These perceptions add up to wanting just to quit, or, if you manage to stay, continuing with a halfhearted, hangdog attitude. Looming somewhere in your mind are messages like "What's the use," "This performance is terrible," "I've already failed in achieving my goal," or "Let's get this over with as quickly as possible."

First, realize that there is always a strong possibility that your negative perception is just plain wrong. Your nervousness has warped your judgment about the performance and, were you an objective observer of exactly the same performance, you would evaluate it quite differently. This may sound like unfounded optimism, but let me relate the following personal experience.

Several years ago I was scheduled for an important solo piano recital in a major city. I knew that the concert had attracted a capacity crowd to a prestigious venue, that music critics would be reviewing the recital for the following morning's newspapers, and that the concert would be broadcast live. I had scheduled performances of new, recently learned repertoire, something that for me always adds an extra measure of pressure. As I left home for the concert hall, I set up recording equipment that would automatically tune in to the radio station and record the concert at the appointed time.

That night I was just plain miserable from the moment I walked onstage until the last note of the concert. My physical responses seemed to me sluggish and strained. The hall was so crowded that some of the audience was on the stage, sitting too close to the piano for my comfort. Every piece impressed me as being mechanical, as well as teetering on the verge of total collapse. I reached the end of the concert with a great sigh of relief. Although I was vaguely aware of the fact that the audience seemed responsive, I was convinced people were just being polite. The program had been a bit long, so I used that fact as an excuse to myself, wimped out, and graciously (?) refused to play an encore. I greeted well-wishers backstage with as much enthusiasm as I could muster, while trying to cope with the sinking in the pit of my stomach that signaled I had just turned in a sizable turkey.

I was so upset when I returned home that sleep was impossible. I anticipated scathing reviews, and so I decided I might as well stay up and face the situation by listening to the air tape of the concert. As the tape began to roll, I was overcome with a sense of total disbelief. What I was hearing could not have been the same concert I just played! Yet it was. The hell I had gone through simply didn't come across. There was not a trace of what I had perceived as sluggishness, rigidity, and emotional constipation. The fact that I had been so uncomfortable and my conviction that the flow of the performance was on the brink of collapse were not detectable. I might, indeed, be critical of a few things here and there, but listening to the tape forced me to realize that the concert was simply much better than I had perceived at the time of performance. Incidentally, the reviews the following day were raves.

That experience dramatized for me the fact that at the time of performance, we are poor judges of the effect we create. Because we are caught up in the act of the performance, we cannot be both the generator and the receiver. Also the emotional tone created by pressure distorts our perception of what is actually happening. Thus the desire to give up during a performance may be a totally inappropriate reaction to what is actually taking place. Remembering this fact is in itself a weapon against the impulse to surrender.

Resist thought patterns other than those of complete dedication to giving your very best. Life is not a string of unqualified successes. There will be times when you will look back knowing a given performance does not represent your maximum potential. When you have to deal with such a reality, you should at least be able to say to yourself that you summoned up your courage and energy and gave it the very best shot you were capable of at the time. In other words, you can spare yourself the agony of looking back and facing the fact that you not only fell short of your potential, something that sometimes happens to everyone and seems beyond control, but also wimped out in the process, something that you need never let happen.

Moments may arise when it is hard not to cave in. At such times, use your will power to stay the course. Alter your physical state with a movement or a breath. Remind yourself that it's not over until it's over. Renew your energy mentally in the face of whatever negative factors have loomed up. Whatever the cost in terms of effort, remain absolutely intrepid in your determination to give it all you've got.

Competitive Challenge

A special case of resolve is needed when you face a competitive challenge. If successive performances are compared and the best selected, then dealing with adversarial distraction means simply putting on mental blinders, giving the best performance you can without reference to what others might be able to do. Doing this may require an extra measure of concentration on your part, but it does not require you to alter your preparation plan. Even so, the competitive environment may generate negativism, not only in your perception of your own shortcomings, but also in the power you perceive in your competitor.

In sports, getting revved up to meet your opponent is a time-honored technique. Pep talk is the classic example. A good coach gives the team a pep talk before it enters the playing field and continues to stimulate motivation for maximum effort with more pep talks on the sidelines or at halftime.

Exercise

Following this example, engage in self-generated pep talk from an imagined alter ego. Just before a performance, exhort yourself aloud to achieve your personal best. During the actual performance, keep up a stream of positive images. These may be fleeting and sporadic, because your main focus is on performing, but they can act as a guardian for your mental state, warding off the attacks of fear or negativism that well up as a result of your fear or your competitor's effectiveness.

When contemplating the competition you must face, exorcise rumor. One can work oneself into near panic by listening to street talk. Inexperienced performers frequently fall prey to beliefs that emerge from such talk. Adjudicators are thought of as possessing formidable powers of perception, as well as an appetite for tearing apart performances. Audiences are conceptualized as a group of inordinately critical individuals who hope for performance failure or disaster. Competitors are glorified to be powerful, tireless, or invincible. Finally, a cursory view of someone else's rehearsal or warmup is often blown out of proportion and taken as evidence of the spectacular and flawless qualities of that person's performance. Remember this saying: "Everyone sounds wonderful through the practice room door."

Don't get caught up in this emotional treadmill. Instead, focus on what you must do, not what your competitors may or may not do. In general, do not attend rehearsals or performances of your competitors just before your own performance, unless you can do so with a coolness that permits you to study the strategy of your opponent and learn something to enhance your own performance. If you're not sure you can maintain this objectivity, then stay away. This does not mean that you have to play ostrich, hiding your head in the sand regarding the challenges you will meet, but you can strike a balance that will permit you to assess the strength of the challenges you must face but stop short of buying into negative thought patterns.

Being Creative under Pressure

Now let us consider techniques you might use for being creative under pressure. We have already discussed using adrenaline to increase effort and energy during a performance. But what about using the excitement of performance to generate on-the-spot creativity? Just as using adrenaline to summon extra force has both pluses and minus, so does trying for an extra measure of creativity. First, remember that creativity can and does occur naturally, but usually without conscious adjustment on the performer's part. The heightened sense of awareness and excitement that unnerves you before a performance is also the agent that adds extra luster to what you do. Thus the very fact that you are adrenaline-filled at the time of your performance will provide an unusually sharp creative edge. Your job is simply to throw yourself into the performance, giving it the best concentration and energy you can. Do that, and the additional smarts, the extra punch, the extraordinary glitter will be there for you.

Still, you might ask if it is possible in this highly energized state to search for even more creativity, muster up an even greater force, and push your psychic accelerator to the floorboard. It is possible of course, but also risky. The very fact that you are already charged up may impair your judgment as to how far you can go successfully. As with the drinker to whom "one more for the road" seems harmless, the additional push could send you out of control, and there is no simple way to assess how far you might go in revving up a performance in progress. If this particular performance is new for you, it is probably wisest to let the adrenaline do its job without further conscious enhancement. If it's a performance you've successfully executed many times, then you may, indeed, be ready to be creative under fire. Perhaps adding flourishes is just what you need to spice things up at this point. Performance experience will help give you a sense as to how much on-the-spot creative improvisation is possible and effective. Remember, however, that the extra push may mean that you have extended yourself to the point where you are operating at the outer edge of your potential. In this case, what you are able to do successfully may differ from performance to performance.

Risk Factor

Having dutifully noted the caution with which one must approach tampering with the prepared performance when under fire, we must also recognize the fact that sometimes seasoned performers consciously court a risk factor in order to push themselves. In doing so, they seek to enter a rare state, one in which maintaining balance seems infallible, improvising imaginative nuance or detail seems effortless, and the risk that attends virtuoso display pays off and is both recognized and relished by the audience. When a performer enters this mode, the effect is breathtaking. However, as with falling asleep, you get into this state indirectly, holding the concept in the back of your mind but knowing that you have to let it happen rather than embrace it directly.

Those who court this state know that the conditioning process for entering it is important. In preparing to go to sleep, you must relax by getting physically comfortable and divert your mind from the cares of the day. In conditioning yourself for an overdrive performance, you must become alert physically, create genuine enthusiasm for the content or process of the performance, and generate enough aggressiveness to relish the adventure itself. Then you need to step back mentally from what you are attempting to achieve, throw yourself into the performance, and hope that the overdrive kicks in.

Seasoned performers know that when it does kick in, awareness of it must remain subliminal, at the outer edges of the consciousness. The moment you cry, "Look at me" is apt to be the moment when this high-flying state tumbles to earth. Rather, simply enjoy the ride, keep your focus, and utilize your tension. Experienced performers also know that this rarefied state is elusive enough not to be on call all the time. In fact, much of the time a performance will simply be fine but not graced with on-the-spot creativity and inspiration. In such cases, accept gratefully the performance that was possible and wait for the next time. And sometimes trying to tap the risk factor doesn't work at all, and the performance is more flawed than if more caution had been used. In such cases, realize that playing with a risk factor is indeed a risk, and that by definition an adventure has an unknown resolution. If things turn out less satisfactorily by your having taken the chance, it is part of the package.

Here too you must exercise judgment. The intoxication that comes from constantly taking risks and making every performance an adventure can become addictive. Some performers risk too much too often in their attempts to bring off spectacular performances. In these cases, not only do solid results become sporadic, but a pattern of erratic, inconsistent performance is established. A performer may even get a reputation for being "wild" or undependable. Should this pattern become entrenched, it is difficult to change. Its antidote lies in the preparation stages, and such performers will have to reshape basic techniques, both mental and physical, and rethink and reorganize basic information to approach performance with a greater measure of control and calm.

Attempting to use the risk factor is like working with high voltage. You will have to assess whether or not you are experienced enough and prepared for the accompanying dangers and, if the performance turns out badly, whether or not you can afford the price. For many performers, just giving a performance that correlates with the preparation will be enough of an achievement and will ensure satisfactory results. For a few, the siren song of achieving the magnificent will lure them into taking risks and living with the consequences. And indeed, such performers, on occasion, achieve performances that become legendary.

chapter twelve
Evaluation after Performance

Your performance may be evaluated in several ways and on several levels. First, immediately following the performance, you'll have a sense of how you have done. There may also be a sense of relief. Your psyche registers automatically the fact that, at last, the performance has taken place and the pressure is gone. Your sense of relief from tension may, in fact, swing too far, so that you feel a temporary sense of loss or even depression.

Mingled with these immediate reactions will be an instant evaluation, which may or may not be objective and accurate. To some extent this instant evaluation will be based on your perception of your performance. This impression is still probably too new to be in proper perspective. It will also be influenced by your basic self-image. The degree of truth you can expect in your self-assessment will depend in part upon how balanced and realistic your self-image is.

External factors sometimes confuse or delay the immediate perception of your performance. For example, rituals of various kinds follow performances: congratulations by well-wishers; receptions or parties; media questions or interviews; traveling; having to change clothes or take down equipment. These are actually useful, for the most part, for they provide diversion at a time when many performers are extremely sensitive. Some will celebrate and maximize their feeling of elation. Many may focus on performance flaws or indulge in self-denigration. Usually this highly sensitive state will pass fairly rapidly, and the psyche will cool down after a few hours. But in some cases it may take up to several days before enough balance is restored to be able to regard the performance with a high degree of accuracy and objectivity.

During this highly sensitive period, one often grasps for clues as to how the performance went. Your own perception has, of course, been formed,

129

but it is still clouded by subjectivity. Many performers tend to interpret even the most innocuous comments as holding profound wisdom or hidden meanings. This pattern is so widespread that a whole vocabulary of wickedly amusing aphorisms has sprung up among those who perform on stage. Performers interpret such noncommittal comments as "interesting" or "fascinating" as the kiss of death. These are seen as a sign that the observer could find nothing positive to say. Comments about content without mentioning the quality of execution is interpreted as admiration for the content but not the performance. Thus such comments as "What a splendid program!" or "What a great work!" or "I am so happy to have heard such and such!" are viewed as ways to sidestep addressing the quality of the performance itself. Even out-and-out compliments can be twisted by this warped sense of perception. So even when a well-wisher rushes forth with an enthusiastic "Your Brahms was terrific," the performer responds with a worried "Oh my, then I suppose that means that you didn't like my Mozart."

Official judgment may also come right after the performance. In competitive events, one either wins or loses. Adjudication in competitions is often swift, and you know immediately how well you did in comparison to others who performed. Audition results sometimes take a little longer to learn, but usually within a few days you know whether or not you achieved your goal. In all of these cases, pushing past the results to assess what you did as a performer is desirable but may have to be delayed until the impact of the consequences subsides.

Evaluation of a performance is especially difficult and emotionally charged when the performance must be repeated very soon. It is especially difficult if press reviews appear within a few hours and you have another performance the next night. In these cases, there is enough time only to attempt to correct any mistakes with some superficial drill and to refocus your concentration to gear up for the next event. Deeply probing evaluation is not possible and probably not wise at this point. In some cases you must summon considerable courage and tough-mindedness to repeat the performance that received harsh judgment by the media.

Thus you can begin to understand that evaluation is not usually characterized by the luxury of sitting back in a detached manner, calmly counting the pluses and minuses of your performance, and, if necessary, instituting changes to make the next performance better. It does not often take place as an orderly process and is tempered by external circumstances and shifting emotional reactions. Yet you need to think through some basic points:

- Reflect on the performance.
- Prepare and improve any scheduled repeat performance.
- Relate your evaluation to your long-range plan.

A series of questions will help with this task. The first set of questions relates specifically to the performance, the second to future performances that will be essentially the same or similar, and the third to overall direction and goals. After you examine your own reactions through these questions, we will turn to external evaluation: critical appraisal from other professionals or teachers, media reviews, competition scoring, and adjudicators' comments.

Questions about the Performance You Have Given

- How did I get through the performance with regard to continuity? Did I keep it going reasonably well once it had started, and did I persist through to the end?
- How did the performance score in terms of what I had planned?
- How did I feel during the process?
- How would I assess the effect of the performance if I were an objective observer?

Continuity

Continuity is an important part of all staged performance. Since it represents your ability to sustain a complete performance, it needs to be looked at honestly in retrospect. Keep in mind that most performers will not score perfectly in this area. In reviewing your performance, you can probably recall instances, possibly vividly and painfully, where there was a glitch of some kind, not only a passing mistake, but a breech in the flow or some miscalculation that left you fighting your way back to a more balanced flow. Examples include external distractions, memory lapses, or blockages in physical processes that support your performance. In the best cases, this glitch came and went rapidly, so that the casual observer detected nothing at all, or else interpreted the momentary aberration as individual flourish or personal style. In the worst cases, everyone at the performance was aware of your trouble and waited to see if you could get it back on track.

Although most performers will not achieve a perfect flow, neither will most accept glitches without attempting to improve subsequent performances. Correcting this problem is often elusive, however, because the breakdowns seem to manifest themselves only under the pressure of performance, and in a variety of places. Typically, you can check the details of preparation beforehand time and again and find that everything seems in good working order. The techniques that support your performance appear to be adequately practiced and flow nicely. Memorization seems solid. Rehearsals give a sense that the performance is, indeed, secure and virtually impervious to breakdown.

But all these positive signs cannot be trusted. Lurking within the demands of a real performance is the danger that a pattern of breakdowns might suddenly loom up full force. Awareness of the insidious nature of this breakdown pattern can be a plus if it motivates you to drill the performance well past the point where it gives every appearance of being secure.

Experienced performers are well acquainted with the constant threat of breakdowns. They habitually review basic information to achieve deeper understanding, continue to drill the basic physical processes to garner a greater measure of security, and repeatedly check every detail of memorized material to ensure virtuosic levels of recall. Getting back on track swiftly and unobtrusively becomes second nature if you create artificial stops and starts through the segmentation and intermittent practice techniques discussed in chapters 6 and 7 on repetition and memory. In this way a network of safety procedures is in place should a lapse in continuity appear at any point in the performance. A plan has been conceptualized and rehearsed for getting things stabilized and moving ahead once more.

With this hedge of safety devices in place and continually drilled, the subconscious will eventually stop fearing breakdowns. When that realization sinks into the subconscious, the breakdown pattern recedes slowly but surely, and performances virtually free of breakdowns begin to be possible. Thus the battle is over, but the war is never won. Working to prevent breakdowns is an ongoing process, and the sometimes tedious, excessive drilling is necessary to keep breakdown or glitches at bay. This is simply a necessary part of performing at a high level of continuity.

How Your Performance Scored

Ask yourself how your performance scored when compared with what you intended to do. Where winning or losing is an issue, the temptation will be strong to simply say to yourself: "Well, you won (or lost), didn't you? So what else counts?" However, if you intend to engage in the performance again, comparing what you did with what you planned is valuable. It provides an instant reference through which you can begin to improve for the next performance. Furthermore, if you did not win, it offers an avenue of analyzing the performance. In this way, you can recognize that winning is not everything, that *how* you performed *is* important, and that improving your performance for the next time is a worthwhile investment of time and effort.

As was discussed in the preceding chapter, garnering an accurate insight into how faithful the performance was to the concept you had planned is difficult because of your involvement during the performance and the effects of pressure. You are apt to exaggerate mistakes and insecure moments during performance whereas you were apt to underplay or forget similar mistakes in rehearsals. In addition, the overall impact of your performance on an audience is apt to remain elusive, because you cannot be both the giver and receiver of the performance. Moreover, you know the content of the performance so well that it is impossible for you to experience the freshness brought to your performance by observers or judges. Without that freshness, you are likely to weigh your assessment more toward detail and technique, for this is, indeed, what you spent your time preparing. The fresh observer will likely be able to assess overall content and effect more easily.

Notwithstanding these drawbacks, the comparison of what you think you did with what you prepared or know yourself to be capable of can be valuable.

Exercise

Consider the first few moments of being on stage, your opening segment, be it an aria, a short prelude, or a sonata movement. Construct a list of questions about the first segment, keeping a successful rehearsal model as your point of reference. Here are some sample questions:

- What kind of a first impression did I make?
- Did I give an overall appearance of being confident, relaxed, and warm?
- Was I able to meet initial challenges of strange environments or adversaries?
- Was I able to focus on musical content and effect communication early on?
- Did my physical responses stabilize under pressure?
- Was I able to change my state if physical responses started to slip?
- Did I brush aside initial mistakes or lapses and gain momentum?
- Was I able to create anything special in the first moments?
- Was the opening segment better or worse than my rehearsal?

After you apply this exercise to the first segment of the performance, apply it to each segment in turn, right to its conclusion. You may balk at making such a detailed examination of each segment because you know the high subjectivity of your perceptions. Yet organizing your thinking will focus your evaluation more effectively than randomly recalling a series of good or bad impressions.

How You Felt

Take another look at your emotional state during the performance and ask yourself if that state served your purpose and if you wish to improve on it. You may not want to remember or relive certain aspects of that state: anxiety, nervousness, tension. To be sure, those feelings were part of the package at the time of performance. Indeed, you tried to deal with them then, and you might well ask what purpose is served by digging them up now for scrutiny. What you need to evaluate is the more fundamental attitude underlying the tension, your mind-set during your preparation time, the one that you hoped you could hang onto throughout the vicissitudes of the performance event.

Exercise

Here are some questions to ask about this underlying state of mind:

- Did some part of me continue to relish the challenge and excitement of the deed?
- Did I insist on being courageous in meeting challenge or opposition?
- Did I continually attempt to approach the performance positively?
- Did I consistently try to reach out and communicate during the performance?
- Was I able to activate my sense of humor when the going got rough?
- Did I attempt to be creative even when I was frightened?
- Did I sustain a high level of energy and concentration throughout the performance?

These questions are not so much about results, but rather the degree to which your mind-set attempted to support your goals. We cannot always control what happens, but we can control the mental attitude we adopt toward what happens. This evaluation deals with your underlying attitude, something over which you can have control no matter what is actually happening.

The Effect the Performance Created

Step back and attempt to conceptualize the effect the performance created, scanning the entire event in your mind's eye.

Exercise

Imagine that you are an impartial observer who just happened to wander into your performance but who had no idea who you were, what your background, experience, or preparation had been, or even what you hoped to gain from this performance. As you imagine this chance encounter, ask yourself the following questions:

- As this performer stepped on stage was my impression a positive one?
- Did this performer seem to be enjoying the performance?
- Was this performer able to reach out and communicate with me early on?
- Was this performer able to appear confident throughout the performance?
- Did this performer, in fact, seem to know what he or she was doing?
- Did this performer sustain momentum or create excitement?
- Were there any obvious mistakes or glitches, and, if so, how were they handled?
- Did this performer seem inventive or creative?
- Did this performer ever touch me or move me emotionally?
- Would I like to repeat my experience with this performer?

Again, answering these questions may seem so subjective that it renders the resulting profile meaningless. Just put aside such hesitations for the moment and do the exercise. Forcing yourself to do so brings you to realizations about your performance. Although the profile will be quite personal, this exercise can help you become as objective as possible in your evaluation and often leads to meaningful insights.

Questions Pertaining to Evaluation for Future Performances

Now we can turn to questions that address how you will want to alter future performances of the same musical works. How soon such performances will take place is important. How to gear up to repeat performances that are scheduled almost immediately has already been discussed; there may be very little time to do anything more than make a few corrections and reset your psychological state. If, however, there is enough time between performances to reenter the preparation mode and make some fundamental improvements, you might want to consider the following questions:

- Are there segments of the performance that need rebuilding rather than correcting?
- Can overall basic techniques that support the performance be improved?
- Was there adequate preparation designed to control nervousness?
- Do I need simply to strengthen creative aspects, or do I need to refocus them?

Rebuilding Rather Than Correcting

You need to focus on things in the performance that didn't work well. Ask yourself, do you simply need to train yourself to execute that particular thing during the performance more efficiently, or does that segment need to be completely rethought? You may have messed up perfectly good ideas in the heat of performance, in which case you need to straighten out the presentation in your own mind. On the other hand, you may have discovered that your basic concept didn't work very well. The tension of a crescendo never took hold; the repose of a tender moment was never fully established; the pacing of a transition seemed erratic; the effect you thought would bring down the house turned out to be a dud. In such cases, you may need to adjust your climax, perfect your timing, or practice a physical response so that it flows more smoothly under pressure, or perhaps replace the effect. You may even need to learn a different physical response altogether, because the one you had prepared proved inadequate in the face of the performance challenge.

If you decide to replace segments of the performance, be sure you know clearly what will replace the old, and be sure you have enough time to rip out the old and establish the new. It is one thing to know that concepts or processes have to be replaced. It is another to determine exactly what replacements will serve your performance more effectively. Once you've decided on the improvements, you still need to put the replacement in the context of your performance. Rebuilding physical responses may require extra time, because you now have to undo the automatic response that you had worked so hard to instill in addition to establishing an automatic response for the new skill. There may be a period of time when your confused response system reverts to the original pattern even though the mental signals you send order up the new.

In assessing how much time these changes will take, reflect on the amount of time it took you to learn the original. It will not necessarily take an equivalent amount, for a crossover facility will likely make learning the new pattern more efficient. On the other hand, the very fact of such facility may lead to underestimating the amount of time required to make changes.

Just as you formulated a timetable the first time you prepared the performance, you will find it helpful to construct a revision schedule, projecting what it will take to get the performance back in good working order in time for the next deadline.

Improving Basic Technique

This part of the evaluation calls for a return to fundamental procedures to strengthen them. You need to drop back to an earlier process of preparation. Doing this suggests an extra measure of preparation time, and there is often reluctance to take that extra time to return to an entry-level activity that seems far removed from your completed performance. To motivate yourself, you must be convinced that the improvement you seek will ultimately enhance the quality of new performance. You may feel reduced prestige in returning to basics, but try to transform that deflation into a feeling of efficacy.

Let us be more specific. At the time of your performance, you had presumably reached the point of performing at levels that represented a synthesis of musical and technical skills. It may seem like a detour to return to practicing basic materials (such as scales) or concepts (such as legato), yet doing so may bring your technique and musicality to a new level, one that will considerably improve your performance of all music. Similarly, returning to the score to observe every mark of expression or embarking once again on repetitive, slow, or sectional practice to enhance fluency are patterns that most great musicians build into their daily routine.

Many believe in the value of this practice so completely that they may bring to it a sense of pride rather than a sense of duty. The patterns drilled have often been developed to a high degree of efficiency, so repeating them at this point to improve their form and flow often engenders an overall feeling of security which can be captured and applied to rehearsal of less familiar material.

Having noted the benefits of returning to basics, you should also be aware of a possible down side. Some may have a tendency to use the comfort of familiar territory as a safety zone and be reluctant to return to the real world of performance. Therefore don't linger too long in the security of perfecting basic techniques without testing them in practical situations. Those who fall into the pattern spend too long practicing and perfecting scales or legato without applying them in the complex context of a musical composition. They spend inordinate amounts of time on exercises and developing isolated technical skills but reluctantly synthesize these well-oiled bagatelles. Spending time improving basic skills is a valuable investment of time and effort but needs to be limited to a specific amount of time. When the time is up, postpone further general improvement until the next preparation session and return to the business of improving the performance under consideration.

Controlling Nervousness

You also need to focus on how better to control the nervousness during your performance. Ask yourself whether you really prepared adequately for the stress you experienced during the performance. If the performance was a new one for you, you may not have been able to assess in advance the degree to which your psyche would experience nervousness. Having lived through the first performance, you now have some sense of the degree of tension attached to this particular activity. With that knowledge, ask yourself if your physical and mental states were brought up to high enough levels of strength, if your drill was intense enough, and if you planned enough dress rehearsals to sense what giving the performance was really like.

Remembering the stress of your performance may lead you to feel that there can *never* be enough preparation and rehearsal! Valid as this notion may seem at first, realize also that a calculable margin of safety does exist. Once you have invested enough time and effort in preparation to cross into that margin, the odds for turning in an integrated, acceptable performance become good.

You must realize, however, that you build that margin of safety through seemingly endless drill. You have to accept that you must habitually work at a level that by popular standards might be regarded as tedious, if not downright boring. But if successful performance is to be a significant part of your life, you need to integrate these patterns so completely that you simply get the work done without emotional baggage, garnering an appreciation for detail and a reverence for the quality of each repetitive act.

Similarly, you must acknowledge time and again that you must plan trial performances, execute them with as much simulation of the real thing as possible, and solicit feedback. Sweep aside inertia in the face of logistical difficulties or stress avoidance, for scheduling many such trial runs creates the safety margin that will see you through the performance. Thus if, after experiencing the initial performance, you determine that your existing dress rehearsal schedule is inadequate, be prepared to beef it up next time.

We all have a tendency to feel weak, helpless, or victimized when under pressure. Having been through the fire once, you know that enduring the discomfort of being nervous is part of performance. Knowing that enduring such tension is part of performing, adopt a more detached, philosophical, and impersonal attitude toward nervousness. Such an attitude is born of a specific line of thinking. As part of the human race, some tribulations are destined to be shared with others. If you must undergo surgery, you will feel pain. When a loved one dies, you will grieve. If you give birth, you will pass through a period of intense discomfort. To this list you must also add the inexorable truth that if you perform, you will experience nervousness.

Having invested so much in preparation, many of us tend to develop a highly personal sense of responsibility when we step up to a performance and thus tend to regard anxiety attacks very personally. Resist the irrational perception that you have been singled out by some malevolent universal power for a particularly torturous version of stress. Instead combine your philosophical acceptance with a tough attitude toward any predilection to dramatize your plight. Insist on cutting such nonsense short and immediately substituting all the techniques you now know for warding off nervousness. Suppress flights of fancy that give free access to panic. Inculcate into your consciousness the truth that, like others, you will endure. Summon up courage in the face of your worst anxiety; breathe deeply and engage in movements to keep physically flexible; invoke humor at your predicament, and even attempt to relish the excitement of the moment. All of these techniques will not alleviate nervous tension completely, but you must make the choice either to capitulate or to fight, and notwithstanding your momentary feeling to the contrary, fighting does make a substantial difference in both reducing the intensity of the tension and in performing effectively.

As you evaluate your battle with nervousness and realize that it will attend all performances in some form, you may ask yourself if living with these demons is too high a price to pay for the performances you want to give. Some individuals answer this question in the affirmative. Some suffer so much from performance tension that they conclude they cannot endure such trauma on a regular basis. They often decide that performance challenges cannot be a recurring part of their lives. They must live with the disappointment of giving up performance, but they prefer to endure this disappointment rather than the trauma of nervous tension.

Of course, many others don't relish the nervous tension yet willingly pay the price in order to perform. They learn they can fight the battle, handle the demons, and take their performance rewards. These individuals can consider themselves fortunate in that their tolerance for stress is strong enough to support their motivation to perform.

Assessing Creativity

Seasoned performers know that in performance, one tries to capture some of the energy of the moment and use it then and there to attain a new level of creativity. In its best version, ideas you never knew you had come pouring forth, heretofore unsuspected strength and endurance are suddenly at your command, and the emotional or dramatic aspects of your presentation may be driven to new heights.

Expert performers strive to achieve such transformations by using performance energy. The desirability of the process should not, however, prevent you from assessing the quality of what actually took place. Such an assessment may indeed reveal wonderful on-the-spot creativity that you will attempt to incorporate as a permanent part of subsequent performances. If this is your assessment, take measures to define and analyze your inspiration to preserve it for the future.

On the other hand, you may also look back and have to admit that, on balance, what you created in your ad hoc excitement is not something you want to keep. In such cases, you may find that the excitement engendering your creativity also spawned an exaggerated or overblown product. Often such qualities seem appropriate when they burst forth in the heat of the event but seem less effective after they have cooled down. Sometimes such brilliance can be achieved only in the face of the performance challenge.

Moreover, some of that inspired creativity will turn out to be as fragile as a wildflower, and the moment you attempt to preserve it, its characteristic radiance withers. Effect your evaluation; incorporate what is of quality; and preserve what is possible. But let the rest go without regret, taking heart in the knowledge that creativity under pressure took place and probably it will return with full force to inspire you during your next performance.

Questions That Relate Your Performance to Long-Range Goals

Let us now turn to how any given individual performance served your overall development or your long-range goals. Several queries apply in this context:

- How much of a milestone was this performance?
- Can remembering this performance positively support long-range goals?
- Do I need to refocus long-range plans as a result of this performance?
- How might external criticism or adjudication affect my future plans?

Milestones

First, assess how significant the performance was. Was it a milestone? In one sense, every performance is important. Every time you gear up to do your best under pressure, you want exactly that to happen: to do your best, to be as good as you can be, to be as inspired and creative as possible. Aiming for anything less can lead to the unraveling of the performance. Almost all performers always strive to perform at an optimum level.

Still, looking back, you should have an awareness of how significant this particular event was in the overall scheme of things. First performances are almost always pretty important, for they test the effectiveness of your preparation. Some performances are significant by virtue of the difficulty of the challenge, such as an unusually taxing repertoire. Some single performances can have fairly far-reaching consequences, such as auditions or major venue appearances. Other performances are important but allow for editing or retakes, such as most recording situations.

You need to formulate a realistic concept of the importance of the consequences of a given performance, because the pressure may have loomed so large during the actual performance that you have exaggerated its importance in your own mind. After having undergone the trauma and noted the strengths and weaknesses, place the performance in a large-frame perspective. Doing so often relieves the sense of being smothered by the intensity of the last performance and provides psychological elbow room to make necessary adjustments and plan for the next time. As you assess significance, you will see that many performances will fall into part of a larger pattern. Like stitches in a tapestry or pearls in a necklace, you may soon regard them as merely making a small contribution to the overall picture.

A first performance will remain important for a while. As you become a veteran of many performances, however, the first will diminish in significance. Although it may ultimately not count for very much in your overall career, it will always have a special place in your memory because it marks the beginning of a long-time activity. Even those performances you regarded as highly significant are apt to undergo conceptual change as you develop. You need to regard all performances as important at the time, but none is so significant that their effects, good or bad, will endure forever.

There is well-known saying: "You're only as good as your last performance." The final two words of this saying might well be changed by many experienced performers to read "next performance"!

Supporting Your Long-Range Goals

This brings us to the next question: does your recollection of your last performance create a positive image in support of your long-range goals? If the performance was successful by external standards, there is probably little or no problem in experiencing a positive feeling when you look back on it. If you won the competition, were accepted as a result of the audition, or got wonderful reviews in the media, your psyche will latch on to these external signs. If, on the other hand, the performance was not so successful by those standards—if you lost the competition, failed the audition, or got bad reviews—then bringing yourself to remembering the performance objectively enough to glean positive things is more difficult.

You need to be able to regard every performance as contributing in some way to an underlying growth that ultimately will help you develop into the kind of performer you want to be and build the kind of career you want to sustain. Thus, where remembering a performance carries negative baggage, focus on what you learned from the experience. Search diligently for the successful aspects of the performance and place it in a context in which it contributes toward your long-term development. Remind yourself that it is indeed possible to turn in a wonderful performance but lose the competition, or to have a very good audition but fail to be selected. You may sense that you created pleasure and garnered appreciation from a large audience, but you still got negative reviews. If you are painfully aware of shortcomings that caused you to lose, fail, or draw criticism, regard the experience as one in which you learned valuable information, garnering points for your next performance that could not have been gained in any other way.

It is easy to dwell on the negative aspects of what took place. Some part of you might argue that attempting to transform your perception of such a performance into something positive is really engaging in extreme sophistry. Override these mental objections. Remember all the old saws about learning from your failures, forging victory from defeat, getting back on the horse after being thrown off. Try to add some much-needed humor by turning your seemingly traumatic or painful plight into a funny situation. In other words, do whatever is necessary to break up the pattern of remembering your past performance as a negative blot.

Doing so will accomplish several things. You will pick up pointers that will improve your performance and thus may be able to identify strategies that failed or creative ideas that misfired. As a result you will be better prepared for the next performance, have more effective strategies, and create more successful ideas. You will also be able to reset your psychology to a great extent before the next performance. You may not rid yourself totally of the residue of a past unfortunate performance, but you can regroup and build a new, more powerful game plan. Finally, in terms of your long-term perception, you can begin to acquire a perspective that will permit you to absorb the passing bumps in the road without losing the forward momentum that will ensure your ultimate success.

Refocusing Long-Range Plans

Occasionally, assessment of a past performance may cause you to alter your long-range plans. Refocusing your goals should not be contemplated lightly; yet careful consideration of your past performance may offer revelations that lead you in this direction.

- You may decide that you are no longer attracted to performing.
- You may uncover an ancillary activity that you deem more attractive.
- You may come to believe that you are not gifted enough for ultimate success in performance.

No Longer Attracted to Performing

As children we went through phases of being attracted to all kinds of adventuresome, romanticized careers. From one day to the next we might have wanted to become astronauts, police officers, entertainers, doctors, lawyers, fire fighters, inventors, or whatever idol struck a responsive chord. As we grew up, we refined our perceptions, a process that usually changed the degree of attraction to different careers. We realized that the images on which we based our desires were fictional or fragmented. We almost always perceived the glamour without the grit, and when we later encountered the grit, we realized that such a career was quite different from what we had imagined.

We were unprepared for the hours of research that go into many professions, or the physical stamina required, or the tedium of drill that attends many others. When these realities began to dawn on us, we revised our thinking with regard to the desirability of that professional goal. Deciding that you are no longer attracted to performing may come about as a result of the fact that your initial perception of it was, in fact, in error. If you have conceptualized a performance, prepared for it, and given it with some measure of success, then you have a good taste of what it takes to pursue a long-term performing career. Yet such experience does not necessarily guarantee that you will want to make this a keystone in your life. Should you eventually realize that in fact you do not, you need to rethink your long-term goals.

Reaching this decision may then translate as follows: I have mounted a few successful performances; I value the experience as a short-term achievement; I do not want to continue to devote large segments of my life to mounting similar performances. The world is full of people who have at one time or another enjoyed intensive activity in sports, acting, dancing, or debate but who do not end up as professional athletes, actors, dancers, or lawyers.

Ancillary Activities

You may also discover that some slightly different activity is more attractive—often one that is similar to performing—and may decide that you prefer the ancillary activity. Whenever shift takes place, the process of preparing and giving performances makes for a solid foundation of insight. Many musicians who set out to be performers end up serving the profession in some other way. Those teachers or coaches, managers or producers, who were performers at one time have in-depth knowledge of the problems the players must face. Those with this understanding have a distinct advantage when conceptualizing, coaching, and even marketing musical performance.

Possessing Aptitude or Gift

You may begin to contemplate a change of focus if you begin to believe that you do not have sufficient aptitude for performance. Here you are entering an area that is not only very difficult to define clearly, but also highly subjective. First, you may not have a realistic overview of the gifts of successful performers, and you may not be objective enough about your own strength. When we are attracted to musical performance, we often focus on role models, men or women whose performances exemplify everything we want to achieve. These models seem like titans, embodying all the attributes we would like to possess, including natural aptitude. Our adulation may cause us to feel that we could never match their performances, not even after a lifetime of hard work and effort. We believe that, in fact, we are not that gifted.

There is the off chance we may be right, but odds are that we are dead wrong. Our idol probably has a host of rivals who possess equal or greater ability. And it is difficult to imagine what the beginning stages of development were like for these highly accomplished individuals. Thus, although we seem to sputter and falter in our early stages, we may be more talented than we understand.

Yes, there is such a thing as not having talent for musical performance. We all have different gifts, so we will exhibit a natural facility for some things and considerably less for others. It is entirely possible to desire achievement in an area for which we do not have an outstanding natural aptitude. Sometimes the desire for achievement and the knowledge that hard work will eventually be rewarded with improvement may lure an individual into pursuing musical performance even when eventual prowess will be a long time in coming and even then the results may be modest when compared with those of peers or competitors.

Even when this limitation is evident, deciding to shift goals may be a tough call. Every individual is entitled to choose how to spend the time allotted on this earth in accordance with personal wishes. Therefore ruling out an activity that is one's heart's desire seems both imperious and foolish. After all, what constitutes happiness is a very personal matter, and if pursuing a given activity offers that euphoric state, perhaps it is best just to leave well enough alone. On the other hand, one can argue that such bliss may eventually be tarnished by the realization that one's personal best falls considerably short of a generally accepted standard of excellence, and that others will always seem to be able to turn in performances deemed superior with greater ease.

If there is a serious question of degree of talent, advice of those experienced in the field can sometimes be of help. Even for experienced individuals, however, assessing talent in its embryonic form is highly elusive, especially when so much depends on growth and development. Even experts can be mistaken. The roster of successful musicians contains the names of men and women who were told somewhere along the way to give it up for lack of talent. Thus, if you do seek the counsel of the experienced, get many opinions, enough for a consensus to emerge. Even that consensus may be so ill defined and conditional that it will offer only a vague sense of where you stand with regard to talent.

If you are very talented, experienced observers will spot your talent easily and probably be quick to inform you. Having talent does not excuse you from the long investment of hard work and effort, but the knowledge of it offers both motivation and fuel to push past the sticking points in your development. If you have questionable gifts, on the other hand, few counselors will be confident enough to suggest that you seek fulfillment elsewhere. Most will use caution because they know an accurate prediction is difficult or because they want to spare your feelings. If several experts seem to hedge a lot, offer advice laden with qualifications, and focus on the competition or the downside of the field itself, then they may be trying to tell you that they do not perceive outstanding natural ability or that your gifts seem meager when compared to those of others.

You still have choices. If pursuing your musical goals is the only thing that will offer fulfillment, then obviously you must follow your dream. At least you will have been forewarned that some experts have reservations about the extent of your natural ability. If, on the other hand, you do not feel passionately about pursuing this activity, you might change your direction toward something for which you have greater aptitude and that will still offer a high degree of personal satisfaction.

Finally, there are a large number of aspirants who sense that they have some talent and compare reasonably well with their peers but they are still not sure of the extent to which that talent will support them. Gnawing questions may plague those with high ambitions as to whether their talent is sufficient to achieve the level to which they aspire. They may ask themselves such questions as: I know I am good enough to be admired by friends and family, but will I be good enough to sustain a career in a marketplace where judgment is tougher? I know I am good enough to perform well, but will I garner a reputation of being outstanding? I know I am competent enough to be accepted as a competitor, but do I stand a chance of walking away with any medals or prizes? I know I have enough talent to be good, but will I ever be great?

The urgency to answer such questions most often comes after initial performances. You have stayed the course long enough to complete a performance or two and are now faced with preparing repeat or new performances. You know what it feels like to complete the cycle of conceptualizing, preparing, and executing a performance, but now you need assurance that you possesses enough basic talent to warrant building such performances into a significant segment of your life. You are seeking assurance that you have the potential to be outstanding.

Such assurances may be hard to come by in any measure that will bring satisfaction. Most experts are loath to offer predictions when it comes to sustaining a career, defeating the competition, winning honors, or achieving greatness. There are simply too many unknown elements even for experts, especially if they have witnessed a myriad of developmental patterns or career profiles through the years, some with surprising twists and turns. At best they may offer the opinion that you have the potential if you continue to work hard, develop at the rate you have already exhibited, and do not run into major hurdles. You will also need to have enough good fortune to garner some degree of recognition at key points along the way.

This type of feedback may be unnerving if you had hoped for more definitive answers. If, however, you feel you have been blessed with some basic aptitude, and if you still desire to develop and achieve after weathering the trials of initial performances, then even modest assurance should be enough to send you on your journey. You are faced with a host of iffy conditions and lurking perils, but this is, after all, the state in which we live our lives each day. We follow our desires, keep a watchful eye out for probabilities, and move forward with enough adventure in our hearts to take the necessary risks.

And what if you never get the gold medal, the highest recognition, accolades from all sides that you are the best, the brightest, or the most phenomenal? Recognize that such honors are of transitory significance even for those who seem awash in glory at some given point in their life. Focus on the more personal considerations: how you will spend your time, hour after hour, day after day, and how you will look back on that investment as your life nears the completion of its cycle. If at the end of your life you realize that you have spent your days in pursuit of your heart's desire, if you have answered the call of your innermost dreams, then you can be counted among the most fortunate of human beings.

External Evaluation

It is important to find a healthy way to deal with external evaluation of your performance. This evaluation is generated by a person whose job it is to render some kind of judgment on what you do; it includes those who determine the results of auditions, adjudicators at competitions, media critics, and professionals whose advice you seek. This group is vested with an authority that has inescapable consequences. The judgment will in some measure affect how you regard your performance, and you must deal with it, both as a practical matter and as a psychological force.

Obviously if the judgment handed down is more or less to your advantage, then content or consequences support your performance efforts and goals. Learning you are selected, being chosen as a winner, being praised in a public forum, or hearing favorable commentary are all reasons to rejoice. If documentation attends these judgments, it will probably be positive, allowing you to take the occasional reservation in stride, since the criticism is set in the midst of positive overall commentary. It is easy, in this case, to respond to suggestions for improvement, for they can be considered in a generally supportive environment.

If, on the other hand, the judgment suggests you are mediocre, or if it is downright negative, then dealing with both the judgment itself and its consequences can be quite emotional, combining hurt, anger, and fear. Sorting it all out and regaining your balance can become one of the most traumatic aspects of performing and needs to be examined in some detail.

As a first step, separate the actual consequences of the adverse judgment from the barbs it carries. Deal with the consequences as an issue unto itself, assessing the damage, and determining what courses of action are open to you. If, for example, you are turned down as a result of an audition, place this rejection in the context of your overall course before you dwell on its fairness or unfairness. If you were passed over for something you deem important to your career, assess what action is open to you for auditioning again or for working around this breech. If you are not declared a winner in a competition or if you receive negative media coverage, place it in the context of your overall efforts as quickly as possible. In some cases, no actual damage has been done. You simply auditioned for a spot that you did not win; or you simply entered a competition in which you did not place; or you gave a performance that some critic didn't particularly like. These may not be the results you wished for, but they may also not be of particular consequence in the context of your long-range goals. Place adverse judgment in the most realistic context possible to keep things in perspective as you deal with the content of the adverse criticism.

You will undoubtedly question the source of the criticism. You may have knowledge that leads you doubt the fairness or wisdom of your critic. Media critics, for example, often get reputations for panning performances. Adjudicators and judges get reputations for liking or not liking certain kinds of performers or performances. Nevertheless, although rationalizing that you were the victim of prejudice or personal eccentricities may seem therapeutic, such thinking is ultimately unproductive and frustrating. After all, the possible bias of your critics notwithstanding, the judgment was rendered, and all the rationalization in the universe cannot undo it. Furthermore, unless you can prove a case of unfairness beyond question, you only appear to yourself and others to have a "sour grapes" attitude. Even if you feel that your suspicions are well founded, it is wiser to direct your focus toward other aspects of the situation, such as dealing with the consequences that you must face and looking at the criticism as a means for improving your next performance.

Similarly, attempting to justify your performance in response to specific criticism also tends to be unproductive. You may be genuinely surprised that certain details were not perceived by your critics as you thought they would be. But taking the attitude of "How could he/she/they possibly have thought that when I was doing such-and-such" doesn't change the fact that some impression was conveyed that invited criticism. For instance, you may think you were convincing in your interpretation, but apparently you were not convincing enough to forestall doubts. You may think your technique was brilliant, but apparently you did not dispel the impression that it was faulty. You may think you were expressive, but apparently you were not poignant enough to move your critics. You may think your were better than your competitors, but apparently you were not able to influence the decision in your favor. Simply put aside the temptation to argue these points mentally, for you can drive yourself to distraction with this inner debate for no good purpose.

Finally, look at the critical comment squarely, putting aside your emotional reaction as much as you can, and see if, in fact, something in it can be used to help you prepare for subsequent performances. Assume for a moment that your critic did not have any particular axe to grind. Then ask yourself why this reaction emerged in the array of reactions open to the critic. There must have been something that, indeed, caused the critic to focus on this or that detail. Discovering what it was that triggered such reaction may lead you to discover something valuable and help institute adjustments that will improve the performance.

This process may lead you to ask hard questions and seek answers that are not easily fathomed, especially if your critics used impressionistic rather than precise words. Your interpretation may simply have been termed "unconvincing," and it will be up to you to try to figure out why. Similarly, your performance may have been described as "wooden," "uninvolved," "half-hearted," "overblown," or any of a number of such general terms, and it is up to you to discern exactly what called forth this reaction. Sometimes you can sense what it is you need to change; sometimes you have to call in others to help solve such riddles; and sometimes you simply have to give up. Giving up is a last resort, but you may not be able to glean enough specific information from general criticism, and in a few cases the criticism may be so vitriolic that trying to deal with its content is simply not in your best interests. In the majority of cases, however, you can make enough effort at understanding what your critic was expressing to say that you have honestly tried to learn what you can from your critics.

Recognize also that legitimate differences of opinion do exist. If your critic bases the criticism on values that you have considered and rejected, then you may simply need to recognize that not all taste is the same. You have run up against someone whose parameters are at odds with your own choices. Different aspects of your performance will lend themselves to this kind of liberalism in various degrees. Many indications on a musical score, for example, are either correct or incorrect in that they were either observed or not observed. Interpretation of such indications, on the other hand, may be open to different approaches. Competition results are most often irrefutable. The fact that someone else's performance in the competition was better than the excellent one you gave may, indeed, become a matter of perception. Almost all performances that aim to entertain or move an audience are open to speculative comment as to effectiveness. Therefore it's valuable to learn from criticism on the one hand, but also measure suggestions for future performances against your own standards and criteria.

There is also a type of criticism directed at who a specific performer is as an individual; attempting to change in response is, in fact, trying to change your defining characteristics. Use careful judgment if you tamper with these components to any great degree. In any case, it may be impossible to make fundamental changes. Basic personality traits define each individual, setting the tone of much of what an individual undertakes. These traits appear as a part of any performance that individual gives. They must simply be accepted as part of the package, although they can be toned up or down to some degree, or incorporated into the performance in a way that supports the performance goal as much as possible.

Some critics will always be on a different wavelength than the performer and will consistently offer adverse criticism. In such cases, you have to recognize the basic divergence of taste and move on. Let us take a few examples.

Suppose you have an effervescent and excitable nature. You will likely always turn in performances with a high degree of volatility. For some critics, any such performance will be deemed too emotional or unstable. However, trying to turn yourself into a placid performer just isn't possible, and if you push too hard, you are apt to distort your natural bent to such a degree that the result is grotesque or forced. Rather, it is better to harness this tendency toward volatility to add life and energy to the performance, but control it so it does not result in overblown moments or throw your performance off track.

Or you may tend to be conservative by nature. For some critics, your performances will probably always seem lacking in excitement or inherently square. Yet there is only so much excitement you can attempt in a performance without compromising your fundamental integrity. Trying to wring an emotional, high-voltage performance from yourself will probably result in an impression of a basically conservative person trying to be glitzy. The effect is apt to turn comic, and, indeed, many a farce has been based on just this premise. Rather, attempt to use the conservatism to enhance qualities that are natural and desirable in any performance, such as security, orderliness, and depth of content. Structure your performance toward those qualities, and at the same time enliven your delivery with enough energy to ward off dullness or predictability.

We can construct similar paradigms using other personality traits: for example, penchants for being intellectual, charming, hard-driving, laid back, aggressive, or demure. Although these traits may not define an individual completely, they do represent the impression given by that individual.

These qualities need to be recognized as fundamental and underscored to play into the performance. Moreover, recognize that these qualities cannot be eradicated completely or even altered to a great extent; trying to do so will only result in an artificial aberration. Whenever criticism suggests tampering with these very fundamental personality traits, regard it with caution and use it only to the extent that it is helpful in enhancing or polishing the contribution these traits make to a performance, but not to an extent that would attempt to destroy or replace them.

In summary, dealing with evaluation and critical feedback requires considerable skill and experience. Acquiring the know-how to handle it may seem disorganized and laden with subjective and emotional reactions. But recognize that it is very human to have a high degree of sensitivity with regard to performance. You have invested a considerable amount of time and effort and have exposed your efforts in an open arena. Moreover, its success may be an important measure of your progress toward long-range, significant goals.

Evaluation is most valuable when it offers specific suggestions for improving the content of or your ability to cope with future performances. Evaluate the evaluation in these terms first of all. A critique is least helpful when offered with cavalier negativism, especially if it focuses on extremely personal traits and offers no corrective suggestions. Such evaluation often serves the ego of the evaluator more than it assists the performer. You may find it difficult to divorce yourself from the hurt of such evaluations, but train yourself to be tough-minded. That is also part of the growth process. Indeed, sorting out what you can use in an evaluation and what you need to throw away lies at the very heart of making evaluation work for you.

Finally, remember that performance is a growth process, and therefore changes every day. Criticism that may be valuable today may not apply tomorrow, not only because of changes in you as a performer, but also because of a variety of fleeting external or environmental factors. Learn what you can from evaluation, consider making changes, and after thinking about them, make them if they seem appropriate, but always protect vigilantly the dream that originally motivated you.

That dream may seem in jeopardy when you are dealing with adverse criticism. But it is possible to strike a balance, listening and learning on one hand from the adversity while keeping alive the belief that this trial is nourishment for growing into your goals. You can even psyche yourself up to relishing critical evaluation as part of the adventure on the road you have undertaken.

Above all, even as you make changes, persevere with a determination that will take into account your long-range aspirations. Remember that if you project your overall goals against your life span, you will quickly realize that living the adventure is at the heart of life's meaning, even more so than arriving at the destination.

chapter thirteen
Performance and Human Interaction

Performance goals tend to be all consuming. In order to achieve them, we busily examine our strengths and weaknesses, set our goals, chart our course, go through various stages of preparation, gear up to the performance, give it, evaluate it, and most likely plan to repeat the cycle. This pattern tends to be extremely self-centered, and properly so, for after all, it is *you* who will be in the hot seat when performance time arrives. Without intense focus on your own ability and preparation, the probability of success would be diminished.

By the same token, it is very easy to become so caught up in the challenges of this cycle that you lose a realistic perception of its meaning in your own life and the lives of those around you. One must constantly strive for balance. Without such balance, it is very easy to assume postures of importance that at best reflect poorly on you and what you do, and at worst lead to neglect of other important aspects of living.

If your pursuit is in the realm of historical (i.e., "classical") music, for example, balance communication of its meanings and emotions with some awareness as to how rarified your field of study is. Remembering how human those who created this music were in their own lifetimes can give your own re-creation relevance and verisimilitude. Such thinking will also probably save you from egocentric displays of temperament that are ridiculous and offensive. Prima donnas may be tolerated, but their excesses are seldom loved.

Should you spend a portion of your efforts giving something back to society in maintaining a balanced lifestyle? Should you seek ways to serve others? If your answer is "yes," you will need to assess exactly how and how much to give or serve. First, however, let's address the issue of whether you need concern yourself at all.

153

Singleness of purpose and unrelenting drive go a long way toward ensuring success in reaching performance goals. We often admire go-getters who do not permit anyone or anything to stand in the way of achieving their goals. We hear stories of how singly focused the world of creative genius often becomes. Thomas Edison is reputed to have neglected his wife to perform experiments. Ludwig van Beethoven is said to have forgotten to feed his cow to create and perform music. Never mind the fact that such men had little time for anything but their work, it could be argued. Look at their glorious achievements!

A strong element of truth resides in such a point of view. The twentieth-century philosopher and writer Ayn Rand argued that only by satisfying our "selfish" goals can we create the abundance that benefits both ourselves and others. Moreover, Rand insisted that those acts of giving or charity we choose are a "selfish" way of preserving the values we hold dear. The corollary to such reasoning would dictate that you pursue your goals with little or no conscious concern about others. If it turns out you do something once in a while that might fall into the giving or service categories, fine. But if it also turns out that you center your life around your performance goals with an intensity that leaves little or no room in your life for much else, that's okay also.

This attitude may seem fine at first glance. There are, however, reasons to consider tempering a singleness of purpose to make room for other values. Fullness in living for most human beings consists of being fulfilled in more than one area of life. If you identify areas of value other than achieving performance goals, you will have to nurture those areas. Doing so will generate benefits that will, in turn, feed the quality and veracity of your performance.

Consider for a moment the fact that in virtually all performance activities the goal is to communicate with other human beings in some way. This connection is obvious in the concert hall or opera house, but is also very much present in recording, writing, editing, and teaching.

Preparing for a performance must include becoming sensitive to the dynamics of interacting with other human beings. You must open up your sensory receptors to tap a continuing flow of information about how people react, feel, think, to the point of sensing not only what *has* happened, but also what is *about* to happen. Such sensitivity does not presuppose that you can or even want to control such interactions, but being aware of human reaction brings another valuable spectrum to your performance, and as a result your work will acquire new dimensions.

This line of thought may impress some as bordering on the metaphysical. If such focus seems too off the wall, consider the following for a moment. Most great entertainers acknowledge the feelings they experience from various audiences. They talk about "cold" audiences, even when those audiences applaud. They bemoan the fact that an audience was "difficult" to perform for, even when external evidence of success seems present. They also sense when an audience is approving, sometimes even before any kind of demonstration. They play to approving audiences with a special measure of élan, to "feed" them. They may even "toy" with audiences in such cases, teasing them, testing the measure of their approval, laughing with them.

An audience clearly comprises a group of individuals, each with individual reactions and feelings. Arriving at the concept of a *persona* for the collection of individuals requires a stretch of logic. Yet crowds of people do indeed take on characteristics, and group actions often manifest themselves from a prevailing mood generated either by the majority of those present or by a segment of activists.

Thus it is not so far-fetched to focus on aspects of your own development that will render you sensitive to interactions with others both individually and collectively. This sensitivity helps garner self-confidence during performance, as well as the ability to make on-the-spot adjustments. Therefore developing such awareness becomes an avenue for more effective performance.

Perhaps the most obvious example of interaction occurs regularly in teaching. There are many teachers who simply cast information in front of the students. Often such a teacher is a highly successful performer outside the classroom and relies on personal example to motivate and instruct students. Such teachers often thrive on the admiration of their students. By the same token, they take very little interest in their students, espousing an "it's up to them" attitude.

By contrast, some teachers are highly aware of the interaction that must take place in the learning process. They believe that the effective instructor must take into account the needs of the students, their desires, and their level of knowledge. This concern does not necessarily mean pandering to students, but rather balancing motivation and capabilities with challenges and goals. Such teachers believe that assessing and utilizing these factors will result in better and faster learning.

Experienced musicians and entertainers have learned to take their audiences into account as they perform. We sometimes see shyness or self-consciousness in inexperienced, often very young performers. We exhort them to smile, look at the audience, and move confidently, adopting body language that belies their insecurity as they walk on stage. These actions not only enhance the first impression, but help the performer begin the process of reaching out to an audience.

Those who study public speaking are trained to look directly into the faces of those assembled, sometimes picking individuals with whom to establish eye contact and being sure to look at the entire audience. Similarly those who work in front of a camera learn to address the lens, that impersonal "eye" that will convey what it sees, often to vast numbers of people.

There is, however, a fine line between being sensitive to an audience and impeaching the integrity of what you have to offer. There will always be some who do not particularly like what you do. This is a matter of taste or values and is not dependent on the quality of the performance. Balance the desire to reach an audience with an awareness of the limitations inherent in what you are able and willing to do.

The line of demarcation between playing to and pandering to an audience will differ for every performer, and social attitudes as to what is permissible vary from case to case. For example, in our society we are not surprised at the fact that politicians cross the line all the time. In speaking before groups with special interests, they adopt positions that they later change, or they make promises they are unable to keep. Public opinion would probably cite expediency as the reason behind these inconsistencies. But the public also recognizes the politician's need to be a desirable candidate to as many different groups as possible in order to win the election. Thus our society regularly regards the politician's foibles with a measure of tolerance seldom extended to others.

Similarly, lawyers want to win legal battles for their clients, and we understand that in the process they may make statements that are misleading, adopt strategies that use the letter of the law in ways probably not intended, or assume positions in order to win the confidence of jurors. Those working in sales also sometimes push the envelope. For some, making the sale is the only goal that counts, even if it means assuming postures, bending facts, or ingratiating themselves to a potential customer. Others will not exceed certain limits, those defined by honesty, truthfulness, and personal dignity.

Physicians, ministers, teachers, and public service representatives, however, are held accountable for representing themselves accurately and completely. We perceive direct connections between what these professionals do and our own lives. If they pander to their audience, irreparable damage could result. Thus these professionals are held rather strictly to a standard of integrity, honesty, and complete truthfulness, neither expecting nor permitting deviation from that standard to court favor from an audience.

Historic ("classical") music is one of the most fascinating fields to observe, for what is perceived as appropriate has changed dramatically over the past few years. Several decades ago there was a widespread belief among classical musicians that participation in commercial projects was "artistic prostitution." Thus pianists who played snippets of Chopin or opera singers who sang miniversions of arias in Hollywood musicals were often harshly criticized by purist colleagues. Defenders of such performances cited the virtues of indoctrinating the broad audience of moviegoers to musical classics, while critics rebutted that the performances did not represent the art well and thus could not woo a substantial audience.

Fifty years later, it is a nonissue. Classical musicians have relaxed their attitudes. Like most musical styles, classical music is available through a multitude of avenues, both formal and informal, to whatever audience it can attract. More and more students who study to become professional musicians learn to perform in many different styles, combining both the traditional and contemporary, the esoteric and the popular, in the hope of interacting with a larger audience. Thus developing skills considered heretical by the purists a few decades ago is encouraged in today's young musicians.

Such skills include not only performance in a wide variety of styles, but also improvising, making music "by ear," and performing in venues where music serves as background to other activities. The purist attitude of yesteryear is now regarded as not only rigid, but historically unfounded. For example, the eighteenth-century European tradition that produced such musicians as Bach, Mozart, and Haydn mandated versatility and creativity, including playing and improvising in popular styles of the period. Musicians of today are thus trained to produce high artistic performances but also to create and lead a resounding performance of "Happy Birthday" at Aunt Minnie's party and perhaps provide some easy, relaxed listening for friends and family after the cake has been cut.

Those who would disdain preparation for such service on the grounds that it might demean their lofty artistic goals are dead wrong on two counts. First, they ignore the practice of the very musicians whose work comprises the tradition they love so much. Second, they restrict the effectiveness of their own artistic efforts by failing to reach out in ways that both build sensitivity to and garner benevolence from the society around them.

Such a philosophy does not, of course, rule out the fact that every serious performer will develop a line not to be crossed to maintain their own artistic integrity. Some may refuse to perform music edited or cut to meet commercial time limits. Others may find certain venues, environments, or types of audiences unsuitable for trying to communicate the material they have prepared. Even so, it is probably better to court adventure and try something new with the hope that your artistic efforts will sprout seed rather than to cling protectively to tradition and pass up opportunities to expand horizons for both performer and audience.

So, we see opera sung in restaurants. Puccini heard while one is eating spaghetti may not carry the same dramatic impact it does in an opera house, but it has reached some ears for the first time and maybe even made a few converts. Beethoven played in shopping malls will probably not carry the great humanist message it does in the concert hall, but maybe some child will ask for music lessons because of that exposure. Wagner as background to the antics of cartoon characters may seem irreverent to opera lovers, but such usage also immortalizes thematic motives that might otherwise have remained relatively obscure, buried deep within an art form appreciated by only a few. Singing a Schubert lied in an evening of karaoke may seem out of place, but perhaps as a result some other participant who never gave much thought to Schubert will go out and buy his music.

Each of us will adopt different guidelines for reaching out with performing activities. The important thing to remember is that your performance needs to be shared with an audience comprised of human beings just like yourself. You may want to claim their attention and communicate with them in some way. To do this best, you need to not only prepare and give your performance, but also open yourself up to being sensitive to their needs and desires. In doing so you set up a two-way communication between yourself and your audience, a circle with the potential to take on a life of its own, growing and building.

As you begin to think about the audience for your performance skills in this way, you may conclude that there are ways you can relate to a larger segment of society. If your performance typically deals in lofty, serious subject matter, you may discover that you can build a play area into your performance. It may mean collecting jokes about your profession, learning popular repertoire, recounting human or amusing aspects of your career, or simply bringing levity, warmth, and cheerfulness to an otherwise somber endeavor. Finally, armed with audience sensitivity and a way to reach out to a broader audience, you can use your performance skills to give to others, bringing happiness or comfort to fellow members of the human race.

Virtually every famous body of philosophy in the world has noted that giving to others is an essential part of our own fulfillment. Not only is giving fulfilling on a personal level, but it has a way of multiplying and returning to the giver an unexpected and abundance of blessings. Best of all for those whose lives are centered around performance, such giving strengthens and deepens your own humanity, thus nourishing your performances and the way you feel about them.

chapter fourteen
The Career Challenge

As we perfect our musical skills and develop regimens with which to achieve successful performance, the world around us changes. So it is quite possible to emerge from our focused activities to face a reality that is different from the one we anticipated. In some cases, we find that society no longer regards what we have worked so hard to achieve as relevant, or has relegated our hard-won achievements to a small, relatively unimportant corner.

Those who study of "classical" (art) music probably recognize early on that there is only a small percentage of the public that enjoy what they do. These musicians may be frustrated by the public's preference for contemporary popular styles. They may even encounter disdain for the music they love so dearly. One radio station announced proudly in its billboard advertising: *No music by dead guys.*

Those who work in an area of music that has a popular following must often face the fact that popular favor is short-lived and that today's popular styles are often replaced within a decade or two. In the United States, jazz styles popular during the first half of the twentieth century were replaced midway in the century by rock. Rock, in turn, saw its popularity eroded in later decades by disco and then hip-hop (rap). Although the earlier styles retain some popularity, they no longer top the charts, and their performers attract smaller numbers.

The advent of music technology has made the scene more complex. Music technology advances at a dizzying rate, and each change carries two powerful influences: the impact of new sounds on public taste, often force-feeding new aesthetics; and the ease with which technology produces music, relieving music-makers from learning traditional music skills. The first influence can be noted in media background music, orchestrated the-

159

ater and church music, and environmental music. The second is reflected in the music created by anyone who can read a few directions and punch a few buttons and, with a few additional steps, realize performances, print, record, and market such music. As computer programmers continually expand the capabilities of electronic instruments, an increasing number of aspirants can unleash musical product in torrents.

Traditional musicians need to come to terms with these changes, evaluating the significance of what they have to offer and the extent to which they can earn a livelihood. One can begin by looking at the role musicians have played historically in Western culture and remembering that the tradition of art music was shaped by men who interacted with relatively small segments of the population. Before the industrial revolution, nobility and the Church were the primary patrons of music, and most of the names we honor composed and performed for these audiences: J. S. Bach, Mozart, Haydn, and Beethoven, for example. With the rise of the mercantile class, composers such as Liszt, Chopin, Wagner, and Brahms found audiences in small, well-to-do, upper echelons of society. Notwithstanding these sources of support, many famous musicians faced financial problems throughout their careers: Mozart, Schubert, and Schumann, for example.

Communications technology in the early twentieth century made music available to mass audiences, and a new kind of stardom came into being. First, motion pictures and radio made it possible for actors to become household names. Many classical musicians made the mistake of assuming that they could achieve similar fame, overlooking the fact that the content of mass entertainment is usually less serious and complex than the music they wanted to market. In seeking mass appreciation, the advocates of classical music embarked on programs to "educate" large segments of the population. Such programs were somewhat successful, but they did not fundamentally change public taste. By the mid-twentieth century huge concert halls were built with the expectation that they would be filled by the newly enlightened masses. The concert halls remained half empty for most events.

As new waves of technology brought more choices to large audiences, interest in classical music waned even more. Those who earlier in the century might have attended a live concert now stayed home and watched television. Later, the computer offered yet another set of leisure-time activities. As the expectations of classical music advocates became increasingly unrealistic, many predicted virtual extinction.

In this context, it is comforting to remember that historically large segments of the population were never significant consumers of serious music. Yet every generation produces individuals who fall in love with the beauty of art music. Some of them become musicians, but most become listeners, counting art music as one of life's pleasures. It is difficult to calculate the extent of this core. Estimates have ranged from between less than 1 percent to as much as 3 percent of the population. Such estimates remain elusive because individuals develop diverse patterns of consumption. A few confine their listening to classical music. Many others enjoy a larger menu of styles, and easy availability encourages variety. We see the physician who travels halfway around the world to hear a performance of Wagner's *Ring* cycle but also collects Duke Ellington recordings and memorabilia; the lawyer whose video collection includes virtually every available Hollywood musical but is also a regular subscriber to the Los Angeles Philharmonic; the teenager who downloads hip-hop and Bach in equal amounts, both being deemed "cool."

So how are you as a performer of serious music to evaluate this complex scene? Have your years of preparation been poorly invested? Are your hard-won achievements to be stillborn? The following ideas may help clarify your thinking and perhaps help you forge a plan for your future:

- Broaden your skills.
- Get involved in appreciation.
- Project your image.
- Run your business.
- Use technology.

Broaden Your Skills

Great musicians of the past provide many examples of occupational diversity. Most of them taught at some point in their careers. Most of them were able conductors of their own works, and many pursued careers as conductors, such as Mendelssohn, Liszt, Brahms, and Rachmaninoff. J. S. Bach, Mendelssohn, Liszt, Fauré, and Rachmaninoff were academic administrators. Villa-Lobos became involved with music education in the schools. Brahms and Debussy earned money as collaborative artists. A few famous musicians had alternative careers in fields outside music: Rimsky-Korsakov and Roussel were naval officers; Borodin was a physician and chemist; Ives was an insurance salesman.

These examples teach us that we can sustain diverse interests and still become outstanding musicians and performers. The extent of such diversity is a personal matter, but encouraging it within oneself leads to greater marketability and often paves the way for a deeper musical understanding. True, cultivating alternate activities takes time away from pursuing your main performance goals. However, you can often garner time to develop a secondary field through careful organization of periods you are *not* using for performance preparation. These segments of time may be small, so you might see slow growth, but consistent long-term effort will give you usable alternate skills. In many cases, skills you are developing in your performance cross over. Therefore it is important to identify as early as possible what ancillary activities appeal to you, which ones are possible for you, and to what extent they can supplement your lifestyle as a performing musician.

Exercise

Here is a list of activities that many performers have incorporated into their lives, annotated as to possible pluses and minuses. You may not agree with the pluses and minus noted. That's fine. The purpose of the exercise is to get to you to think. Check off the ones that might serve you, keeping in mind that the activity should hold some measure of personal attraction.

- Teaching
    - \+ Ready market in almost any locale, especially teaching children
        Monetary return is immediate
        Utilizes skills you are developing anyway
        Possibility of developing meaningful interaction with students
    - − Students may lack motivation or time to prepare lessons
        Monetary return may be modest
        You may feel frustrated or bored teaching lower-level skills
- Service Collaboration (Accompanying)
    - \+ A good market in areas where other musicians are active
        Monetary return is immediate
        Utilizes your musical skills
        Possibility of meaningful interaction and performance
    - − Must have excellent sight-reading and rapid learning skills
        Monetary return may be modest
        Selection and interpretation of music is made by collaborator(s)
        Possibility of performing with inept musicians
- Church Work
    - \+ A good market
        Monetary return ranges from modest to substantial

Utilizes music skills; may require new ones (conducting, organ)

Possibility of meaningful interaction and performance

- You may compete with musicians who are specialists

  Music selection may be dictated by liturgy or congregational taste

  May require working with performers of limited musical background

  Rehearsal time is frequently limited because of church service schedule

  May encounter complex administrative environment

- Lounge/Hotel/Restaurant/Party Gigs

  + Work available is based on reputation

    Monetary return ranges from modest to substantial

    Utilizes music skills, often new styles and repertoire

    Possibility of performing in interesting venues

  - It may take time to build a reputation

    Developing skills and repertoire may be time intensive

    It may be annoying that your music is background

    Venues or instruments may be substandard

- Writing/Editing

  + Staff positions pay salaries

    Publication often enhances performance career

    You can often choose your topic and timetable

    Possibility of significant contributions and relationships

  - Intense competitions exist for staff positions

    Nonmusical skills must be developed to a high level

    Professional journals pay little for freelance submissions

    Research is often time intensive

    Professional market is crowded with submissions

- Technology Assistance (Recording and MIDI services)

  + A good market in areas where other musicians are active

    Monetary return is both immediate and good

    Work sharpens sensitivity to acoustic and musical values

    Possibility of significant contributions and relationships

  - Investment is required in both equipment and training

    You may have to compete with specialists in the field

    Constant updating of knowledge and skills is required

    Need to physically move and set up equipment

- Education Administration
  - + Salaried and titled positions

    You may be able to influence curricular significance of music

    You may be able to set educational standards for music

    May lead to community leadership role
  - − Personal performance may not be included

    Complex personnel interaction may prove frustrating

    Goals may be frustrated by limited financial support
- Management/Performance Service Organizations
  - + Salaried positions are available in management firms

    You will be a part of the performance scene

    Your skills can be used for your own performance career
  - − Personal performance may not be included

    Successful management of others may result in frustration.

There are numerous examples of individuals who have supplemented their performing career with one or more of these activities. The following are real-life profiles, one for each of the fields listed:

- Naomi earned a doctorate in piano performance. She targeted local and regional piano teacher organizations for her performances. Soon she earned a reputation as a performer and was invited to give a recital at the national convention of a music teacher organization. This performance gave her national exposure, and as a result, a university sought her out for its faculty. The teachers she performed for now send her their best students for college work. She is one of the most celebrated college-level piano teachers and continues to perform and teach both on and off campus.

- Michael earned a Master of Music degree. At college he earned money by playing orchestral reductions of standard piano concerti for his classmates, so he developed a large repertoire in this specialized area. He settled in an urban area where many concerto competitions for pre-college piano students are scheduled every year. As an experienced collaborator, he provides brilliant accompaniment for the soloists in these competitions. Within a few years, his reputation became such that he earns most of his income from this activity. He continues to perform as a soloist and chamber musician.

- Lillian grew up singing in her church in the midwest. She acquired a large repertoire of solos popular at Sunday worship services. She selected a university music school in the heart of a metropolitan area and submitted a sample CD and her repertoire list to area churches. She began to be regularly engaged as a soloist for services, weddings, and church activities. With this work she was able to enroll part time at the university music school and eventually earned two degrees. By that time she had received an offer from a church to become the minister of music. Over the years she held several such positions, each representing an increase in prestige and salary. Now she performs constantly and directs the music program of a large urban church.

- Sally always enjoyed played popular music at high school parties. As she earned a Master of Music degree in classical piano, she continued to work on her popular repertoire and arrangements. When a lounge at a local hotel advertised for a pianist, she got the job because during the audition she asked the lounge owner what his favorite song was. It was not only in her repertoire, but she had developed a showy original arrangement of it. As her career grew, she did a season on a luxury cruise ship, one at a resort in the Caribbean, and one at a ski resort in Switzerland. She finally took up residence at the lounge of a celebrated West Coast hotel. She married a man who was able to record and package her lounge acts. These CDs caught the attention of a national distributor, who signed her as one of their artists. Now she and her husband spend all their time producing CDs, and Sally makes occasional live appearances at very high fees.

- Martin was regarded as a model student during his university years because he was not only a fine performer but also a dedicated scholar. As a singer, he enjoyed programming music by neglected composers. His research led to uncovering an early publication of some art songs by a little-known nineteenth-century German composer. He included them in his junior recital and created a new, annotated edition of them, which was accepted by a prominent music publisher. Martin went on to get a Master of Music degree and fielded a job teaching voice at a small college with a weak music department. He felt frustrated because it was difficult to be innovative with repertoire choices, since his students were not very advanced. In a professional journal, he spotted an opening for a junior editor at the publishing firm that had accepted his earlier edition. He applied, got the job, and in recent years has developed an entire catalogue of specialized repertoire, much of which he uncovered and edited himself. He presents recitals of this music regularly at a local art gallery.

- At university, Gwen dated a boy from the engineering school who was involved in electronics and had acquired some professional recording equipment. Together they began to record the senior recitals of the music school's students. As a bassoonist, Gwen had the musical training to offer advice with regard to microphone placement, CD organization, and editing. Within a few months, Gwen and her boyfriend found they had a booming business. Upon graduation Gwen stayed at the same university for graduate work while her boyfriend enrolled in a graduate program at a famous engineering school 2,000 miles away. They drifted apart, but Gwen's interest in technology continued, and she took all the courses offered in MIDI, then got part-time work in a local commercial sound studio. Gwen had developed as a first-rate bassoonist, but neither teaching the instrument nor orchestral work attracted her as much as arranging and creating music through technology. She began to present seminars for local music teachers in the use of technology in their studios. One of these caught the attention of a major manufacturer of electronic instruments. She now heads up the education department of that organization. She plays bassoon weekly in a community symphony orchestra.

■ Irene married during her first year as a graduate student in piano performance. She was an able pianist and was able to continue into the doctoral program. Her work was interrupted each time she became a mother, and by the time she finished her degree, she had three children. Irene taught at home for a few years, something she was able to do while raising her children. As they reached school age, Irene became concerned about the quality of the music being taught in the public schools of her city. An activist by nature, she began urging parents' groups to consider the quality and quantity of music in the curriculum. Soon she became known as one of the most significant voices in the city for music and the arts. She was asked to be on the board of both the philharmonic and the art gallery. Meanwhile, the school board hired her as a consultant to guide the selection of new materials for the music curriculum. Irene selected some materials and designed others. The city's leading conservatory approached Irene about becoming its new administrative head. She now leads a school that offers music instruction privately to pre-college students of all ages, and she continues as a music consultant to the public school system.

■ Oliver is a fine string player. During his college years, he formed a string quartet with three other students. He worked constantly to find bookings for the group at retirement homes, weddings, and other social events. In his senior year he entered the group in a national chamber music competition, where they took third prize. A few concerts followed, but even with Oliver's industry, the group was not able to earn a living wage for its four members. Oliver tried to get a noted concert management firm to add the group to its list of artists. He was unsuccessful, but his presentation was so impressivethat he was offered an entry-level job in the organization. A decade later Oliver became the director of an international music festival. He works with the most important musicians of our time, is able to assist young talented musicians, and creates musical events that are attended by large audiences. He is also an active chamber musician and plays frequently in area ensembles.

Note that in each of these cases, the ancillary activity was born of genuine interest and developed slowly, alongside growth as a performer. You should not regard these cases as compromises. In each case, the individual preserved performance and integrated it into a broader lifestyle. Moreover, these individuals relish the mix of performing and broader professional interaction, and they feel their contributions to music and its role in our culture are greater as a result of broader career profiles.

Get Involved in Appreciation

You undoubtedly feel passionate about the music you perform. You probably believe that everyone should experience the pleasure you derive from this music, and when you encounter indifference, you are dismayed. We begin to understand such indifference when we think about the number of activities that compete for our attention. Each day is filled with sound we do not listen to, screens we do not watch, and noise we shut out. We learn to concentrate on important things by keeping distractions at the edge of our consciousness. To get audiences intensely involved in your music, you must find ways to focus your listeners, setting the music apart from the myriad of daily sounds and highlighting its beauty.

Seek ways to create understanding between the music you perform and your audience. Traditional music appreciation classes analyze various elements of the music to develop more perceptive listeners. This approach is effective when time is available to examine details, and you should practice explaining structural, melodic, and rhythmic characteristics of your music as simply as possible. When you are not allotted enough time for such detailed consideration, look for human interest "hooks." Relate some tidbit about the composer, perhaps at the time the composition was written, about the performance tradition of the piece, or about your experience preparing it. Plan what to say ahead of time, so that our comments are focused, and limit the talking to only a few minutes. Present this information as a verbal program note just before performing the music. Audiences respond well to such informality. It personalizes the music, the composer, and you, as the performer.

Some musicians go even further by creating a theatrical experience, using costumes and characterization. For singers who are preparing an opera role, rendering an aria in character comes naturally. One pianist I know appeared as Franz Liszt, letting his hair grow long like Liszt's, playing the composer's music and affecting the staging and gestures history reports Liszt used. Another appeared as Clara Schumann, playing her own and her husband Robert's music, chatting about the Schumann children between numbers.

Other musicians have used performance preparation as a basis for motivational lectures. One musician has successfully marketed seminars outlining motivation and organizational principles as exemplified by the preparation of a Schubert sonata. A performance of the complete sonata climaxed the day-long workshop. Another has highlighted social history, discussing the role of African-American music in the culture of the United States and singing a program that includes spirituals, hymns, jazz, and freedom songs. Still another creates programs for children consisting of the music that J. S. Bach, Mendelssohn, Schumann, Debussy, and Chick Corea wrote for children.

Develop your own version of such programming. It is well worth the time and effort, for such presentations offer distinction for the performer, involve the listener, and build audiences for the future

Project Your Image

There is an old saying: "Build a better mousetrap and the world will beat a pathway to your door." Many musicians seem to believe this. They feel that if they are good enough, they will somehow be discovered by a large audience and achieve fame. So they prepare performances, give them, repeat the cycle, and wait expectantly. This pattern is comfortable, for it permits them to remain modest and avoid the responsibility of selling themselves.

Such a pattern will probably result in extremely slow career growth, because we live in a competitive society, one in which promotion abounds. Remember that the marketplace is crowded with alternatives to your music-making. So unless you project your image as a musician, you will likely not attract much attention, no matter how beautifully you perform. Yet many musicians find projecting their image difficult; they feel uncomfortable selling their art or are fearful of becoming overbearing.

You can deal with this reluctance by learning to talk about the music itself, trying to convey your enthusiasm for sharing it, and building a repertoire of musical trivia. Such an idea shouldn't make you self-conscious, but if it does, consider the following:

- Someone enthusiastically shares a recipe at a dinner party. You would like to try it, and you remember the person as someone who loves to create delicious food.

- Someone discusses what they will plant in their flower garden. You would like to see it when it blooms, and you identify this person as someone who loves natural beauty.

- Someone tells a funny story about a customer who mistakenly ordered item A instead of item B, and of how the situation had to be straightened out. You laugh, but you remember how the raconteur earns his living and that he cares about his customers.

Exercise

Practice answering the following questions aloud, including the indicated detail:

- What music are you preparing currently? Are you finding it difficult? Fun? Humorous? Exhilarating?

- What have you been reading about the composer of the music you practiced today? Can you tell an anecdote about the composer?

- Where do you plan to perform the music you are practicing? Is the date set? Is the venue interesting? Will the audience be a special group (children, seniors, adjudicators, faculty)?

- What music are you dying to learn next? What concerto would you like to play with an orchestra? What operatic role would you love to create on stage? What tune would you like to arrange?

- What music do you love to listen to? When you are in the car? When you are studying or reading? When you are getting dressed? Do you have a favorite radio station or TV music channel? What music do you download?

- What musical artists do you admire? Do you know something about their lives or careers that you can share? What have they recorded? Where have they appeared recently? Have any scandals attended their careers?

Now think of conversational openers and rejoinders, and once again practice them aloud, pretending you are conversing with someone in a social situation. Here are a few models:

- "You know I am an enormous fan of XXX, and I was listening to their performance of XXX the other day and was wondering just how they manage to create the impression of . . . ."

- "Do you happen to know of a violinist by the name of XXX? No? Well, he is a musician I admire very much because . . . ."

- "Do you read much biography? Well, I am into the life of XXX, because I am learning a piece by him, and when he was a child something unusual happened to him . . . ."

Think of ways in which you can add a musical component to a topical conversation. (This might require some research):

- If politics is the subject, be able to talk about composers whose lives were affected by political events, such as Beethoven, Schubert, Chopin, Liszt, Paderewski, Bartók, Rachmaninoff, the Soviet composers.

- If human rights is the subject, learn of the struggles faced by poor European musicians (Mozart, Beethoven, Schubert, Liszt), African-American musicians (Samuel Coleridge-Taylor, Scott Joplin; Marian Anderson), and women composers (Clara Schumann, Fannie Mendelssohn).

- If jokes are being told, be ready with a repertoire of funny musical stories.

You must use judgment with regard to how much you center your conversation on music. Obviously, you do not want to become so focused on who you are and what you do that you become tedious. Most classical musicians, however, court anonymity. They may fear that nonprofessionals are not interested in classical music. In fact, just the opposite is usually true. Almost everyone either has studied music or has a family member who has done so. Thus classical musicians enjoy enormous respect in most circles, and often nonprofessionals want to share their experiences with music as well, as students, relatives of performers, or aspiring performers.

By projecting your image, you weave a web of connections. You may not be able to trace how strands of this web lead directly to more opportunities to perform, but over time they will. Those with whom you come in contact will know you as a performing musician, and at some appropriate moment they will speak of you. Moreover, as you live your role as a musician, you will wear your professional mantle with ease, take increasing pride in what you do, and will be able to open up more as a performer.

Run Your Business

Many musicians do not regard their profession as a business. They regard the term *business* as suggesting something impersonal and profit-oriented, and they believe that these characteristics are incompatible with creative, artistic goals. Such musicians should realize that reticence to regard their profession as a business and to adopt standard business practices robs them of opportunities to market what they do and earn a secure living. Here are a few examples of standard business practices you should incorporate:

- Create attractive business cards, and develop the habit of using them.

- Develop brochures. These should be attractively designed and should include a short biography, a striking picture or two, possibly a sample program, and press reviews.

- Create a website. Professional help is both easy and cheap. Your website should contain sound bites from your performances, at least one human-interest item, both formal and informal photos (if possible, pictures of you in performance or of your audience intently listening).

- Develop a series of demonstration events: small performances that show you off. Service clubs, health care facilities, senior facilities, public libraries, and art galleries often welcome these programs. These demonstrations will be unpaid performances. Regard them as the equivalent of the free seminars or promotional dinners mounted by investment firms and real estate developers.

- Become active in professional organizations. Most of these are oriented around teaching, but many will also offer opportunities for you to perform, especially if your presentation includes talking about the music.

Two additional items that should be on this list need special consideration. The first is advertising. Many musicians eschew personal advertising, and it is regarded suspiciously in the profession. Advertising in professional journals, particularly in annual directories, is acceptable, but such exposure is noted mostly by fellow musicians and managers. Advertising to the general public suggests availability to anyone who will pay the price, and many feel this arrangement renders their artistry commonplace. Moreover, advertising broadly is expensive and inefficient, because targeting potential entrepreneurs who will arrange performances is difficult. Therefore whether or not to use advertising is a personal decision, and those who decide to try it need to study the marketplace carefully.

The second item is seeking representation. Many performers would like to have management, but finding a satisfactory manager is problematic. Managers with good track records are inundated with aspiring performers who want to be on their rosters. As a result, these managers usually consider only those who have already established a reputation, have outstanding reviews, or have won an important competition. You can find less reputed representation, but often these managers have difficulty securing performances because they must compete with their more powerful counterparts.

Still, many musicians seek some level of management to provide marketing guidance and a shelter from having to tout their own virtues. If you decide to look for representation, keep in mind that finding it requires both persistence and a measure of luck. Before you begin your search, remember that any arrangement with a manager is likely to require financial investment, certainly for materials and office costs incurred in your behalf and, in many cases, an up-front retainer.

Use Technology

Mounting an argument for the use of technology to whatever extent possible seems unnecessary. Technology has, after all, permeated all aspects of daily living. Over the past decade it has not only become omnipresent in our lives, but also, for the most part, it has proved the nay-sayers wrong and has converted the recalcitrant. In certain areas of musical performance, philosophical or aesthetic debates still exist over the efficacy of technology, and there are still individuals who, for a variety of personal or professional reasons, prefer the older models to the new.

Musicians whose chief area of interest is classical music value much that is old. The music they usually perform was written from decades ago to centuries ago. Stringed instruments created hundreds of years ago are the most highly prized. Song texts often come from historic periods of literature. Opera features period costumes and settings. Performance practice is often steeped in tradition. As a result, these musicians learn to cherish the past, often viewing contemporary change with alarm or distrust.

It may well be, then, that technology is here to stay, but without necessarily supplanting traditions or patterns that served us well in the past. Ultimately the coexistence of the older and newer modes, the slower and the faster, the comfortably old-fashioned and the sleek modern, will not depend upon evaluation by the current generation, which witnessed the rise of technology. Rather new generations of performers will pass judgment on older models and patterns simply by continuing to find them fascinating or not. Those who knew the old methods in their heyday learned to love specific qualities and have valued associations with the past. New generations will not have these associations; sentimental ties will not exist; so intrinsic value of some sort will have to save the day if the old is to survive.

In the meantime, those who value the old should not assume the worst. There are many examples of the old holding its ground and continuing to coexist with the new. As a pianist, I take heart in the relationship between music technology and the piano. One would have to look hard to find an area of human endeavor in which technology has been resisted with more determination.

The piano took a little over a century to evolve into the instrument we know today. It was invented in about 1710, and its major improvements were all in place by about 1850, that period seeing the birth of several of the manufacturers whose names are still prominent today. Since that time, the piano gained in popularity, and over the next century it became not only a leading concert instrument but also the tool for musical events and rehearsals of all kinds. It became a ubiquitous presence in theaters, schools, dance studios, churches, community centers, restaurants, bars, hotel lobbies, banquet spaces, and of course many homes. It was, in fact, the instrument on which most children learned the fundamentals of music, whether or not their skills as keyboard players continued to develop. Thus a great segment of music instruction took place on the piano's keyboard.

Along with its multiple practical uses, the piano also became one of the primary vehicles for musical expression. This tradition was fed by a long list of distinguished European composers who themselves were primarily performers on the piano: Mozart, Beethoven, Schubert, Schumann, Chopin, Liszt, Brahms, Debussy, Ravel, Rachmaninoff, Prokofieff, Bartók, Scriabin, Stravinsky, and others. Thus much of the historic ("classical") music of the past two centuries of Western civilization involved the piano in some way, either as a solo instrument or collaboratively with singers, other instrumentalists, or orchestras.

During the nineteenth and twentieth centuries, moreover, an entire culture developed around presenting the piano music of "great" composers. Superstars of this culture toured the world as celebrated performers and garnered demonstrative fans. These pianists were regarded as messengers of beauty and high artistic purpose, thereby gaining acceptance into elite social circles. Even a brief representation of distinguished names would extend over two centuries and be as long as a dictionary. Of the many mid-twentieth–century icons, Claudio Arrau, Walter Gieseking, Dame Myra Hess, Vladimir Horowitz, Alicia de Larrocha, Guiomar Novaes, Artur Rubinstein, Rudolf Serkin, and Artur Schnabel come to mind.

Moreover, many popular musical expressions of the twentieth-century also involved playing the piano with a high degree of technical skill as well as artistic goals. Well-known "popular" musicians who were pianists included George Gershwin, Scott Joplin, "Fats" Waller, Duke Ellington, Art Tatum, Oscar Peterson, Bill Evans, McCoy Tyner, and Herbie Hancock, among many others.

With so many role models in a wide variety of musical expressions, it is no wonder that the the piano attracted a number of aspiring young people in each generation. The fact that the life of a performing star was demanding in terms of preparation, required constant traveling with frequent inconvenience, and offered limited security at best were all insignificant deterrents in light of the excitement of the music, the piano, and the glamour. As each young generation stepped up to this challenge, a small industry formed to offer instruction, instruments, and counseling. Piano teachers, piano manufacturers, piano stores, piano festivals, and piano competitions all flourished. Even though audiences for piano recitals were being weaned away by the many other entertainment opportunities, the piano industry was still considered alive and well by its practitioners.

Then in the latter part of the century a great plague began to develop. The electronic piano was introduced. As with most plagues, the beginning stages didn't seem very threatening. The electronic piano sounded tinny, had a shorter-than-normal keyboard, pedals that worked poorly, and keys that depressed insensitively. That it was portable, unlike the piano, didn't seem enough of an advantage to offset its shortcomings. But then, technology, never at a standstill, really went to work. By the 1980s attractive "digital" pianos, as they came to be called, had overcome many of the faults of the earlier versions. Manufacturers could "sample" piano sounds accurately enough to produce good likenesses. Full-sized keyboards of eighty-eight keys were commonplace, and many aspects of piano action were copied well enough to garner tolerance by a lot of players. Pedal action was much better, cases were made attractive, and portability improved. Pianists could carry their instruments around with them and perform anyplace they could plug in.

Moreover, a technological marriage of great significance took place at about the same time. *Synthesis,* music generated by electronic means, first came on the scene in the 1940s when composers built large electronic generators as instruments with which to compose and play music. These generators could imitate traditional instruments as well as produce qualities of musical sound that were distinctly electronic. Initially often bulky and requiring large spaces, these instruments, like computers themselves, quickly became compact, acquiring both versatility and flexibility. Until the 1980s, however, "playing" these instruments required plugging and unplugging electric cords, turning dials, manipulating levers, or using open hands to control electronic fields. Then in the 1980s came a tremendous breakthrough: synthesis control was combined with the traditional piano keyboard. Within a few years keyboard-controlled synthesis was by far the most frequent type encountered.

The world of the traditional piano faced a double threat. Not only was the piano itself in danger of being replaced by a reasonable and serviceable, portable substitute, but also that substitute could do a lot of new tricks. If you wanted a substitute piano, the machine could accommodate you. But if you wanted a substitute oboe, drum set, guitar choir, or sounds like those heard in the most recent space movie, it could also provide those things. With only the flip of a switch, programs soon allowed the keyboard to create literally hundreds of sounds, both imitations of traditional solo instruments and a host of exciting new sounds.

To add insult to injury, for a few extra dollars you could get a built-in "sequencing" program, a computer program to record and store music digitally. By selecting various sounds in sequence and recording each in turn, you could combine a series of sound "tracks" in a way that would enable you to build your own orchestration of whatever material you play and record. Moreover, this whole package in its deluxe model could be had for a fraction of the cost of a traditional piano. In addition, kids found it fun and trendy as part of the new tech world.

Is it any wonder that the piano world went into a state of panic! Rehearsal halls, churches, community centers, restaurants, bars—you name it, no longer needed those big pieces of furniture that always required tuning and took up too much space. Youngsters found they didn't have to practice Bach and scales in order to sound like *Star Trek*. Mothers and fathers could afford a new TV set, because junior's piano keyboard synthesizer wasn't as expensive as a piano, and also could enjoy the quiet to watch the new TV by telling junior to plug in the earphones when practicing.

During this period there was a lot of defensive rhetoric from the piano world. Since the new technology was associated with music typically found in popular entertainment, piano aficionados frequently pointed fingers and raised issues of "quality" or "standards." They conveniently forgot that some of the icons of their tradition were subjected to the same charges by the conservatives of their own time. They also talked a lot about the "touch" of electronic instruments "ruining" sensitivity to piano touch, conveniently forgetting that many of their icons played more than one keyboard instrument—harpsichord, organ, and clavichord, for example—all with vastly different touches.

Simultaneously, however, some of the less conservative members of the piano community began to realize several things. First, touch issues on digital pianos notwithstanding, computer programs that were hooked up to digital keyboards could make use of highly effective teaching software in areas of music fundamentals. Thus the tools of technology rendered the teaching of harmony, ear training, and basic functional skills easier, more enjoyable, and more effective. Second, students were fired up to create music with sequencing programs. Thus skills of improvisation and composition, often relegated to the back burner in piano studios, were wondrously restored to the level of exciting creative experiences. Third, playing together as musicians became both practical and pleasing to the ear. Digital pianos were space and cost effective in numbers, so each student could have an instrument for collaborative music, and computer software could provide professional-sounding backup. Thus collaboration ended up sounding glorious.

The most remarkable discovery, however, took place more gradually. Piano students had their fun with technology but then looked forward to *returning* to the piano in the teaching studio to continue their study of piano music, even sometimes to do their composing. As the novelty of electronic sounds wore off, students returned to wanting the real thing: the piano. In music schools that specialize in providing commercially oriented training, the best jazz and rock keyboard players began to exhibit yearnings to improve their *piano* skills.

Now a decade later, the panic has abated. Piano teachers flourish, piano sales have stabilized, and a new generation of young pianists seek training to become professionals. What happened? The answer lies in the quality of the piano itself. With all of its mechanics, its wood and felt, its hinges and flanges, the piano is an imperfect but individual instrument. The sound of each piano falls a little differently on the ear; the touch of each piano keyboard seems to have its own individual character; each piano has its strengths and weaknesses. Pianos need care, to be tuned and adjusted.

In short, they, as devices, seem to have many of the characteristics we associate with being human. We perceive them in some ways as we perceive other human beings. We "like" or even "love" certain pianos. This piano has a better "touch." That one "sings" wonderfully. This one is more "powerful." That one is "sweeter." Thus many musicians feel they can express themselves more personally, with more flexibility, and with a greater degree of touch control at the piano. This is a deeply rooted affinity, and it seems to indicate that the piano has weathered the storm and will coexist with its more modern technological keyboard cousins. The piano seems to have staked out its claim in a corner of our world, whether because of physical or acoustical phenomena or a psychological identification with fundamental variants, the "human" aspects in each instrument.

That technology will continue to change our lives is certain. That each of us will incorporate different modes of technology into our performance process is also certain. There is bound to be constant learning, adjustment, growth, and change, all generated by a technological revolution that seems to be accelerating. Each new wave of wondrous gadgets will bring fascination and influence fashion. Fascination wears off, however, and fashion constantly changes.

Thus we are reminded of the fact that technology is focused primarily on upgrading the means by which we achieve our goals. The goals themselves, conceived by the human mind and born of the human condition, do not change. The basic content of the thought processes that drive our lives will remain the responsibility of the individual. The level of our achievements continues to be determined by each of us. Technology can assist, facilitate, and make it possible to do things heretofore impossible, but after the excitement has died down, it is we who are in charge of selecting what we do, charting how we do it, and maintaining the quality of its content.

As performing musicians we must find a place in society and a way to earn a living, like the generations of musicians before us. There is no known formula with which to do this, but, just as we rely on our creativity in making music, we can use it to broaden our career horizons, develop and involve our audiences, project our role as musicians, market our product, and incorporate appropriate technology around us. We need not be intimidated by this challenge but should regard it as an integral part of the excitement inherent in choosing to live the life of a performer. In so doing, we form a bond with the great men and women of the past who loved music and being a musician to the fullest measure possible.

chapter fifteen
Physical Challenge and Performance

Dealing with physical challenges is part of living. At some point in life almost everyone encounters a setback that mandates a healing process and possibly an adjustment to what can be done physically. Some minor maladies result in short periods of delay, such as the flu. More serious ones can result in prolonged recuperation, such as mononucleosis or a full-blown case of tendinitis. When these periods enter the picture, it is often difficult to drop one's productive work patterns in an attempt to support the healing process.

Moreover, the malady itself or the medicine prescribed for its cure sometimes induces atypical or distorted mental states. Thus reflecting on one's state during these periods is unwise and can be even downright damaging. Rather, if you are in this situation, reiterate your long-term goals frequently and remind yourself continuously that healing, although sometimes frustratingly slow, will eventually take place. Assure yourself that you will be able to return to the main highway of progress.

Keeping things in perspective sometimes requires being persistent and tough-minded, but such a mind-set is possible, and you need to muster the discipline to maintain it. If your mind seems muddled because of disability or medication, withdraw your focus from your work; suspend goal-oriented thought until you can think clearly enough to envision a return to some degree of normal activity. Substitute thoughts that support the healing process, even if they seem benign. Refuse to project your present state into the future or against any kind of timetable, for the rate of healing cannot be mandated, and putting yourself on a schedule invites disappointment and frustration. If you surprise yourself and your doctors with a rapid recovery, so much the better, but learn to support general concepts of recovery without imposing timetables or conceptual demands.

Others face more enduring physical challenges. Should disability be a permanent part of one's life, it seems somehow insensitive to urge a simplistic process that smacks of being a quick fix. Often these seemingly rational solutions don't really deal with the frustration, anger, or discouraging fallout. Yet after the inevitable emotional flailing upon discovering a permanent disability, the immutable fact remains that there is nothing to do in the long run but to accept what cannot be changed. Acceptance should be linked with adjusting with as much grace and dispatch as can be mustered, and with envisioning new goals within the framework of what is possible. As devoid of feeling as such advice may seem, it likely remains the only course of action open, and as such is best acted upon while one is trying to minimize continuing emotional turmoil.

There is reason to take heart. Recognize and celebrate the fact that in today's society, a disability is not regarded as a reason to withdraw from the mainstream of life's activity, and achievement at all levels is both recognized and applauded. For example, those confined to wheelchairs participate in marathon races and basketball games. Paraplegics paint works of art with their teeth. Outstanding blind keyboard players have been celebrated since the fourteenth century. Thus many physically challenged individuals experience and continue to effect remarkable, even spectacular, demonstrations of prowess in a wide variety of activities. These achievements provide inspiration for everyone, especially for those who seek role models to help face their own problems and aspirations. Indeed, such models become fountainheads of motivation and light up the path to be traveled.

The one infirmity that besets everyone is aging. This process comes on us incrementally, so that, although its onset may be gradual, its effects are continuous after we have reached maturity. Thus it is not possible to effect a one-time solution to its challenges, but rather we must face a series of endless adjustments, most of them regarded as compromises. Aging, of course, is an inescapable part of life; every living thing must face it. When it is our turn to give up something we used to be able to do, however, most of us respond emotionally. For some this response is negative, resulting in depression, despair, or resignation. There is a tendency, furthermore, to overreact, fighting back with a degree of petulance. This position takes hold, telling us that if it is no longer possible to play the game as we once did, then it is best not to play the game at all.

To some extent society supports withdrawal from the game as we get older. The concept of retirement suggests a life without pressure, a leisurely pace, being able to take it easy. "Golden years" are subliminally equated with sunsets and rest. Retirement activities are often conceived as somehow less consequential than activities undertaken during one's "working" years. Senior health plans advertise images of retirees who are pleasantly but mildly motivated. They contemplate "what the black keys on the piano are for," or "traveling to places one can't pronounce," or "teaching the puppy who's boss"—all with a kind of bemused detachment that suggests that even the participant doesn't really care whether any of it takes place or not.

The fact is, individuals start aging from the moment they are born and must make adjustments throughout their life, and so facing the changes at the end of life need not and should not be regarded any differently than those they have have been facing all along. When you were an infant, you could probably put your toes in your mouth. As an adult, unless you are a contortionist, you can no longer do that, but you have adjusted to this inability without regret. You have long since decided that chewing on your toes need not be one of life's irresistible diversions, so it doesn't really matter that you can't do it any longer. As silly as this example may seem, it illustrates the process by which we can successfully meet the limitations aging imposes.

Two rules of thumb operate hand-in-hand at this point. The first might be stated as "Do as much as you can for as long as you can," and the second "When you can't do something any longer, learn to generate equal passion for whatever you can do." Both maxims have been put into practice by a large number of older men and women. Doing so frequently breaks the mold of expectations for those of retirement age. Some of these individuals never enter into a "new" state called "retirement." They choose to work for as long as they are physically active, putting into practice the first maxim of "doing as much as you can for as long as you can." These individuals generally have managed to combine their work with a lifelong love for the thing they do. They continue playing another concert, going to the office, doing another show, producing the product, or offering the service with an inner joy that often sustains their motivation and energy.

Performers are often among this group. Performers, moreover, often seem to conjure up mysterious longevity when they engage in their specialty. Stepping into the spotlight yet another time, and another, and still another seems to invigorate the human spirit and create an aura that defies the aging process. At times, even physical infirmities seem to be magically set aside during a performance, the performer becoming so focused that an aura of youthful energy is generated, one that belies actual age and physical condition.

Other individuals, who lacked as strong a love for their work, may indeed find that the "retirement" years offer opportunities to change their life, and they sometimes discover new passions. In such cases, the maxim of "doing as much as you can for as long as you can" still holds true. They may have to learn a great deal about a new field of endeavor, but learning is invigorating when combined with desire and undertaken at a reasonable pace. Adjustments may have to be made at the outset, however, if the "new" pursuit has a strenuous physical component. Even in these cases conventional wisdom is often proved wrong. An abundance of success stories suggest that individuals of retirement age can and do gear up to participate effectively in physically taxing activities.

Even for those whose life has been dedicated to performance, the dreaded moment inevitably arrives when it is impossible to do one's thing at a customary level of excellence. Fingers become less agile, voices eventually lose their characteristic vitality, muscles weaken, sight dims, or hearing is less precise. Age limitations come to us all, but for performers the process can be unusually traumatic; it means stepping aside from the activity that has fueled creativity and passion for decades—a hard realization to face, but inevitable.

At this point it is vitally important to realize one's passion can be fed vicariously. When you can no longer physically execute a given activity, you need to work in other ways. You can still become an expert on the preparation, training, achievements, and archives of the field. Technology and research can become gateways that permit total immersion in any world of human endeavor. That immersion, in turn, has the potential to generate the joy and passion needed for continuing to live a vital life.

Thus the second maxim of "generating passion for whatever you can do" becomes the next challenge. As we encounter turning points in the process of aging, we will undoubtedly have strong emotional reactions as we realize that normal activity is no longer possible. At such moments we may not accept our state easily, and we may find it difficult to regard the "next best" as satisfactory. There may well be times in which frustration or resentment run rife. When such emotions are full-blown, they tend to take over completely, and there seems no relief from their intensity. However, they too eventually wax and wane. In those windows of time when the emotional pain subsides, you need to consider what degree of involvement is possible and will bring you into close proximity to the activity you love. This process requires a considerable degree of tough-mindedness, for you must assess honestly your own strength, resist self-pity and futility, and garner enthusiasm for those avenues still open to you.

If you can no longer perform, set aside disappointment and teach or coach. If you can no longer be a player, stop whining about it and be an active watcher, analyzer, critic, or commentator. If your days of public achievement are over, don't expend energy wallowing in memories of past glory, but rather use this energy to create alternate ways in which you can still contribute. In short, work to accept as quickly as possible what can't be changed, and get on with what is still possible.

Turning your thinking around will not happen all at once, and indeed the first few attempts may seem futile. But repeated effort at resetting your mental focus will eventually yield results. In the long run, continued movement in this direction will even make it possible to extract satisfaction from the knowledge that you are doing everything you can to be close to the world that excites you. In the process you may discover other aspects of that world for which you can develop new passion and that might have gone unnoticed had you not been forced to make changes.

Finally, if you are blessed with a very long life, you will eventually have to deal with that stage where activity is highly restricted because of weakness or infirmity. If this point arrives, know that there is no shame in living happily and comfortably with your achievements from a former time. Curtail living in the past as long as other activity is possible, for living in the past inhibits what is possible in the present. By the same token, if you reach that point when you are able to manage only a basic daily routine, then you might well draw nourishment and solace from the memories of previous challenges, adventures, and achievements. When this point in life comes, you need to turn a deaf ear to the often-heard approbation of "has-been" status. At this point in life, you must indeed heed the old folk-rhyme:

> I'd rather be a has-been
> Than a might-have-been, by far;
> For a might-have-been has never been,
> And a has-been was once a star.

And in this context, every one of us who has lived the adventure of performance can, indeed, establish a claim to stardom.

chapter sixteen
Performance Careers in Retrospect

As we conceptualize, prepare, give, and evaluate performance, we envision the road we expect to follow. We know that we will likely experience detours and bumps, as well as some smooth stretches. Yet we hold fast to the thought that the road will lead us to the destination we desire, that one performance will follow another until we feel seasoned and expert. Those who have gone this distance can confirm that, if they envision their journey with half-closed eyes, taking in its contour without much regard for detail, they can conceive of the overall dimensions of their journey.

If, however, their scrutiny becomes the least bit detailed, they quickly realize that the journey has seldom held a steady, single course. Rather a series of influences and pressures have rendered most small segments of the journey highly erratic, in terms of both direction and forward motion. Thus successful pursuit of a performance career has depended heavily on repeated correction and intrepid persistence, with frequent need simultaneously to overcome frustration and futility.

Some of the influences that pull at us during our careers are inherent to all human beings and appear naturally; others are born as a result of activity we initiate consciously; still others seem to be thrust upon us by our fate. They form into patterns with which we become thoroughly comfortable. Looking at these patterns evokes ideas we have encountered in other contexts. Yet examining concepts with a variety of approaches is valuable, for new revelations often emerge, like the new designs and colors revealed as a kaleidoscope is held to the light and rotated. Here are three such patterns:

- Plateaus
- Burnout
- Changing self-images

185

Plateaus

Nature prefers irregular growth cycles. Plants shoot up for a period of time and then require a period during which they change little before the next period of noticeable growth. Similar patterns of sporadic growth can be observed in animals and humans. The seeming nongrowth portions of the pattern that take place in learning development are often referred to as plateaus. This imagery suggests that we reach points where we have to go along at the same level for a period before we can climb again.

We may recognize this pattern in theory, but in practice it is difficult to be objective enough to know when we have entered such a plateau. Thus we often feel a sense of frustration or bewilderment, because although we seem to be working just as hard and effectively as ever, growth seems to have all but stopped. We have a tendency at these points to try to determine what we are doing wrong, when in fact the answer may be that we are simply crossing a plateau.

If you realize that you are experiencing a plateau, it may be easier to accept that you will have to wait for the next obvious spurt of growth. However, a performer's question is likely to be: how long will it take to get to the point of noting improvement again? The answer depends upon too many incalculable factors to be able to predict: how difficult the next climb is; how intently you continue to work; how much fueling up you need to be ready for the next upward thrust. Clock-watching, moreover, won't help. Instead, try to diffuse frustration and impatience, for doing so will almost always hasten getting across the plateau. Try to continue to work at a steady, intense pace, holding firm to the belief that growth is taking place in invisible but necessary ways.

By the same token, you must not go so far in accepting a plateau that you become complacent. Some performers bask in the security of a given work routine, comfortable in a plateau mode and not expecting to see any growth. Announcing that you are *crossing a plateau* or reminding yourself frequently of this state, usually with an underlying glow of knowing satisfaction, can be a symptom that you are using the plateau pattern as an excuse for not showing signs of growth or improvement. Thus patience with plateaus must be combined with a watchful eye and perhaps a bit of gentle prodding to keep you moving toward growth and improvement.

Burnout

Burnout is a conviction that creativity is waning as a result of deeply rooted boredom. You perceive little excitement in your performance work, having lost earlier enthusiasm. You may be continuing to throw yourself into the tasks at hand with energy and purpose, but there is an underlying sensation that your accomplishments are uninspired, ordinary, or less than first-rate. You may even be able to point to growth and development, but without being able to shake the feeling that the product is less than your best. Short-term loss of motivation was addressed in chapters 5 and 6, with suggested techniques for climbing out of these doldrums. The burnout state, in contrast, is more deeply rooted and almost always opens up serious questions about long-range plans and objectives.

This state is most often encountered after a long period of performance or preparation. It is frequently experienced in conjunction with a sophisticated regard of one's area of endeavor. You convince yourself that you've seen it all, been there, done that, all of it many times over. Nothing surprises you; nothing thrills you; nothing sweeps you away. No future prospect, plan, or challenge fires you up. Hard on the heels of this jaded world-weariness comes an inner bewilderment that keeps asking if this is all there is—if you should expect yourself to go down life's road repeating over and over again the same pattern of preparation, performing, and bowing. Something whispers that if this is all there is, then you would just as soon, and maybe rather, do something else.

Burnout often overcomes those who are at a midpoint in their careers. It is usually associated with a midlife crises, when one is looking back over fifteen to twenty years and seeing approximately the same period of work ahead. Degree of success may be a factor but often lies outside the central issue of whether or not one wants to spend the remaining years of one's life doing the same thing.

For some, this ennui is so pressing that change itself is regarded as a panacea, even if it means turning away from activities that have been close to the heart. If such disenchantment erodes the romance of your endeavors sufficiently, you may be willing to flirt with giving up pursuits that you had deemed central to your very existence. The trials and tribulations of having achieved some degree of success may have worn you down to the point where you ask yourself if following your dream is worth the price. Or perhaps you have simply become weary with the familiar patterns of your performing life to the extent that you seek relief even if it means forsaking something very dear to you.

For others this crisis is brought on by the fact that the work they have devoted their life to is not their innermost love. Somewhere along the line, they gave up their heart's desire in favor of earning a living, providing for a family, or answering some other pressing need that was persuasive at an earlier time. If this is the case with you, you must now face the fact that you are tired of your choice and, having succumbed to burnout, you can no longer convince yourself that you are on the right track.

The unnerving realization may emerge that you must change your direction without delay or your entire life will be spent pursuing activities that aren't what you really wanted to do. You become convinced that someday you will experience a profound sense of self-betrayal over not having followed your dream and that it will be too late to do anything about it. You fear that at some moment near the end of your life you will look back over your time on this earth with a sense of frustration rather than satisfaction, with the realization that the summing up of your life is deeply disappointing.

Sorting all of this out is not an easy task, and taking action does not necessarily guarantee relief. Some experience burnout, change the course of their lives or careers, and find that their repressed spirit is indeed liberated. They end up engaged in activities that restore their zest for living, look back on the change in direction as a refreshing adventure, and wonder why it took so long to make it.

On the other hand, burnout can be treacherous. It can goad you into making changes without having given enough thought to either the consequences or a realistic consideration of what a new activity entails on a day-to-day basis. Careful consideration is the key. Contemplate change with your eyes wide open and your head cleared of half-formed, romanticized misconceptions. Such consideration may act like a bucket of cold water on the flame of your adventure, but not necessarily so. It might strengthen your resolve to take the plunge.

Here are three exercises that will help in such consideration:

Exercises

- Do your research. Ask those who work in the area you propose to move toward how they spend their days, their hours; what special joys and frustrations they experience; and if they experience the satisfaction you hope to bring into your life. You are contemplating an important life decision, so it is well worth the time and effort to halt the flow of your life a few days to inundate yourself in the reality of your new existence. If possible, take some vacation time and go live in your dream world, simulating as much as possible the daily existence of that lifestyle.

- Calculate the cost. Ask how the change will affect the lives of those you love; whether the new activity will give you enough for an acceptable, even if modest, standard of living; how much, if any, pain you will experience in leaving your present activity behind.

- Imagine the twilight. Visualize yourself at the end of your life and ask how you will feel about the change in retrospect, first focusing on the change by itself, without expectation of success or failure. Then, if you find that success or failure patterns cannot be ruled out of the total picture, ask yourself about the degree of success it will take to give you the satisfaction you want to look back on.

The dose of reality generated by such exercises may cool your impulse to change course. If it does, then you will likely conclude that things are better than you had thought. The burnout will probably have been demolished in the process, and most or all of your former energy and creativity restored. If, on the other hand, after doing the research, considering the cost, and imagining the long run, you find yourself only more fired up, then go for it.

If you want to be extra cautious, set up a short period of time as a buffer zone, wait it out, recheck, and then proceed, if that is your decision. This is the real life equivalent of that window that appears on your computer screen asking if you are "sure" after you have executed a command. If after careful consideration, you still want to move ahead with your adventure, wait several days, perhaps no fewer then ten and no more than thirty, before you leap.

During that time, shelve your obsession and try to spend very little time thinking about the great decision. Go about your daily tasks with as much emotional detachment as possible. After the waiting period is up, check your results once more, as well as your emotional thermostat. If the cooling-off period has diminished your infatuation so that moving ahead with your dream no longer seems imperative, wait even longer. If, on the other hand, your compulsion still burns brightly, consider yourself "sure," and get going.

Some individuals who experience a period of burnout would like to move out of it but are by no means giving serious thought to a fundamental change of direction. They know that they are doing what they want to be doing, that their overall life's endeavor is focused right where they want it to be. Still they are faced with temporary weariness with their work and find it difficult to inject it with enthusiasm and meaningful creativity difficult. Antidotes to classic cases of staleness are well known, and we already considered some of them in the context of short-term stalling. Let's review several in regard to burnout:

- Change your environment or physical state.
- Get physical.
- Start a new project.
- Use your work in a way that will serve others.

Changing Your Environment or Physical State

Perhaps the most obvious and most common way to change your environment or physical state is to take a vacation. Vacation works as an antidote to malaise to the extent that the normal pattern of day-to-day life is interrupted and you must deal with a new environment. Staying at home and relaxing is therefore less effective than going out of town. Going out of town to a professional convention is not a vacation because, although your environment may be altered, your focus remains unchanged. If you cannot afford the time or money to leave home, then at least tell all your friends and associates you are gone. Shut yourself off from all the usual avenues of communication (except perhaps for an occasional check in for emergencies). Dedicate your days to activities that are completely different in content from the usual and that take you to a new environment, even if it is local.

Either by means of an out-of-town vacation or an at-home break, you are trying to effect a psychological break with your day-to-day patterns and the setting in which you execute them. The break must be long enough so that when you return to your usual activities, you experience a small psychological jolt. You should feel that you need to reacquaint yourself with the content and dimensions of your world even though your mind knows logically that this is familiar territory.

You may reenter your home and look at it with fresh eyes, remarking on your new perception of its good and bad points. Sometimes the space in which you normally move seems "larger" or "smaller." Your physical environment seems momentarily foreign, as if you were living and working in it for the first time. All of this "strangeness" will undoubtedly be fleeting, but in the instant that that shadow of disorientation passes across your consciousness, you can grasp new insight into your normal world that will dispel feelings of burnout.

Getting Physical

A special application of changing your state is doing something that changes your physical being: your pulse rate, your metabolism, your degree of muscular contraction, and so on. We all know the value of exercise for our bodies, but we may not realize how physical exertion engages us psychologically. It alters our focus. Not only do we get rid of physical poisons, but as we return to our normal psychological focus we do so with a different perspective.

For physical activities to be effective as an antidote to burnout, several conditions should prevail. To begin with, you must throw yourself into the activity with enough dedication to dispel looking over your shoulder at the work you left behind or begrudging the time it is taking. Once you have embarked upon a period of exercise, dedicate the time it consumes willingly, regard it as play, and rev up your energy to hit it hard. The exercise must be vigorous enough or prolonged enough to consume your being totally, at least for a few seconds or minutes.

There should be some small period of time in which it seems like doing this activity is all there is, and nothing else matters. Your pulse rate needs to increase. If possible, you need to perspire. These indications signal that your physical state has been altered and that you must return to a more normal condition at the end of your exercise period. As you return, you have a window of time for renewing the mental attitudes you have built up around your work.

Starting a New Project

Starting a new project often renews enthusiasm that can dissolve burnout. This endeavor sometimes works well, if you are at a point in your work where beginning something new is natural and appropriate. There is, however, some danger in using this technique. Once the newness of the project wears off, you will enter into a prolonged period of work during which all the same patterns that resulted in burnout in the first place reappear. Thus you still must address the issue of rejuvenating the underlying enthusiasm for the substance of your activity. For example, if you feel weary because you cannot achieve a secure performance of a piece of music, starting a new piece may relieve the frustration, but you must still perfect the first piece, and eventually you will face the same problem in the new one.

Moreover, instituting new projects at inappropriate times in your work cycle can result in too many things going at once. If this happens, you may find that significant progress on any one of them becomes difficult. Furthermore, the fact that previous projects have not been completed may trigger bothersome psychological feedback. Although using new projects to rectify burnout can sometimes be effective, use it with some degree of caution as to its timing and ultimate consequences.

Serving Others

Dedicating some portion of your work to the service of others was considered in chapter 9 and remains one of the most effective ways to give new meaning to whatever you do. It may seem at first glance that finding the time and energy to engage in service is both impossible and foolhardy. For many, this perception belays any effort to incorporate a service component into their professional life. After all, giving is ultimately a personal matter. If, however, you pass up opportunities to give, or if you do not create ways in which the fruit your efforts might benefit others, you will end up ignoring one of the most powerful and enduring fountainheads in the universe.

Few people experience the call to lead a life of total dedication to good causes. Most of us pursue goals of our own design and get caught up in traveling paths that are both personal and essentially self-serving. To argue against such self-fulfillment flies in the face of most of the patterns we observe in nature. All life is essentially self-sustaining, and nature mandates instinctive behavior that serves this principle.

Even so, those who have relegated some measure of their time and effort toward activities that benefit others find, often to their surprise, that their perspective changes. As you see the difference your efforts make, you find new value attaches itself to your performance work. Moreover, service often provides opportunities to perceive how your efforts are regarded by a world foreign to your own. As a result, you may reorder priorities within your own world. You might see that some aspects of your work that you consider ordinary are extremely meaningful in the eyes of those you contact, while some that you deem important generate relatively little notice. For example, you might regard yet another performance of a musical chestnut as mundane, but performing that familiar music in a hospice could result in an intense emotional experience for you and your audience, whereas your brilliance in more esoteric music is not nearly as effective.

Encountering such foreign perspectives is apt to interrupt your own patterns of work and generate a shakeup of values, often resulting in change. As you return to your own routine, you may do so with a fresh viewpoint and some ideas for improvement. Thus investing in service for the benefit of others results in the paradox of your garnering renewed energy and creativity for the very activity that means so much to you. Such a paradox may seem mysterious, but those who have become so engaged testify without exception to a newly discovered fulfillment.

Changes in Self-Image

Let us now turn to the changes in self-image you may encounter during your journey. Imagine that you have conceived and prepared your performance, given performances, perhaps many times, dealt with feedback, and even envisioned long-term career-like patterns based on your performances. Throughout this journey you dealt with your self-image, sometimes focusing on it directly in an attempt to alter or improve it, and sometimes simply being subliminally aware of its presence and importance. If you have enjoyed a reasonable degree of success, you have probably settled on a self-image that, while perhaps not perfect, has been sufficiently positive and appropriate. You may be aware that your self-image has become stronger as you have grown from novice to experienced performer. Furthermore, you may have formulated several defining aspects of your self-image.

For example, the level of recognition you have achieved will influence your belief as to who you are and how you fit into the larger picture. You may be recognized as a star, whose achievements are widely acknowledged in your field. Or you may have carved out a solid, productive niche for yourself within your field. Or you may recognize that, on balance, you are one of many who work in a given arena of music, providing performance that is useful and personally rewarding but not particularly outstanding. Teaching others too may be an important part of your role.

These perceptions may or may not be accompanied by a feeling of security. Indeed, in some areas of performance whatever you achieve from an artistic standpoint is vulnerable to competition or lack of recognition. In some arenas you may have safeguards built in, such as seniority, tenure, or union protection. You may or may not have ample remuneration for your work, depending on the market value placed on your success and the way you have positioned yourself within that market. You may or may not look forward to longevity, depending on the extent to which your contributions are sought and, often, upon the degree of physical prowess that is inherent in what you do. For all of us, aging inevitably becomes a factor.

Alongside efforts to achieve and improve our performance are myriad external forces that affect our ability to realize our goals and our self-regard. As a result, our self-image is constantly undergoing transformation, sometimes slowly and other times very rapidly. All of the reflective attributes we have fought so hard to accrue and preserve must be continually reestablished, often with a totally different set of challenges. This never-ending demand for self-evaluation is inherent in life. It is the fountainhead of our frustrations and our joys, the force that drives us to achieve our finest moments and ultimately to deal with our own mortality.

Notwithstanding the buffeting of life's external forces, somewhere within you is a core being that is the essence of how you regard who you are. As we have observed, trying to achieve insight into this central, inner entity is both awkward and elusive. Maintaining balance as you contemplates the ingredients of your psychological makeup often invites wishful thinking in some areas and self-denigration in others. Yet if you persist in reflecting with as much objectivity as possible, you can garner a list of qualities that emerge consistently no matter the external characteristics at any given point in time. A series of questions can often act as a catalyst for the realization you seek:

- Are you fulfilled by what you do, enjoying a high degree of satisfaction from just being engaged in it without regard to the degree of success you experience?
- To what extent can you characterize yourself as a survivor? Or to put it another way, when you have faced what seemed like insurmountable setbacks, have you been able to pick yourself up and do whatever was necessary to get yourself back into operating mode?
- Do you feel that you help, serve, or please others through your work?
- How proud are you of your work? Do you represent some standard of quality or achievement in your own thinking? Does what you do set an example for others?
- Do you feel appreciated? Do you feel you have to convince others of the efficacy or value of your work? Do you regard what you do as experimental, controversial, or innovative?
- Do you see yourself as efficient, energetic, and upbeat in your day-to-day work, or as pressured, harassed, and burdened?
- How much humor, playfulness, charm, or wit do you exude as you work?
- If you could travel again down the road you have traveled, to what extent would you want to change your course?

Of all the areas that you must deal with in trying to achieve self-awareness, it is wise to limit detailed consideration of one in particular: the degree to which you think you are recognized, held in high esteem by others, or celebrated.

Trying to assess the degree to which you are revered depends upon so many diverse factors that it would be almost impossible for even an *objective* source to formulate a definitive evaluation, much less your own *subjective* perspective. We all know the icons of the popular culture. If you could knock on a door in any corner of the world, tell your name to whatever stranger responds, and be assured of instant recognition, you would have popular icon status. If, indeed, such status turns out to be your lot, it is definitely not in your best interest to revel in this fact with self-congratulation or to cultivate dependency upon it for your self-image. The reasoning behind this admonition is obvious: fickleness is inherent in popular culture and your fame will probably be downgraded tomorrow. You will be a has-been the day after; and by next week you will be in the "whatever happened to" category at best or completely forgotten at worst. Moreover, such notoriety is seldom based on carefully considered evaluation of what you have contributed to your area of endeavor, but rather on information gleaned from a cultural grapevine that is neither accurate nor discriminating.

If your status is somewhat less than that of an icon, then determining how well known you are depends very much upon whom you ask. Some will know your work and value it; others will know your work but minimize its influence; still others will not know you or what you do at all. There will be as many shades of variety in these perceptions as the number of individuals who offer an opinion. Trying to get an overview of these attitudes is like the parable of the blind men and the elephant. (In trying to describe an elephant; each man came up with a different description because each felt a different part of the animal's body.) Reality will vary significantly with the perspective of each person. Using such information in the formulation of a self-image is useless, and insisting on such an unreliable process will only result in frustration.

Quite aside from this problem, however, there is something fundamentally contradictory in assessing your own self-image by taking polls of opinions of others. One's self-image, by definition, has to be generated from within. The difficult process of defining the essence of your self-regard should, in fact, eschew widespread input from others, as well as perceptions that depend upon recognition by broad segments of the population. Rather keep your own counsel. Formulate your own set of values with regard to the significance of your contribution. Acknowledge graciously whatever recognition seems forthcoming but remain impervious to its intoxication. Finally, seek to develop a private, inner integrity upon which to base your self-regard, one that will result in your living comfortably with who you are and what you do.

Yet another by-product of a long, successful career is that you feel you are competing with the successes of past performances or with perceptions built on those performances. If you have been able to sustain a performance career, you have undoubtedly turned in impressive, even distinguished examples of your work at various points along the way. Moreover, the reality of the achievement may have been exaggerated as the public and professional grapevines recall the event. Thus as your career progresses, when facing similar challenges, you will have to deal with the reality of what you did in the past as well as the popular perception of what you did. The expectation linked to your next performance may haunt you, whether or not such expectation is well founded and logical.

Let us once again recall the adage "You are only as good as your last performance" and point out that profiles of long, successful careers do not confirm its truth. Virtually every successful performer has undoubtedly had some bad performances, some flops, even entire periods of failure, along the way. Dealing with such low points seems formidable, but love of the work itself and the fortitude to neutralize such rough periods should get you moving again with renewed energy.

Whether gearing up anew after such a period of disappointment, or whether facing a new challenge, the perceptions of your past success or the expectations of your audience may gnaw in the back of your consciousness. Will this time be better than the last? Or even as good as the last? Do I have the stuff to pull away from a past disappointment? Or to generate as great a success as I have already enjoyed? Am I as good as I was? Am I as ready as I was? Will the risk factor work in my favor as effectively this time? Are the odds the same? Are there more handicaps? Do people expect too much? Will people be more critical this time? Are people expecting the wrong things out of this performance, not realizing inherent differences between this and past ones?

The list of questions and hypotheses could go on and on and, quite obviously, to no avail. The reality is, of course, that every performance is different and should be treated differently, and comparisons are pointless. If you have learned from previous performances (preparation procedures, research strategies, how to deal with the performance itself, methods of evaluation), use that knowledge to deal with the challenges of the performance at hand. On the other hand, trying to anticipate results, effects, or outside perceptions in the light of previous performances should be exorcised from your thinking for several reasons.

First, you have limited objectivity in your regard of past performances, even though you may have gone through an evaluation process. Dwelling on past performances is unlikely to garner more objectivity. Second, every performance comes with a whole set of outside variables, your upcoming one included. Assess the variables you now face, overcome the current challenges, and capitalize on present opportunities. Looking at previous performances not only dilutes your concentration on the job at hand, but also tempts you to assume that the variables of the past are identical with present ones, act on that assumption, and end up making serious mistakes. Third, public or professional perception of performance notoriously has been, is, and always will be unstable and unpredictable. The lasting impression gleaned by any given individual or group is often born of some random detail. Thus negative evaluation often persists without a grasp of overall content or merit. By the same token, instant accolades are offered and success heralded even before style has been scrutinized or content carefully considered.

Taking such inconstancy into account, accept with gratitude the accolades when they appear. But targeting them is both dangerous and foolish.

Indeed, calculating how to generate such accolades diverts your attention and often fosters a self-consciousness that, when it does not cause you to stumble outright, will likely keep your performance from ringing completely true. Notwithstanding their own foibles of perception, audiences are quick to sense grandstanding, and although they may feign momentary acceptance, deep down they feel disgruntled when they sense they are being manipulated.

Therefore regard each performance as a separate piece of work and reject mental patterns that conjure up comparisons with past performances or respond to expectations that might be out there. Use the information, the techniques, or the experience that you have amassed from previous performances, but regard such attributes as tools, not as influences or standards. Such discipline not only will preserve the integrity of the current performance, but also will maximize the sense of discovery and adventure inherent in your present enterprise without the baggage of your past or your imagined public/professional standing.

There are, however, ways of looking at the past that can be instructive and beneficial at a somewhat deeper level. This process is best undertaken *between* performance projects. In such periods there is often an impulse to get an overview of where one has been and to assess the overall content or tenor of a number of past performances. Such reflection can sometimes act as a catalyst for trying something new. For, example, you may sense that you have been going in one direction enough, and you feel the need to tackle a different set of challenges.

Such a need may lead to a change of repertoire, venue, genre, or the role you play in the performance. If you have restricted your activity to participation only, you may try teaching, production, or management roles. You might want to think about switching operatic role-types, changing repertoire periods, doing something light or entertaining instead of serious, doing ensemble instead of solo. We all can cite examples of public figures who have effected such a change: opera singers who become coaches or stage directors; instrumental soloists who conduct; concert performers who become media commentators or critics; practitioners who become teachers; front-line contact persons who become planners, managers, or producers.

Moving in these directions offers more rewards than simply changing one's pace to ensure continued vitality. Many changes signal a move toward a new enterprise and often reflect a desire to shape the future of one's field or leave some kind of heritage. Such impulses are frequently born of a deeply felt dedication to the activity itself and an idealistic regard for its destiny. These patterns may lead to work that addresses the public or social issues in a given field of activity. Thus, an opera star becomes the chief executive of a guild that protects the rights of theater musicians. A virtuoso pianist works full-time in the public schools to raise the level of students' music appreciation. Often groups of individuals whose careers have revolved around performance begin to think of themselves as a family of sorts, and attention to the needs of the "family's" children, elderly, or distressed becomes an issue of importance.

Thus, many performers who have met and mastered the challenges of successful performance and who have built strong careers find themselves drawn to activities that harbor positive influences for their profession and its future. They begin to give birth to forward-looking projects, invest in the next generation of practitioners through teaching, or give themselves to work that supports a social need. These impulses to combine their erstwhile ambitions and personal goals with work that is far-reaching often become steps toward a personal reckoning with the relationship that their career as a performer plays in their innermost spiritual life. This relationship is considered in more detail in the final section of this book.

postlude
Performance and Your Spiritual Life

The first indications of awareness of the spiritual aspects of one's work as a performer often manifest themselves in a deepening understanding as to the meaning of the work itself. Patterns that one has followed for years, and that have always been important, begin to take on a more personal and profound meaning. An innermost response begins to awaken and fill your work, endowing it with a new level of authority, significance, and often ease of execution. The response may be difficult to define, for it represents a level of perception beyond technical, intellectual, or emotional excellence. It offers intense personal involvement with conceptual clarity that renders transmission of musical and emotional values both pleasurable and effortless. One is aware that one has, indeed, become a master, and the inner joy and peace one derives from this state is both assured and consistent.

This new inner state does not release you from the hard work of preparing a performance, the creative struggles necessary for reaching your optimum readiness, or the tension involved in giving a performance. It does offer both perspective and a deeper measure of wisdom. Underneath the active dynamics of the performance cycle is the knowledge that you can create and execute a performance of breathtaking quality and effectiveness as an integral part of the person you have become. This sense of unity with the performance itself suggests an identity that seems close to the core of your spiritual being, so close that you begin to regard who you are as the same as what you do.

It is precisely at this point that we might pause to reflect and pose some questions about this newly found relationship. If, indeed, this closeness between who you are and what you do is progressing to the point of being identified as your spiritual life, then you might want to question whether this deepening relationship, wonderful as it is, will ensure your continued

199

spiritual growth and development. Can you approach the final days of your time on earth with the knowledge that the activity that has become your *raison d'être* is enough, or should you attempt to sustain some kind of spiritual life apart from that activity? While the obvious answer is that each person must decide individually, and that answer will vary from person to person, there are some observations that may be helpful at this juncture.

One's deepening sense of identity will naturally be enhanced through repeated, habitual consideration on the meaningful, emotional aspects of the music itself. Repeated performance of that music, adding up to extensive experience, will provide a certain measure of identity, to be sure. But exploring the inner world that attends this newfound relationship will provide an even more intense awareness of it. On the other hand, consciously exploring such inner values is frequently difficult, because as one warms up to the task, one is likely to feel a variety of deterrents, ranging from self-consciousness to bewilderment, and possibly including even frustration and impatience over the amorphous, elusive nature of what we are attempting to focus on.

What is it we are trying to bring into focus? We are often not sure. We know that there is a certain reality to the sense of identity we have come to feel with our development as a performer. We know that who we are, what our destiny is, and what we might hope to leave behind is tied into this performance activity. This much is real to us, although hard to put into words, and harder to frame in abstractions or language that goes beyond what we personally are experiencing. We also sense that studying this aspect of our being more closely would be both interesting and beneficial. Furthermore, many spiritual leaders attest to the fact that time thus spent will in some undefined way reap rewards of great value. We are willing to try, but it all seems too nebulous.

Do we sit down and try to think about the love we have for our work? To what end? Do we try to think of what we can do to turn our work into charitable impulses? Is socialization of our activity really the best use of our time and energy? And even if we decided to try to represent attributes that will be deemed broadly beneficial, how do we underscore spiritual values as we contemplate future performances? Won't such an attempt end up being merely self-conscious or pretentious? Or maybe just useless?

Such questions and doubts emanate from our rational, conscious mind and, as products of purposeful short-term thinking, are well founded. By the same token, all of us are aware that perception and realization of a different sort take place at levels of the mind somewhere underneath the surface we use for day-to-day living. We know that, like falling asleep, contemplation of values or attributes that might be described as "spiritual" have to be approached indirectly and with an attitude that invites psychological grazing and sensitive awareness. Thus we must agree once again to put aside our conscious reservations temporarily and attempt to enter a world that is less than clearly defined. Some temperaments will be comfortable roaming around in this fuzzy state; others will be impatient with it, deeming it a waste of time; a few will even dislike its lack of definition and purpose.

Exercise routines for both beginners and those who are out of shape spiritually are not unlike physical exercises in the way they are approached and the expected results. You do a few simple ones in the beginning on a regular basis. You work daily for small segments of time and set goals that are easy to achieve. Your workout may seem benign and ineffectual in the beginning, but after a few days of regular practice you should begin to sense some positive feedback. Such exercises can take many forms, but for most individuals, the basic procedure is a variation on procedures we touched upon earlier in the context of strengthening our self-esteem.

Exercise

Create a window of time, ranging from five minutes to an hour, in which you become quiet. Attempt to slow the flow of your conscious thought process, and gently direct your mind toward a listening awareness, at the same time slowly feeding your mind from a menu of nonspecific images while targeting the area of interest in a general way. A list of such non-specific images might include concepts of goodness, spirituality, creativity, love, wisdom, intelligence, community, healing, strength, energy, or simply the life force itself. Call up these images and attempt to sense their presence and their power as they intertwine with concepts associated with your work as a performer. As with drifting in and out of sleep, these images will wax and wane, their immediacy sometimes being felt clearly and at other times but dimly.

You might pose questions that aim to tap into fundamental motivation. These too should be kept of a general nature, so that your mind can continue to roam freely and wait expectantly. Examples might be: "If you could set aside the physical, emotional, or environmental limitations you have come to believe in, what would you like to do most?" Or "If you believed all things possible for you, what achievement would please you most?" Or "If you absolutely knew that a Divine Power would grant you answers to your prayers, what would you pray for?" Or "If your creatively were unlimited, what would you like to create, to leave behind as your legacy to mankind?" Or "If you knew you could bring into your reality instantly whatever you could conceive, what would you focus on?"

Such imaginings may bring you face to face with a divergence between what you believe you should want and what you really want. You may find yourself surprised at the fact that certain goals you always assumed you wanted are suddenly attended by reservation, even rejection, in light of the imagined prospect of their becoming instantly realized. You may uncover values you hold that have never been fully manifested. Your imagination may stimulate creativity in such a way that the means to achieve your goals suddenly become clearly outlined, and ideals that you had heretofore regarded as impossible may be brought within practical range.

Feedback may come during the exercise session itself in the form of certain realizations. On the other hand, maybe the only feedback you sense will come in a more diluted form, and at other times. In such cases, you may draw blanks in terms of definable impressions during the actual exercise sessions, although you may experience a feeling of general well-being. Positive results can often be noted in more general ways as you mark an improvement in overall mind-set, unusually energetic and positive moods, powerful and seemingly effortless concentration, or a wealth of highly creative ideas.

As with physical conditioning, results will be sporadic. You will experience setbacks and plateaus. There will be times when your spiritual exercises seem routine and devoid of meaning. When such doldrums are encountered, summon up fresh resolve and attempt to energize your spiritual workout with a combination of will power and inventing new patterns to reengage your attention. There will be times when your emotional palette unaccountably has no taste for engaging in contemplative activity. These patterns too are typical of physical training. Perhaps a short break in routine might be good therapy. After the breather, however, pushing through the barrier might be critical for realizing a higher level of achievement. As with patterns of physical growth, progress may be elusive at times. You will experience moments of both discouragement and encouragement.

All of this diverse, seemingly zigzag activity does, however, add up to a highly significant result: you have a spiritual life. Imperfect and sporadic as it may seem, it becomes an ongoing component of your existence as a human being. The testimony of millions of men and women who have attempted to sustain such a spiritual life is that unmatched strength and good result from such efforts. Most of us will not, in fact, become philosophers, seers, or priests, but through persistent efforts you can be sensitive to the metaphysical heartbeat of your universe. In so doing you will give full range to your talents and be able to contribute to the world as a result of developing your potential to the optimum.

Sustaining a spiritual life will also provide its own unique reward. Whether it is called breakthrough, realization, revelation, inspiration, or transfiguration, something seemingly miraculous will at some point come into your experience. The characteristics of such an event vary considerably from one person to the next. It may be dramatic and emotional, or it may take place in the midst of profound, meditative calm. The event may be sudden and fleeting, like a lightning flash or, like the coming of dawn, be gradual and deliberate. The impression it leaves behind may be crystal clear and definable, or it may be hazy but leave a residue of well-being or change of a more general nature. You may be able to identify the insight garnered from such an experience and build on it, or you may be left trying to recapture the brilliance of the instant. You may not even be sure it happened, or, if you have the perception that *something* took place, you may not be quite sure how to define it.

In any event, however, embracing the event, believing in its efficacy, and continuing to reach for the enlightenment it promises will generate a fertile environment to stimulate further visitations, more frequently and with clearer content. Such moments cannot be programmed, but patience and expectation will produce results. There may be controversy over the source of this experience, some relating it to a universal power or God and others insisting it is merely an offshoot of the activity of our own subconscious. In fact, you likely will never be able to be completely sure about the source and nature of the power you are tapping into. By the same token, you can sustain a relationship with this power, build an inner life, and reap its benefits either without defining it at all or defining it in a way that is in tune with your personal philosophy. The important bottom line is to attempt be a player, to set your mental antennae for receiving, and to practice regularly those exercises that focus on your inner self.

Like living itself, however, sustaining a relationship with your spiritual life is not a journey without hardships. Usually you will be able to enjoy a relatively trouble-free relationship with your inner self in the early stages. It is as if some wise overseeing power recognizes the fact that the early stages of spiritual life are fragile and early growth has to take place without major challenge. Once these early stages have taken place, however, even your spiritual life can become the target of serious setback, and disappear. Such a situation may result from an unfortunate event in your life, an accident, misfortune, or the death of a loved one. It could be engendered by a moral dilemma, some situation for which there seems no ethical or "right" solution. It may even form gradually with the growing realization that certain fundamental questions about life and death lack completely satisfactory answers. Whatever the trigger, the symptoms are usually profound doubt as to the existence of spiritual substance, or, if you are still willing to admit that there is *something* out there, you may find it difficult to believe in its value, efficacy, or benevolence.

Spiritual explorers have described such a period of bleakness for centuries. But its opposite must also be acknowledged, for there are also periods when we seem to be in tune with a fountainhead of creativity to an unprecedented extent. During such times the flow of ideas seems effortless and inexhaustible. Connections are instant and brilliant. Concepts are stunning in theory and work wonderfully in application. Revisions or adjustments are virtually unnecessary, for we aim and score a bull's-eye with every effort. We realize we are on a roll, but we are momentarily convinced it can go on forever.

Such a period might be regarded as a unique reward for the spiritual traveler, a mountaintop from where the view is breathtaking and vast. We drink in the exhilaration and beauty of such an experience in the hope that we can capture its essence in the form of permanent change. Yet notwithstanding the all-consuming power it displays, it does come to an end, sometimes diminishing after a few seconds, sometimes after hours or days. We find ourselves coming down off the peak, returning to a more normal mode of existence, by comparison just plugging along.

Still, we have experienced change deep within us, for we continue to enjoy the benefits of the creations wrought during that period, and we remember the moments of ecstasy as a time when our reason for being was completely understood. We know too that if we continue to travel the spiritual highway, we will find our way to the top of the mountain again sometime in the future and that an instant of such experience is worth however many miles or whatever effort it takes. We are content in the knowledge that we now belong to that brotherhood of mystics who have experienced firsthand, intimate contact with the Source of the universe.

Sometimes, too, another sort of understanding is given to us. This experience is born not of searching in the void nor of surfing peaks of creativity. Rather, it is one in which we are able to glimpse the total of our work and life with enough perspective to perceive a profile that defines once and for all who we are and what we stand for. This vision telescopes both the past and the future. Thus you see your past as a road without bumps, hills, valleys, or detours, but rather as a straight-shot freeway, the means by which you have moved from your genesis to the present. In the same vision you sense the direction the rest of the journey will take.

In an instant you realize that your dreams, work, preparation, performances, successes, failures, and achievements all add up to something more than a compendium of your activities. Taken as a whole, your efforts have created a field of energy outside of yourself, one that will continue to affect the world and those in it long after you are gone. These are your spiritual children, and if you have nurtured them well, they will continue to honor you. You will then experience a profound inner peace in the irrefutable knowledge that the performance you gave in living your life to the fullest was your greatest.

Selected Bibliography

Baum, Kenneth, Richard Trubo, and Karch Kiraly. *The Mental Edge: Maximize Your Sports Potential with the Mind/Body Connection.* New York: Perigee, 1999.

Bernstein, Seymour. *With Your Own Hands: Self-Discovery Through Music.* New York: G. Schirmer, 1981.

Blumenstein, Boris. *Brain and Body in Sport and Exercise: Biofeedback Applications in Performance Enhancement.* Hoboken,N.J.: John Wiley & Sons, 2002.

Bruser, Madeline. *The Art of Practicing; A Guide to Making Music from the Heart.* New York: Crown Publishing Group, 1999.

Caldwell, Robert. *The Performer Prepares.* N.p: Caldwell Publishing Co., 1990.

Cameron, Julia. *The Artist's Way: A Spiritual Path to Higher Creativity.* New York: J. P. Tarcher, 2002.

Desberg, Peter. *No More Butterflies: Overcoming Stage Fright, Shyness, Interview Anxiety and Fear of Public Speaking.* Oakland, Cal.: New Harbinger Publications, Inc., 1996.

Desberg, Peter, and George Marsh. *Controlling Stage Fright: Presenting Yourself to Audiences from One to One Thousand.* Oakland, Cal.: New Harbinger Publications, Inc., 1988.

Elson, Margaret. *Passionate Practice: The Musician's Guide to Learning, Memorizing, and Performing.* Oxnard, Cal.: Regent Press, 2002.

Emmons, Shirlee, and Alma Thomas. *Power for Singers.* New York: Oxford University Press, 1999.

Ferguson, Howard E. *The Edge: The Guide to Fulfilling Dreams, Maximizing Success and Enjoying a Lifetime of Achievement.* N.p.: Getting the Edge Co., 2001.

Freymuth, Malva S. *Mental Practice and Imagery for Musicians.* N.p.: Integrated Musician's Press, 1999.

Gallwey, W. Timothy. *The Inner Game of Music.* New York: Doubleday, 1986.

———. *The Inner Game of Tennis.* New York: Random House, 1974.

Green, Barry. *The Mastery of Music: Ten Pathways to True Artistry.* New York: Broadway, 2003.

Green, Don. *Audition Success: An Olympic Sports Psychologist Teaches Performing Artists How to Win.* New York: Routledge, 2001.

———. *Fight Your Fear and Win; Seven Skills for Performing Your Best Under Pressure.* New York: Broadway, 2002.

Green, Don, and Julie Jandsman. *Performance Success: Performing Your Best Under Pressure.* New York: Routledge, 2001.

Judy, Stephanie. *Making Music for the Joy of It.* New York: J. P. Tarcher, 1990.

Liebermann, Julie Lyonn. *You Are Your Instrument.* New York: Hui Ksi Music, 1997.

MacKinnon, Lilas. *Music By Heart.* Westport, Conn.: Greenwood Publishing Group, 1981.

McCamy, John C., and James Presley. *Human Life Styling; Keeping Whole in the 20th Century.* New York: Harper and Row, 1975.

Nachmanovitch, Stephen. *Free Play: Improvisation in Life and Art.* New York: J. P. Tarcher, 1991.

Parncutt, Richard, and Gary McPherson, eds. *The Science and Psychology of Music Performance; Creative Strategies for Teaching and Learning.* New York: Oxford University Press, 2002.

Ristad, Eloise. *Soprano on Her Head: Right-Side-Up Reflections on Life and Other Performances.* Moab, Utah: Real People Press, 1982.

Salmon, Paul, and Robert Meyer. *Notes from the Green Room.* Indianapolis: Jossey-Bass, 1998.

Shainberg, Nancy. *Getting Out of Your Own Way: Unlocking Your True Performance Potential.* N.p.: Luminous Press, 2001.

Shockley, Rebecca Payne. *Mapping Music: For Faster Learning and Secure Memory; A Guide for Piano Teachers and Students.* Middleton, Wisc.: A-R Editions, 1997.

Werner, Kenny. *Effortless Mastery: Liberating the Master Musician Within.* New Albany, Ind.: Jamey Abersold Jazz 1996.

Westney, William. *The Perfect Wrong Note and Other Musical Breakthroughs.* Pompton Plains, N.J.: Amadeus Press, 2003.

Index

accompanying. *See* collaboration
adrenaline
adjudication *See* evaluation, external
administration *See* education
    administration
    effect of on performance, 111, 117–118
    effect on tempo, 120–121
advertising, 171
advice. *See* evaluation
African-American music (musicians), 168, 170
aging, 180–183
analysis
    role in memorization, 82
    role in preparation, 62–65
Anderson, Marian, 170
appreciation, by others, 194–195. *See also* music appreciation
aptitude, 145–147
Arrau, Claudio, 173
association. *See* memorization, mnemonic association
attention, as a reward, 28–29
audiences, 154–156

Babe Ruth. *See* Ruth, "Babe" (George Herman, Jr.)
Bach, Carl Philipp Emanuel, 63
Bach, Johann Sebastian, 157, 160, 161, 168

Bartók, Béla, 170, 173
Beethoven, Ludwig van, 143, 157, 160, 170, 173
Borodin, Alexander, 161
Brahms, Johannes, 160, 161, 173
breakdowns. *See* continuity
breakthroughs, 52–53, 204
breathing, 56
Bülow, Hans von, 78
burnout, 186–192
business practices, 171

Carnegie, Andrew, 103
challenge, 26–27
Chopin, Frédéric, 160, 170, 173
church musicians, 162
cocktail musician. *See* lounge musician
Coleridge-Taylor, Samuel, 170
collaboration, 162
competition, 123–124
concert management. *See* management
continuity, 131–132
Corea, Chick (Anthony Armando), 168
creativity under pressure, 124–125, 140
criticism. *See* evaluation, external

Davis, Adelle, 35
death, 19–21
Debussy, Claude, 161, 168, 173
De Larrocha, Alicia. *See* Larrocha, Alicia de

delaying confrontation, 99
digital pianos, 174
disability
    long-term, 180
    temporary, 179
diversion, 107–108, 113
dress rehearsals, 108–112
drill. *See* repetition

Eastman School of Music, 74, 108
Edison, Thomas, 154
editing music, 163
education administration, 164
Ellington, Duke (Edward Kennedy), 161, 173
environment, change in, 59–60, 190
evaluation
    of career goals, 45
    external, 147–151
    following performance, 129–131
    for future performances, 135–140
    of nervous tension, 130–140
    of timetables, 50
exercise. *See* physical exercise
exercises
    for conceptualizing an action plan, 43
    for contemplating a career change, 188–189
    for energy and focus, 55–56
    for evaluating the effect of your performance, 135
    for evaluating your performance, 133
    for evaluating your performance attitude, 134
    for identifying ancillary activities, 162–164
    for motivation, 32
    for pep talk before and during performance, 124
    for performance simulation, 109–110
    for physical coordination, 101–102
    for physical well-being, 36–39
    for positive thinking, 21–24
    for projecting your image as a musician, 169–170
    for speaking fluently, 102
    for spiritual awareness, 201

for varying repeated patterns, 72
for visualizing long range goals, 42

Fauré, Gabriel, 161
fear before performance. *See* nervousness
following through, 93–94

Genhart, Cécile, 74, 108
Gershwin, George, 173
Gestalt, 65
Gieseking, Walter, 173
goals
    diversification of, 43
    long-range, 41–43
    short-term, 43–46

Hancock, Herbie (Herbert Jeffrey), 173
hand stretching exercises, 74
Haydn, Franz Joseph, 157, 160
health. *See* physical state, general well-being
Hess, Myra, 173
Hill, Napoleon, 103
Horowitz, Vladimir, 173

imagery, 101–104
improvising, 157
inspiration. *See* breakthrough
Ives, Charles (Edward), 161

Jesus of Nazareth, 43, 103
Joan of Arc, 43
Joplin, Scott, 170, 173

Larrocha, Alicia de, 51, 173
learning
    patterns, 65–66
    plateaus, 186
Liszt, Franz, 63, 160, 161, 168, 170, 173
long-range goals
    refocusing, 143–147
    supporting, 142–143
lounge musician, 163
love for a field of endeavor, 29–30
luck, 100

management
    as an ancillary activity, 164
    for the performer, 171

Mellon, Andrew William, 103
memorization, 81–89
   and anxiety, 88–89
   and mnemonic associations, 83–85
   and precision levels,
   and time issues, 86–87
Mendelssohn, Fannie, 170
Mendelssohn, Felix, 91, 161, 168
milestone performances, 141–142
motivation. *See* performance,
      motivation
Mozart, Wolfgang Amadeus, 43, 160,
      170, 173
music appreciation, 167–168

negativism. *See* positive thinking
nervousness
   controlling, 138–140
   just before performance, 8
new projects, 191
Novaes, Guiomar, 173

observers, 111–112
opinion, non-professional, 94–95, 112
optimism. *See* positive thinking
outreach to audiences, 157–158
overview, 96

pacing, 120–121
Paderewski, Ignacy Jan, 78, 170
Pandering to audiences. *See* audiences
pep talks, 60–62
performance
   applied to a wide variety of activities,
      4–6
   catalysts of, 8
   defined by external factors, 6–7
   as a means of self-realization, 10–11
   motivation, 25–32
   past, 195–198
physical challenge. *See* disability
physical exercise, 190–191
physical state
   during performance, 121
   during practice, 56–57
   general well-being, 33–39
piano
   characteristics of, 176–177
   history of, 173–174

planning. *See* scheduling
plateaus. *See* learning, plateaus
popularity of musical styles, 159
positive thinking
   assessing degree of, 16
   selecting materials to improve patterns,
      17–19
   at the time of performance, 98, 99
   see also exercises for positive thinking
practice
   open-ended, 51
   structuring, 51–53
precision. *See* memorization, and preci-
      sion levels; rate of work
pretending for relaxation, 57
projecting your image as a musician,
      168–170
Prokofieff, Serge, 173
psychoanalysis, 13
Puccini, Giacomo, 157

quality control, 91–97
questions
   about a performance you have given,
      131–135
   about a performance you must repeat,
      125–140
   that relate your career to your self-
      image, 194
   that relate your performance to long-
      range goals, 140–151

Rachmaninoff, Sergei, 161, 170, 173
Rand, Ayn, 154
rate of work, 92–93
Ravel, Maurice, 171
recognition. *See* appreciation, by others
repetition, 69–80
representation. *See* management, for the
      performer
residual tension, 106–108
reward, 27–29
Rimsky-Korsakov, Nikolay, 161
risk factor during performance, 125–
      127
role models, 44–45
Rosenthal, Moritz, 71
Roussel, Albert (Charles Paul), 161
Rubinstein, Artur, 7–8, 173

Ruth, "Babe" (George Herman, Jr.), 75

scheduling
    interim goals, 46–51
    for performance deadlines, 47–50
Schnabel, Artur, 173
Schubert, Franz Peter, 158, 160, 168, 170, 173
Schumann, Clara, 168, 170
Schumann, Robert, 91, 160, 168, 173
scoring your performance, 132–135
Scriabin, Alexander, 173
security, 75–79, 95–96
self-awareness, 117–119
self-image, 13–15, 98, 192–198
Senancour, Étienne Pivert de, 63
sequencing, 175
Serkin, Rudolf, 173
service to others, 30–31, 191–192
showing-off. *See* attention, as a reward
Socrates, 13
Soviet composers, 170
speed. *See* rate of work
spiritual awareness, 200–204
stage fright, 105–115
    symptoms of, 105
    see also nervousness
starting over, 110–111
Strauss, Richard, 63
Stravinsky, Igor, 173
stretching. *See* hand stretching
    exercises

subconscious mind, 102–104
synthesis, 174–175
synthesizers. *See* synthesis

talent. *See* aptitude
Tatum, Art (Arthur, Jr.), 173
teaching
    interaction with students, 155
    as part of a career, 162
technology
    assistant as ancillary activity, 163
    influence of, 159–160
    keyboard controlled, 174–176
temperament, 100–101
tension. *See* nervousness; residual tension;
    stage fright
timetables. *See* evaluation of timetables;
    scheduling
Tyner, McCoy, 173

Vanderbilt, Cornelius, 103
variation
    of practice order, 58–59
    of repetition patterns, 71–73
    of repetition speed, 70–71
versatility, 157
Villa-Lobos, Heitor, 161

Wagner, Richard, 157, 160, 161
Waller, "Fats" (Thomas Wright), 173
warm-up, 57–58
withdrawal, 121–123
writing about music, 163